Towers of Ivory and Steel

How Israeli Universities
Deny Palestinian Freedom

Maya Wind

VERSO
London · New York

First published by Verso 2024
© Maya Wind 2024
Foreword © Nadia Abu El-Haj
Afterword © Robin D. G. Kelley

1 3 5 7 9 10 8 6 4 2

Verso
UK: 6 Meard Street, London W1F 0EG
US: 388 Atlantic Avenue, Brooklyn, NY 11217
versobooks.com

Verso is the imprint of New Left Books

ISBN-13: 978-1-80429-174-0
ISBN-13: 978-1-80429-176-4 (UK EBK)
ISBN-13: 978-1-80429-175-7 (US EBK)

British Library Cataloguing in Publication Data
A catalogue record for this book is available from the British Library

Library of Congress Cataloging-in-Publication Data
Names: Wind, Maya, author.
Title: Towers of ivory and steel : how Israeli universities deny
    Palestinian freedom / Maya Wind.
Description: London ; Brooklyn, N.Y. : Verso, 2024. | Includes
    bibliographical references and index.
Identifiers: LCCN 2023041708 (print) | LCCN 2023041709 (ebook) | ISBN
    9781804291740 (trade paperback) | ISBN 9781804291757 (ebook)
Subjects: LCSH: Universities and colleges—Political aspects—Israel. |
    Education, Higher—Political aspects—Israel. | Higher education and
    state—Israel. | Palestinian Arabs—Education (Higher)
Classification: LCC LA1443 .W56 2024 (print) | LCC LA1443 (ebook) | DDC
    378.5694—dc23/eng/20230925
LC record available at https://lccn.loc.gov/2023041708
LC ebook record available at https://lccn.loc.gov/2023041709

Typeset in Minion by Hewer Text UK Ltd, Edinburgh
Printed and bound by CPI Group (UK) Ltd, Croydon CR0 4YY

Contents

Foreword
Nadia Abu El-Haj

July 24, 2023: The Israeli Knesset passes a bill that eliminates the "reasonableness standard," that is, an Anglo legal concept that grants the High Court discretion to strike down government decisions and appointments it deems unreasonable. The first step in a broader judicial overhaul championed by the most right-wing ruling coalition in Israeli history, the entire opposition—fifty-six members of the Knesset—boycotted the vote. According to the *New York Times*, among many other English- and Hebrew-language publications, this bill and the larger judicial overhaul of which it is a part threatens to undermine "Israeli democracy." Secular, liberal citizens who have overtaken the streets over the past several months are fighting, we are told, to save Israel's soul.[1]

What if, however, this right-wing "turn" is better understood as the logical culmination of a state that, since its very establishment, has never been able to reconcile its "Jewish" and "democratic" commitments? A settler nation-state founded upon the expulsion of approximately 750,000 Palestinian inhabitants, *Jewish* democracy was predicated on ethnic cleansing. That act was necessitated by the Zionist commitment to establishing a Jewish state: How else would one possibly establish a Jewish majority? What's more, what if its non-Jewish—that is, its Palestinian—citizens, have never been and can never be equal members of a Jewish state? And what if, after over fifty years of ruling over Palestinian *subjects*—military rule and siege over the territories occupied in 1967—Israel's very soul, its institutional and juridical core, is better described as foundationally antidemocratic?

As covered in the US press, the current Israeli political crisis is but one more instance of a more general shift toward right-wing, (proto-) fascist, and antidemocratic political movements throughout the Euro-American world. Writing from my home in New York, the slide into illiberalism and the threats to democratic institutions are on full display, here at home and not just elsewhere. And yet, I want to insist, what is unfolding in Israel should not be integrated, and certainly not seamlessly, into this larger global trend. Israel is not and has never been a democratic state.

Israel is not the state of its citizens. As a Jewish state, a fundamental distinction cleaves the contours of citizenship. While upon its establishment, the state declared it would protect the "religious" and "cultural" rights of its "minority" citizens, Israel was established as the "national home" of "the Jewish people," wherever in the world they reside. Today, with approximately 20 percent of its citizenry Palestinian, with its military rule over nearly 5 million Palestinian subjects who enjoy none of the rights or protections of even an unequal citizenship—and with 68 percent of Palestinian refugees having no right of return—that foundational principle endures. In July 2018 the Israeli Knesset passed a new "Basic Law" that more than just perpetuates but absolutely enshrines Israel as "the Nation-State of the Jewish People."[2] Among other provisions, the law states that "the right to national self-determination" in Israel is "exclusive to the Jewish people"; what's more, it declares, "the state views the development of Jewish settlement as a national value, and shall act to encourage and promote its establishment and consolidation."[3] In response to legal challenges that argued the law is racist and antidemocratic, in 2021, the High Court—that very court purportedly essential to safeguarding Israel's "democratic" character—ruled it constitutional, that is, one presumes, "reasonable."

Israel should not be described as a democracy, "flawed as it may be," now under threat from the right.[4] Structural racism is not unique to the Israeli state, of course. But in comparison to those Euro-American liberal democracies with which Israel is generally compared, there is a cardinal, material difference: racial inequality is written into the law. More accurately, it is written into two separate legal regimes—one civil and one military—both of which differentially govern Palestinian and Jewish citizens and subjects who reside in territories under the state's control. That is why in 2021 and 2022, Human Rights Watch, Amnesty International—as well as the Israeli human rights groups B'Tselem and Yesh Din—declared Israel an apartheid state.[5]

The vast majority of Jewish-Israelis protesting the judicial overhaul are worried, primarily, about threats to their own rights (and driven by an interest in the division of resources among the state's Jewish citizenry)—that is, as secular liberals, as women, as LGBTQ+ persons. What is more, the protest leaders are doing their best to exclude any signs of Palestinian identity and politics from the demonstrations. Whatever the "soul" of Israel's "liberal democracy" refers to, it does not include Palestinians—and the myriad political demands and imaginaries that comprise Palestinian politics.[6] But what if we put the Question of Palestine at the center of what is at stake? What if realizing a democratic state is impossible without grappling with the fact that Israel is a settler nation still in the "frontier stage" of settlement? In a speech before the Knesset in advance of the vote on the reasonableness standard, the minister of justice—Yariv Levin—listed five government decisions the High Court had struck down using that standard: all of them "were about Palestinians and the occupation." As Ben Reiff reports, this should come as no surprise. Levin has spoken previously about the need to "diminish the power of the judiciary" in order to realize the annexation of the Occupied Territories. In short, as Reiff puts it, this is the "judicial overhaul's endgame."[7] There is no "democratic Israel" that can be pried apart from the question of Palestine: this is a settler state. Its foundational commitments and acts—built into its enduring Zionist political imaginary and the operation of its institutions and political parties, liberal and illiberal alike—are racist and antidemocratic down to their very core. At least, that is, if one acknowledges that the lives of Palestinians, both citizens and subjects, and not just the state's Jewish citizens, should be matters of political and ethical concern.

What then might any of this have to do with the topic of Maya Wind's *Towers of Ivory and Steel*? Let me quote from her introduction: "For decades, Israeli universities have been widely celebrated in the West as exceptionally free. European and North American academic institutions maintain research collaborations and joint degree programs with Israeli universities, which are often the only such academic partnerships in the Middle East." But what if they are not "exceptionally free"? What if Israeli universities, far from being bastions of pluralism, academic freedom, and spaces for open political dissent, are in fact "complicit in the violation of Palestinian rights?" Taking advantage of her position as a Jewish-Israeli citizen to gain access to Israeli universities, state and military archives, and libraries, Wind has collected, translated, and analyzed data essential to answering that question. An unparalleled and exceptional book that delves deeply into the history and modus operandi of some of Israel's most vaunted liberal institutions, the result is an empirically robust case for the myriad ways in which such depictions are patently untrue. There is no "institutional innocence" here.

No university is an Ivory Tower—severed from the historical, political, and economic conditions of the state and society in which it exists. Nevertheless, working within what is now widely recognized as an apartheid regime, the close ties between Israeli universities and the state—and the consequences of those ties—take, as Wind masterfully demonstrates, a distinctive form. Beginning in 1918 with the establishment of Hebrew University, the first of the now eight major public institutions of higher learning, these universities have been an integral part of building and maintaining the state as the Jewish national home—including, quite centrally, through technologies and strategies of war, ethnic cleansing, occupation, and siege (see chapter 2). Not only have Palestinian students who are citizens of Israel been structurally marginalized and discriminated against, the universities often do the work of the state itself: they crack down on Palestinian student speech and organizations in the name of "security" (see chapter 5). What's more, they house academic programs tailored to train soldiers and security forces. This is not the equivalent of military personnel enrolling for a university degree on an American university campus, nor, for that matter, is it equivalent to the presence of

ROTC. This is more like having West Point embedded within a US university—an embedding, it is worth highlighting, that "requires" the university, among other things, to establish security zones within the dorms that house such personnel (chapters 1 and 3). For their part, Palestinian universities are subjected to both bureaucratic and military control: the Israeli state determines the number of foreign faculty and students allowed to teach and study at Palestinian universities, and vets them (on political grounds) before granting visas. Universities in Gaza, the strip itself under continuous siege, are cut off from the outside world almost entirely and exposed, over and over again, to aerial bombardment. For their part, Palestinian universities throughout the West Bank, including East Jerusalem, are repeatedly subjected to closures and raids, with their students and faculty arrested and, often, subjected to torture while in detention (chapter 6). Meanwhile, not only do the vast majority of Israeli academics remain silent, so too does the university leadership. There is absolutely no institutional defense of academic freedom when it comes to Palestinian universities. And in the midst of the escalating violence of what is closing in on a sixty-year "occupation," not a single university has severed ties with Israeli military or security forces, let alone with Israel's arms industry (chapters 3 and 6).

July 23, 2023: The American Anthropological Association announces passage of a resolution to boycott Israeli academic institutions by a 71 percent margin.

The law striking down the "reasonableness standard," the AAA's boycott vote: these two events happened on the same day. I juxtapose them here not because I harbor any illusions regarding their respective political impacts. I juxtapose them, rather, because of the nature of the discourse mobilized against heeding the call for a boycott of Israeli academic institutions, in the US and elsewhere—that is, the argument that Israel is a secular democratic state, far less oppressive than many other regimes worldwide. In short, Why "single out" Israel? Such political what-about-ism, as should be apparent to anyone paying attention, is but a tactic to derail Palestinian resistance to the Israeli state. No political project—not ever, not anywhere—has addressed every single possible cause at one and the same time. That is not the nature of politics. The substantive—the more sincere—question is: "Are Israeli universities complicit in the violation of Palestinian rights?" as Wind asks. This expansively researched, empirically detailed, carefully argued book provides a clear answer: "Yes." As demonstrated by the American Anthropological Association's recent vote, the international academic community is recognizing, increasingly, the deep entrenchment and complicity of Israeli universities with Israel's ongoing and fundamentally antidemocratic project of settlement and apartheid. And it is coming to the conclusion that continuing to conduct business as usual with Israeli universities is, decidedly, "unreasonable." To those—liberals and conservatives, on the left and on the right—who oppose the call for an academic boycott, I ask: Is there any Palestinian resistance movement that you might ever—or that you have ever—recognized as legitimate?

Introduction

On the gray afternoon of January 10, 2022, a windowless white van with a Palestinian license plate drove onto the campus of Birzeit University, north of Ramallah in the occupied West Bank. Once the van had cleared the east campus gate, two men in jeans and hooded sweatshirts emerged from the front doors. They began making their way to a meeting of the student council, where the elected heads of the various student blocs were in attendance. Then, suddenly, the back doors of the van swung open, and Israeli uniformed soldiers leapt out—some from the special forces in dark ski masks—armed with semiautomatic weapons. They quickly followed in the footsteps of the two undercover Israeli soldiers and opened gunfire.

Chaos broke out as the students tried to disperse, but the soldiers knew exactly who they were after. They slammed four student association leaders onto the ground. There they lay, face down, as they were handcuffed, blindfolded, and beaten. Other soldiers were directed to aim their rifles at the perimeter of the scene, as students tried to document what was unfolding on their campus in broad daylight.

One of the leading student organizers, Ismail Barghouthi, scrambled up the closed university gate to escape. But soldiers targeted him and shot him in the thigh. He was seized, along with four other students, and taken away in the white van, leaving behind a pool of blood on the asphalt beneath the campus east gate.[1]

The five students were brought to the Ofer military detention center in the occupied West Bank, where they were interrogated for hours by Israeli officers. Three students were released, but Barghouthi and his peer Mohammed Khatib remained in detention.[2] Barghouthi and Khatib were indicted by the Israeli military court system for their activities in their respective student groups, which Israel termed "unauthorized associations."[3] While his case was processed, Barghouthi was detained for weeks. Meanwhile, Khatib was placed under administrative detention—by which Palestinians can be indefinitely incarcerated in Israeli military prisons without charge or trial—for months, until May 2022.[4]

Barghouthi and Khatib are among dozens of Palestinian university students abducted and detained by Israel every year in the Occupied Palestinian Territory (OPT), for membership or activities in 1 of the 411 student associations Israel has deemed "unlawful."[5] They were among the fifty-four Palestinian students incarcerated in 2022 alone.[6]

Just months after the raid on Birzeit University, on April 17, 2022, a demonstration was held near the Tel Aviv University campus, outside the offices of the Israeli Security Agency, the Shin Bet. Organized for Palestinian Prisoner's Day, the protest was held in solidarity with Palestinian prisoners under administrative detention.

Rami Salman, a Palestinian Tel Aviv University student, made his way to the demonstration. A citizen of Israel, Salman wore a kaffiyeh and stood alongside dozens of Palestinian and Jewish-Israeli citizen activists calling for an end to the authoritarian practice of student detention in the OPT.[7] After the protest, Salman headed back to his dorm, located opposite the Shin Bet offices.

He didn't make it far. Salman was followed to the university by Israeli undercover police officers. He was seized on the stairs to his dorm building, beaten, and dragged to his arrest.[8]

Across all the territories under Israeli governance, the university campus is not a safe space for Palestinian students. Israeli universities are not independent of the Israeli security state but, rather, serve as an extension of its violence.

Salman's own institution, Tel Aviv University, announced in July 2023 that it is embarking on yet another partnership with the Israeli military. The university had won the Ministry of Defense bid to house the prestigious "Erez" BA program for officers in combat military units. The dual-major degree includes an academic program focused on military "areas of interest," paired with another program in the humanities, social sciences, business, or engineering.[9] In the Erez program, the military explains, "military and academic training are intertwined," wherein the cadets are transformed "from civilians to elite fighters."[10]

Accompanying the prestige—and substantial state funding—is a fifty-three-page list of conditions from the Ministry of Defense agreement, which Tel Aviv University signed upon winning the bid. The soldiers will be in uniform and permitted to carry their military weapons to campus. They will study most courses alongside civilian students, except for their tailored nonacademic military courses—offered on campus and taught by senior military personnel—which also earn them credit toward their degree. For the academic courses offered by the university to soldiers and civilians alike, the Ministry of Defense suggested a list of topics that they consider "integral" to the Erez program. These include "strategy and national security," "terror and guerrillas," and "contemporary military thought."[11]

Per the agreement with the state, the university commits to reporting to the military any and all "field security issues," should it be required. And, crucially, faculty must now conduct themselves in accordance with military restrictions. The university, the agreement demands, "undertakes to ensure that the academic staff will refrain from offensive statements toward the IDF soldiers studying at the institution, whether it is statements concerning their actual military service in the IDF or whether it is statements concerning them wearing uniforms. This commitment is essential."[12]

Not only, then, will Tel Aviv University take on the additional qualities of a military base, it will now become further embedded in the state apparatuses that sustain the occupation. Armed with military training and a Tel Aviv University degree, combat officers will go on to maintain Israeli military rule and a system of racial oppression over millions of

Palestinians, including university students—like Barghouthi, Khatib, and Salman.

For decades, Israeli universities have been widely celebrated in the West as exceptionally free. European and North American academic institutions maintain research collaborations and joint degree programs with Israeli universities, which are often the only such academic partnerships in the Middle East. Upon launching a dual degree program with Tel Aviv University in 2020—the only such program it offers in the region—Columbia University advertised its Israeli counterpart as one that "shares Tel Aviv's unshakable spirit of openness and innovation—and boasts a campus life as dynamic and pluralistic as the metropolis itself."[13] Speaking at an advocacy summit to grow support for Israel among American college students, Columbia University president and First Amendment scholar Lee Bollinger declared:

> We are committed to cooperating with partners in Israel, to learn from them and to foster global conversations, through which students and universities can help to shape all societies. Experiencing different perspectives, of course, deepens our understanding of different narratives, and also we understand how countries manage everything from pluralism and conflict to illness and drought—all universal issues.[14]

Columbia is not alone in characterizing Israeli universities as liberal bastions of pluralism and democracy, uniquely worthy of academic partnerships in the broader landscape of the Middle East.[15] In 2022, the US-based Freedom House scored Israeli academic freedom as 3 out of 4, contending that "Israel's universities have long been centers for dissent and are open to all students."[16] That same year, the European-based Varieties of Democracy Institute ranked Israel as among the top 10 percent of countries in the world for academic freedom.[17] These assessments mirror Israeli academia's self-narration, as one of "unwavering and unparalleled commitment to excellence, multiculturalism, pluralism, and the cause of peace."[18]

This apparent Western consensus has, however, been questioned by Palestinians. In 2004, academics and intellectuals launched the Palestinian Campaign for the Academic and Cultural Boycott of Israel (PACBI) and called on international scholars to initiate a boycott of Israeli academic institutions. They explained their call to target Israeli universities on the grounds of decades of ongoing institutional complicity in Israel's "regime of oppression" against Palestinians. Israeli institutions of higher education, PACBI contends, "have played a key role in planning, implementing and justifying Israel's occupation and apartheid policies."[19] For PACBI, the academic boycott is not merely a means to an end but rather a strategic targeting of the Israeli academy as "one of the pillars of this oppressive order."[20]

Shortly thereafter, in 2005, 170 Palestinian civil society groups—including trade unions, refugee rights associations, women's organizations, grassroots popular committees, and NGO networks—came together to launch the Boycott, Divestment, and Sanctions (BDS) movement. Inspired by the South African movement against apartheid, Palestinians call for BDS as a means to exert pressure on Israel to meet the three core demands of Palestinian civil society, as stipulated in international law and UN resolutions: first, end the colonization of Arab lands and dismantle the military occupation and the wall; second, recognize the right to full equality of Palestinian citizens of Israel; and third, respect and promote the right of Palestinian refugees to return.[21]

Many in the international community have responded to this call. In North America, some academic associations have adopted BDS resolutions over the last decade, including the American Anthropological Association, the American Studies Association, the Middle East Studies Association, and the Native American and Indigenous Studies Association. So, too, have faculty and graduate student unions, including UAW Local 2865, the University of California student worker union; UAW Local 2110, New York University's graduate student organizing committee; and the University of Toronto Graduate Students' Union.[22] In Europe, the Teachers' Union of Ireland, the British Society for Middle Eastern Studies, and the UK National Union of Students, among others, have voted to endorse the boycott.[23] Sustained by broad coalitions and endorsed in votes on thoroughly debated resolutions, the academic boycott is gaining traction worldwide.

The backlash to this growing movement has been severe. The Israeli government and international Zionist organizations have used lawsuits, lobbying, legislation, and what activists and civil rights organizations call "intimidation and smear campaigns" to intercept, demonize, or even criminalize the movement wherever it gains momentum.[24] The debate over the academic boycott has roiled universities across Europe, North America, Australia, and South Africa and has become central to discussions about race, justice, and the meaning of academic freedom in higher education.

With rare exceptions, Israeli academics have responded to PACBI's campaign with overwhelming and often indignant opposition. From across the Israeli political spectrum, faculty have formed well-coordinated counter-campaigns to any initiative to support the boycott, often backed by funding and talking points provided by the Israeli state itself.[25]

These Israeli scholars—representing Israeli state arguments in international academia's court of public opinion—have by and large converged on a similar refrain: *Injustices committed against Palestinians may or may not exist; but even if they did, this has nothing to do with us.* Writing in opposition to the first referendum on the academic boycott by the American Anthropological Association in 2015, leading Israeli anthropologist Dan Rabinowitz published his outward-facing apologia for Israeli higher education in the English edition of *Ha'aretz*. "Israel does inflict injustices on Palestinians," he wrote, "but making universities accountable for them is ludicrous."[26]

This claim by Israeli scholars that they are but bystanders has become central to their opposition strategy, especially with rising worldwide support for the academic boycott. Anticipating the passage of the resolution to endorse the boycott by the Middle East Studies Association of North America (MESA) in 2022, Israeli academics built their case on both institutional and individual innocence. The Middle East and Islamic Studies Association of Israel asserted that the group is "apolitical" and that Israeli universities are, likewise, not responsible for government policy. Meanwhile, the Association for Israel Studies implored MESA not to "punish" Israeli academics for mere "guilt by association."[27]

Having declared that their universities and academic associations play no part in Israel's oppression of Palestinians—"even if" such oppression existed—Israeli academics have swiftly moved to claim that, in fact, *they* are the ones being repressed. Israeli academics thereby subvert the argument for Palestinian rights—and, specifically, the academic rights of Palestinian scholars and students—for their own ends. At risk of violation, they argue, are the academic freedom and rights of individual Israeli scholars, wrongfully held accountable for injustices for which they bear no responsibility. This claim misrepresents PACBI's call to boycott Israeli academic institutions and not individual scholars. Yet the absolute majority of Israeli academics continue to rally against what they insist is directed at them on a personal basis.[28]

As the debates about the academic boycott have expanded in the Western academic arena, certain Israeli scholars have emerged as particularly effective gatekeepers of the conversation. Curiously, these scholars are often "self-styled progressives" who argue—for an international audience—that they support Palestinian rights yet oppose the academic boycott. In fact, self-identified progressive Israeli scholars and associations frequently hinge their opposition based on this very identification.[29] "Most of the humanistic and dissident voices in Israel," argued anthropologist Baruch Kimmerling, "sound from the ranks of the academy, or are supported by its faculty members."[30] While admitting that not all members of the Israeli academy can be counted among supporters of Palestinian rights, Kimmerling nevertheless insisted that the international academic community refrain from enacting the boycott, so as to safeguard Israeli universities as a platform for progressive mobilization.[31] Most recently, in 2023, the Israeli Anthropological Association came out in opposition to the second referendum on the academic boycott at the American Anthropological Association, claiming it would be counterproductive to boycott Israeli universities that are, in fact, "at the forefront of the struggle to maintain democracy and equal rights."[32]

Liberal Israeli scholars, then, join with their right-wing compatriots in their opposition to the academic boycott, arguing that Israeli universities and their faculty are being mistakenly—and therefore unjustly—targeted. They do so based on the foundational claim that Israeli universities must be institutionally distinguished from the Israeli state. For too long, the Western academic community has taken these claims at face value.

This book therefore begins with the question posed by Palestinian civil society, and which Israeli academia has endeavored to foreclose: Are Israeli universities complicit in the violation of Palestinian rights?

The book seeks to answer this question by revealing how Israeli universities are entangled with Israeli systems of oppression. It does so by drawing on the extensive research conducted by Palestinian scholars and civil society organizations, as well as by making the evaluation of the data about the complicity of Israeli universities—which has been kept principally as an internal Jewish-Israeli conversation—subject to international debate.[33]

My position as a white, Jewish-Israeli citizen awarded me ready access to Israeli state and military archives and libraries, where I read official policy documents, state and military memos, government-sponsored research reports, newspapers, books from Israeli academic presses, and unpublished master's and doctoral theses approved by the Israeli universities themselves. This vast trove of papers demonstrates, in great detail, Israeli universities' many ties to the Israeli state, including to its apparatuses of violence. It offers abundant data about the theories, expertise, infrastructure, and technologies developed in and through Israeli universities to support Israeli territorial, demographic, and military projects. Yet, such archives exist almost exclusively in Hebrew and remain mostly inaccessible to audiences outside of Israel. This book, then, translates, synthesizes, and critically analyzes this data and existing research to make it more widely accessible to the international academic community.

My status enabled me to enter Israeli universities and observe conferences and events across campuses. There I could witness the terms under which the discourse on Palestine and Palestinians develops and unfolds, and how Palestinian and critical Jewish-Israeli students and faculty navigate university life and politics. I conducted interviews with Palestinian students and Palestinian and Jewish-Israeli faculty, many of whom were willing to share their experiences and analyses. Yet they consistently asked to have their names withheld for fear of retaliation both within and outside their universities. Honoring this request, I omit identifying information and use pseudonyms whenever quoting or directly drawing on interviews. In the process of research and writing, I also engaged the analyses of Palestinian student organizers, many of whom advocate for transparency about their universities to help build the international pressure that they believe—in contrast with the Jewish-Israeli "self-styled progressives" gatekeeping their opinions from international discourse—is required for these institutions to be decolonized and remade.

This book also draws on critical Palestinian and Jewish-Israeli academic scholarship on the Israeli system of higher education. Palestinian scholars have been interrogating Israeli universities for decades. They have studied and analyzed the limits imposed on Palestinian knowledge production, pedagogy, and expression on Israeli campuses, as well as Israeli violations of the right to education of millions of Palestinians living under military occupation.[34] This analysis has been built upon by several Jewish-Israeli scholars, who have critically examined the universities designed for their own benefit, as well as the mechanisms by which both Palestinian and Jewish anticolonial thought was excluded from academic spaces.[35] This book, a comprehensive study of the Israeli university, builds on this rich body of work to demonstrate the complicity of Israeli institutions of higher education in Israel's projects of settler colonialism and apartheid.

On Apartheid and the Academic Boycott

After decades of sustained research and advocacy by Palestinian scholars, activists, and human rights and civil society organizations, there is growing worldwide recognition of the Israeli regime of apartheid imposed over the Palestinian people.[36] In 2021, Human Rights Watch issued a detailed report concluding that the actions of the Israeli state—the systemic oppression of Palestinians across Israel and in the OPT, the inhumane acts committed against them, and the intent to maintain this domination—together constitute the crimes against humanity of apartheid and persecution.[37] This was followed in 2022 by an Amnesty International report, which likewise determined that Israel operates a system of apartheid against the entire Palestinian people, including refugees, and called for pressure by the international community to dismantle it.[38] Even major Israeli human rights organizations B'Tselem and Yesh Din issued reports recognizing, albeit within their own conceptual limitations, Israel's regime of apartheid.[39]

Leading Palestinian human rights organization Al-Haq has documented an increase in discussions of Israeli apartheid in the United Nations Human Right Council (UNHRC), and growing official recognition of Israeli apartheid by state governments, such as South Africa and Namibia.[40] Notably, the UNHRC Commission of Inquiry's first report on Israeli discrimination against Palestinian citizens of Israel, Palestinians in the OPT, and Palestinian refugees and exiles abroad, also cited the 1973 International Convention on the Suppression and Punishment of the Crime of Apartheid.[41]

On the heels of this emerging consensus, there is growing recognition in the international community of how Israeli practices are rooted in settler colonialism. This is evident in the 2022 report of Michael Lynk, former UN special rapporteur of human rights in the Palestinian Territory occupied since 1967. In his report, Lynk determined that Israel's political system in the OPT qualifies as apartheid, which, he acknowledged, directly resulted from Israel's settler-colonial project in the West Bank, including East Jerusalem.[42] The current UN special rapporteur, Francesca Albanese, similarly noted that Israel's practice of intentionally seizing Palestinian land and seeking to replace indigenous Palestinians with Jewish-Israelis in the OPT is not only a war crime under the Rome Statute, but a "hallmark of settler colonialism."[43] Albanese concluded that the comprehensive view of Israeli practices of apartheid required recognition of its settler-colonial "root causes."[44] Building on years of research and advocacy by Palestinian scholars, legal experts, and civil society organizations, Al-Haq in 2022 detailed in a comprehensive report how Israeli military occupation and apartheid are tools of Israel's decades-long project of settler colonialism. Palestinian civil society coalitions argue that Israeli apartheid cannot be fully dismantled without recognition of Israeli settler colonialism, which they regard to be as old as the Israeli state, and are calling for the academic boycott as an essential step toward decolonization.[45]

In January 2023, the Palestine Liberation Organization (PLO) joined the BDS Movement, the Palestinian NGO Network, the Palestinian Ministry of Justice, and the Palestinian Human Rights Organizations Council to issue a historic anti-apartheid statement and call to action. Collectively, they called for building a global front to end Israeli settler colonialism, apartheid, and occupation and advocated for Palestinian rights as stipulated in international law and UN resolutions.[46] This broad Palestinian coalition explained apartheid as both a tool and manifestation of Israeli settler colonialism, which must be dismantled so that Palestinians can exercise their inalienable rights, as stipulated in international law. They called on the international community to participate in the BDS movement, including the sanctioning of complicit Israeli academic institutions.[47]

Palestinian civil society has thus drawn for Israeli universities a clear road map to decolonization. They have called on the international community to guide its implementation by at the very least "ending complicity" in the system of oppression.

Yet despite repeated calls by Palestinians to hold accountable the very institutions implicated in Israeli violations of international law, even the growing global recognition of Israeli settler colonialism and apartheid often overlooks Israeli universities. This book intends to contribute to international conversations about holding Israeli universities accountable, by documenting the material ways in which they are implicated in the systemic violation of Palestinian rights and academic freedom. Israeli universities have often been exceptionalized by scholars in the Western-dominated academic community and have been shielded from many of the criticisms directed at peer institutions in other settler states. Yet it is precisely in this that Israeli universities stand apart. As academic institutions directly and actively implicated in what has overwhelmingly been recognized as a regime of apartheid, Israeli universities are continually exempted, or "singled out," from the Palestinian demands for justice.

This exemption is all the more striking considering the degree to which Israeli universities are embedded in the Israeli state's systems of oppression and racial domination against Palestinians. Tel Aviv University's Erez program and institutional ties to the Israeli security state are by no means exceptional. There are eight major public Israeli universities. They are all directly governed by the Israeli Council for Higher Education and largely funded by its Planning and Budgeting Committee.[48] As this book will show, all eight universities operate in direct service of the state and serve critical functions in sustaining its policies, and thereby constitute central pillars of Israeli settler colonialism.

The Settler University

Settler-colonial states are founded through foreign invasion, with the objective of eliminating Native inhabitants and establishing a settler nation on Native land. Settlers seek to replace the Natives and claim the territory as their own.[49] Settler colonialism is therefore understood as a distinct form of colonial governance, because it centers domination over land, which, in effect, becomes domination over life. To maintain their settler state and make the place their home, settlers must continually reassert their exclusive claim to the land, making the violent campaign to disappear the land's Indigenous peoples into an *ongoing* process of invasion and dispossession rather than a single or historical event.[50] As Audra Simpson illuminates, this settling of land and of consciousness continually builds "moral and political worlds," as well as physical ones, "atop the worlds of others."[51]

The logic of elimination and replacement that typifies settler-colonial states is constitutive of the Zionist movement and the Israeli state.[52] The stated mission of the Zionist movement was to settle in historic Palestine and establish a Jewish majority as the basis for a Jewish state. From the dawn of the movement and for decades afterward, Zionist leaders, organizations, and institutions openly called their project the "coloniza-tion" of Palestine.[53] For Zionist leaders and later for the Israeli govern-ment, this has entailed pursuing a deliberate strategy of Jewish migration and settlement, with the aim of expelling the indigenous Palestinians and altering the land's racial composition. The planned and incremental dispossession of Palestinians by the Zionist movement over half a century was consolidated and accelerated with the 1948 mass expulsion during the establishment of Israel, what Palestinians call the Nakba (catastro-phe).[54] With Israel's founding, the state continued this territorial and demographic program of replacement, officially terming it "Judaization."[55] In the decades since, Israel has worked to maintain a demographic supe-riority and population distribution, so as to undermine Palestinian claims to their lands and to self-determination.[56]

From the start, Israeli academia has been entangled in this territorial project of replacement central to Israeli state building. Indeed, before even the founding of Israel, the Zionist movement founded three univer-sities, which were explicitly to serve the movement's territorial objectives in Palestine. First, in 1918, Hebrew University was established as a comprehensive university and center for the formation of a new collec-tive Jewish-Zionist identity and nation. Founded at the apex of Mt. Scopus, it was also built as a strategic outpost for the Zionist movement to stake symbolic and political claim to Jerusalem.[57] Likewise, the Technion in Haifa and the Weizmann Institute in Rehovot were estab-lished to advance the scientific and technological development of Israel as a Jewish state in historic Palestine.[58]

In the lead-up to the 1948 war, these three institutions of higher education were directly recruited to support the violent dispossession required for Zionist territorial expansion. The leading Zionist militia, the Haganah, established a Science Corps, which opened bases on all three campuses to research and refine military capabilities. Throughout the 1948 war, the universities helped sustain the Haganah and other militias in their mass expulsion of Palestinians to establish the state of Israel.[59] Faculty and students developed and manufactured weapons, as their campuses, equipment, and expertise were put to the service of Zionist militias. With the establishment of Israel, the Technion and the

Weizmann Institute came to anchor the state's scientific-military capabilities (chapter 3).[60]

Over the state's first two decades, prominent academics further aligned with political leaders, and the government consolidated its power over higher education.[61] By the late 1960s, Israel's "Judaization" program had expanded on multiple frontiers. Now, new Israeli universities were built to anchor this territorial and demographic project, their campuses constructed as strategic regional outposts that impelled both Palestinian enclosure and Jewish settlement expansion.

In the largest city of the Palestinian-majority Galilee, Israel developed and granted full accreditation to the University of Haifa in 1972. That same year, Israel built Ben-Gurion University in the center of the Naqab (Negev), the region most sparsely populated by Jewish-Israelis. Israeli universities created facts on the ground in the form of permanent Jewish settlements in the OPT after 1967. Hebrew University expanded its Mt. Scopus campus into occupied East Jerusalem, while Ariel University received full accreditation in 2012 as the newest Israeli university in the occupied West Bank. Across their localities, these universities were planned and built to serve as pillars of regional demographic engineering (chapter 2).

The 1967 occupation of the Gaza Strip and West Bank, including East Jerusalem, further entrenched how academia produced expertise on behalf of Israeli military governance. Claiming new territory while differentially ruling Jewish and Palestinian citizens, as well as Palestinian subjects living under military occupation, required new and expanded capabilities. Diverse academic disciplines immediately stepped in to produce this knowledge for use by the Israeli state, and in so doing expanded their own scholarly frontiers. Archaeology, legal studies, and Middle East studies, among other fields in Israeli academia, continue to serve the state and its maintenance of a regime of apartheid (chapter 1).

Israeli academic knowledge production developed through ties to the Israeli government and military in the OPT and was often itself steered toward direct military applications. Israeli universities designed—and continue to run—tailored academic programs to train soldiers and security forces to carry out their work and to enhance their operations. The development of Israeli higher education was imbricated with the rise of Israeli military industries, and Israeli universities still sustain them. Rafael and Israeli Aerospace Industries, two of Israel's largest weapons producers, developed out of infrastructure laid by the Weizmann Institute and the Technion. Today, Israeli universities collaborate with Israeli weapons corporations to research and develop technology that is used by the Israeli military and security state in the OPT. This technology is later sold abroad as field-tested or "battle proven" (chapter 3).

The institutional commitment of Israeli universities to the state have profoundly shaped the opportunities and experiences of their Palestinian faculty and junior scholars. After decades where critical research was foreclosed, in the 1980s and 1990s, Palestinian and some Jewish-Israeli scholars created new openings to explore the histories and structures of violence and oppression of the Israeli state. This scholarship and the foundational debates it instigated were immediately marked as out of bounds, with researchers and faculty facing harassment and silencing campaigns. This backlash has escalated over the past two decades, as university administrations aligned with the state and Israeli far-right groups to more narrowly define permissible research, teaching, and discourse on their campuses (chapter 4).

Palestinian students, too, are deeply affected. From its founding, Israel has limited Palestinian citizen access to education, and universities have restrained and conditioned Palestinian enrollment.[62] University administrations continue to curtail Palestinian presence and learning on their campuses, and persistently collaborate with the Israeli government in repressing their Palestinian students, and particularly student organizers (chapter 5). Israeli universities violate the foundational academic freedoms of their Palestinian and critical Jewish-Israeli faculty and students, excluding knowledge production, pedagogies, and expression that challenge the systems of oppression unfolding daily just beyond and within their campuses.

In the OPT, Palestinian higher education has long been under Israeli siege and, currently, is under escalating attack. Since their establishment, Palestinian universities have been governed by the Israeli military, subjugated by the state to prevent them from becoming sites of Palestinian resistance. In the occupied West Bank, including East Jerusalem, Palestinian universities are subjected to bureaucratic restrictions that isolate and obstruct them, as well as recurrent military closures and raids, and the abduction, detention, and torture of faculty and students. In the Gaza Strip, Palestinian universities have been subject to Israeli aerial bombardment and remain suffocated under an illegal blockade. Far from defending the academic freedoms of faculty and students in the OPT, Israeli universities continue to sustain the military system that rules them and to subdue Palestinian student mobilization for liberation and true equality on their own campuses (chapter 6).

Together, the chapters in this book document how Israeli universities actively sustain Israeli settler colonialism, military occupation, and apartheid, as well as their own complicity in the ongoing violation of Palestinian rights as recognized under international law. It is on the basis of these universities' collaboration with the Israeli state that Palestinian civil society, including the Palestinian Federation of Unions of University Professors and Employees, has called for the international community to enact the academic boycott.[63]

Israeli academics are frequently incensed at the BDS movement's call for accountability. They refuse to accept that Palestinian scholars and civil society leaders are making demands on them and consistently foreclose the very conversations that the Israeli academy should instead be undertaking: how to remake their universities as institutions working against—and not in service of—Israeli settler colonialism and apartheid.[64]

These are undoubtedly challenging conversations to initiate, as is always the case when grappling with accountability for violence committed onto others. But as Eve Tuck and K. Wang Yang argue, "decolonization is not a metaphor." The decolonization of universities is and should be unsettling.[65] In the face of the boycott, Israeli academics consistently make "settler moves to innocence"—that is, actions that preserve the structure of the settler state and the violence that sustains it—while denying that they bear any responsibility for their universities' role in violating Palestinian rights.[66] But as Indigenous and other scholars of settler colonialism have shown, colonial education systems are structurally sustained by the scholars who work within them. Inhabiting the settler university, Suriamurthee Moonsamy Maistry argues, is a "state of complicity by default."[67] As scholars of education demonstrate, academics are not "innocent of power" nor exterior to the conditions that make their institutions.[68] They are implicated in perpetuating the coloniality of their universities and cannot simply opt out of this complicity.[69]

Israeli scholars, then, bear structural individual responsibility for their universities. Even so, the Palestinian call for boycott is directed only at institutions. The BDS call has, in fact, extended an "unambiguous invitation" to conscientious Israeli academics to become active participants and partners in the struggle for Palestinian liberation.[70]

In the tradition of the African National Congress in South Africa and other Indigenous movements across the world, Palestinians are holding Israeli universities accountable for sustaining the violent settler regime that rules, dispossesses, and subjugates them. In South Africa, some white faculty and students heeded the call from the ANC—echoed by the international community—and demanded that their universities sever their ties with the apartheid regime and take meaningful steps toward decolonization.[71] Palestinians are calling on scholars across the world to guide Israeli academics to demand the same.

PART I
Complicity

1

Expertise of Subjugation

"We, in Israel, have a major role in developing the law in this area, because we are at the forefront of the fight against terrorism. This is gradually being accepted in both the world and the Israeli legal system . . . What we do becomes the law." —Professor Asa Kasher, Tel Aviv University[1]

"What we do today is a revision of international law, and if you do something long enough, then the world will accept it. All international law is based on the fact that an act that is forbidden today becomes permissible, if enough countries do it . . . When we started to define the conflict with the Palestinians as armed conflict, it was a dramatic switch . . . It took four months and four planes to change the United States's mind on the issue, and if it wasn't for those four planes I'm not sure we could develop the thesis of a war on terror to the dimensions we developed it today." —Daniel Reisner, former head of the Department of International Law, Advocate General's Corps[2]

On December 27, 2008, an Israeli targeted airstrike killed eighty-nine Palestinian police cadets during their graduation ceremony in the Gaza Strip.[3] This strike was no accident. It was planned for months in advance and discussed at length in the Israeli Military Advocate General's Corps, responsible for the rule of law in the Israeli military.[4] Specifically, the proposed airstrike was brought to the Corps' Department of International Law, which has increasingly played a key role in military decision-making, its jurists routinely advising senior Israeli commanders during the planning and execution of military operations. These military jurists thus not only offer legal advice, but shape how laws of war are interpreted and how military violence is waged.[5]

The Department of International Law approved the targeted airstrike, thus initiating Israel's 2008–9 offensive on the Gaza Strip. Under the leadership of Colonel Pnina Sharvit Baruch, department jurists had contended that the police cadets could be considered combatants and, therefore, legitimate targets, because they would likely be absorbed into military forces that fall under Hamas authority in fighting the impending Israeli military offensive.[6] The execution of the Israeli air strike itself, in other words, changed the designation of the cadets it targeted from civilians to combatants.[7] This argument has since been criticized by both international human rights organizations and legal scholars as unduly expanding the definition of legitimate targets and as an unusual if not improper reading of international humanitarian law.[8] Nevertheless, the department sent its jurists to the operation rooms on the Israeli designated border of the Gaza Strip for the remainder of the offensive, sanctioning tactics that were widely criticized by the international community as war crimes.[9]

Not even two weeks after a ceasefire was signed toward the end of the offensive, Tel Aviv University announced it had appointed Sharvit Baruch as a lecturer in its Faculty of Law. Moving directly from overseeing the 2008–9 offensive on the Gaza Strip, Sharvit Baruch was hired to teach a course on international law the following semester.[10] Sharvit Baruch's appointment to the Faculty of Law was broadly celebrated, except for opposition by a few university faculty and student groups who decried her role in sanctioning war crimes and compromising the academic integrity of legal studies.[11] Responding immediately to the criticism, Minister of Defense Ehud Barak contacted the university administration to support the appointment, and Prime Minister Ehud

Olmert preemptively threatened to withhold funding from universities that would reject faculty based on their work for the Israeli military.[12]

Meanwhile, Tel-Aviv University resolutely stood by the appointment and declared that "it does not intend to scrutinize or evaluate the legal, political, and moral positions of its teachers."[13] Yet the university administration did, in fact, evaluate and hire Sharvit Baruch precisely on the basis of her legal, political, and moral positions. She was hired because of this very expertise, which she gained exclusively during her service in the Military Advocate General's Corps.

In her transition from head of the Military Department of International Law to Tel Aviv University, Sharvit Baruch continued her service to the state. As a senior research fellow and director of the Law and National Security Program at the Institute for National Security Studies (INSS), she currently facilitates collaboration between military personnel and academics to develop interpretations of international law that defend Israeli military operations and policy. These interpretations include defenses of military tactics she personally oversaw.

During Sharvit Baruch's tenure, the Israeli military has legalized "roof knocking," a practice of shooting relatively smaller munitions at buildings, ostensibly to warn Palestinian civilians immediately before they are bombed. First put into practice during the 2008–9 offensive on the Gaza Strip, the Israeli military leadership hoped the accompanying legal framework offered by the Department of International Law would help clear it of accountability for subsequent Palestinian civilian casualties.[14] But "roof knocking" was deemed inadequate as a measure to protect civilians, and condemned by the UN and international human rights organizations.[15] Israel nevertheless continued extensively using this tactic in its subsequent offensives on the Gaza Strip in 2012, 2014, and 2021.[16] Even in the face of the international condemnations and investigations that followed, the INSS Law and National Security Program has continued to formulate legal defenses of "roof knocking" to sustain Israeli military doctrines.[17]

This chapter investigates how Israeli academic disciplines have developed in service of the Israeli government and security state, and, crucially, how they continue to materially support state projects. Dominant paradigms in diverse disciplines are entangled with, and structurally complicit in sustaining, Israeli apartheid and military occupation, and their ongoing infringements of Palestinian human rights. Leading departments and scholars across disciplines have subordinated their intellectual inquiry to the requirements of the Israeli state, as illuminated by three representative case studies.

First, the discipline of archaeology constructs evidence to support Israeli land claims through erasure of Arab and Muslim history, and substantiates Israeli use of excavations to expand Jewish settlement and expropriate Palestinian land. Second, legal studies—including ethics, law, and criminology—create a discursive and legal infrastructure to justify Israeli violations of international human rights law and the laws of war, continually developing legal interpretations that shield the Israeli state from accountability for its illegal military tactics and permanent military occupation. Third, Middle East studies produces racialized, militarized knowledge about the Middle East that offers a framework to legitimize Israeli violence against Palestinians, and commits regional and linguistic expertise and academic training to the Israeli military and security state. Through their structural ties and collaboration with the Israeli state, these disciplines have themselves become integral sites of knowledge production that maintain, develop, and refine Israel's systems of apartheid and military occupation.

Archaeology

On the night of August 6, 2022, Israeli soldiers drove into the Palestinian village of Susiya in the South Hebron Hills of the occupied West Bank. They handcuffed and blindfolded Nasser Nawaja, a longtime activist and advocate for Palestinian residents in the region. Soldiers took Nawaja to a military facility, where he was kept—still handcuffed and blindfolded— for twelve hours, before being brought in for interrogation with the Shin Bet. The Israeli officer asked Nawaja about his activism and demanded that he "stop causing trouble," before releasing him home.[18] Nawaja had been through this before. As a leading advocate against the planned expulsion of his community of over 350 Palestinian residents of Susiya, he has been routinely retaliated against by Israeli forces.[19] The primary reasoning behind the impending expulsion of Susiya residents: an Israeli archeological site on village lands.

At Susiya, archeological digs are used to service the expansion of Israeli military control and Jewish-Israeli settlement. Palestinians have lived in the village of Susiya since at least the early twentieth century; the Israeli military government itself initially recognized the village, as well as the documentation validating the Palestinian private ownership of much of its lands.[20] Yet under the aegis of archeological research—and with the aid of Israeli universities—this recognition has gradually been entirely rescinded.

Joint military and archeological surveys and mapping of the area around the village of Susiya began in 1969 and excavations commenced in 1971.[21] The digs were pioneered by the Institute of Archaeology at Hebrew University. The first Israeli academic archeological center, it was established as its own institute, with no coincidence, in the wake of Israel's occupation of Palestinian Territory in 1967.[22] Hebrew University archeologist Shmarya Guttman oversaw the digs, through which Israel claimed to have uncovered the ruins of a synagogue and a Jewish town that date back to the fourth century CE.[23]

Since the first digs at Susiya, archeological research and Jewish-Israeli settlement have expanded in tandem. Akiva London, who participated in the digs under Guttman and would later become an archeologist at Bar-Ilan University, returned to the area in 1981 as one of the founding members of the settlement Carmel overlooking Susiya. Recalling the decision to establish Carmel, London explained that he came to know the location through the archeological excavations and became concerned that the area was "entirely empty of Jewish settlement."[24] In 1983, following the expansion of excavations, Jewish settlers established a settlement adjacent to the archaeological site. In an attempt to erase the contemporary Palestinian village, they named the Jewish settlement Susya and declared that they were "reclaiming" Jewish presence on the land.[25] London was one of the leaders of the development of the archeological site at Susiya and later moved his family to the settlement of Susya.[26]

This explicit use of proximity to an archeological research site to expand settlement construction proved only the first step. In 1986, the Israeli military occupation administration, euphemistically called the Civil Administration, officially recognized Susya as a national archeological site. Following this decision, Israel expelled Palestinian residents of Susiya who had lived there for generations and transferred some of their privately owned lands to the jurisdiction of the settlement of Susya.[27]

Archeological excavation in Susiya led by Israeli academics has continued through the 1990s. The digs at the village of Susiya were expanded by the Israeli Antiquities Authority as well as by Hebrew University professors Yizhar Hirschfeld and Avraham Negev.[28] Ruins of a mosque were also found on the very same site as the synagogue, yet these were swiftly erased from the historical record; there is no mention of them in official documentation or at the site itself.[29] The Israeli state narrative about Jewish and Muslim life at Susiya has been selectively and unscientifically shaped by Israeli archeologists. Israeli research on Susiya has focused almost exclusively on the time between the first Byzantine and the Islamic periods, when the city was settled by Jews. Research and documentation of life in Susiya during the Muslim periods were not conducted, and archeological layers of the site covering the last 500 years of the city—including generations of Palestinian life at the village—were almost entirely destroyed.[30]

This historical and contemporary removal of Palestinians is ongoing. Since Israel's expulsion of the Palestinian residents of Susiya from their original village in 1986, they have resided on their agricultural lands. The Israeli military has since repeatedly expelled them. Each time they have returned to increasingly smaller plots of their lands, because Jewish-Israeli settlers have replaced them. In parallel, Israeli settlers have expanded the settlement of Susya and built two new unauthorized settlement outposts, one of which was established on the lands of the archaeological park of ancient Susiya.[31] Archaeological arguments have meanwhile been repeatedly used to justify the Israeli settler and military occupation of Susiya's lands.

Akiva London, as one of the leaders of the local settler movement from the Department of Land of Israel Studies and Archaeology at

Bar-Ilan University, drew on his status and expertise to undermine Palestinian legal petitions and claims to their lands. Echoing familiar settler-colonial tropes justifying the replacement of Indigenous peoples, London asserted that the Palestinian lands of Susiya had been "totally empty," with Palestinian families living there only seasonally, and that they had settled on Israeli state lands only after the state recognized the archaeological site.[32] Repeating unscientific arguments made by his peers at Hebrew University and upholding the selective preservation used to curate the archaeological site, London claimed that Susiya was a "Jewish city" that has been "almost entirely preserved."[33] Further protecting this historic Jewish town, he argued, required keeping Susiya's Palestinians off the land.[34]

With backing from the Israeli military, Jewish-Israeli settlers keep Susiya's Palestinians away from their agricultural lands through physical attacks and intimidation, poisoning their water sources and destroying their crops and property.[35] Legal appeals by Palestinian residents of Susiya to request a master plan that would allow them to build proper housing and legally reside in their town have been repeatedly denied, and their community remains unrecognized by Israel. The Israeli military and Civil Administration issued demolition orders for the homes of Palestinian residents of Susiya in 2017, and they continue to live under the permanent threat of demolition and complete expulsion from their lands.[36]

Living in this state of violence and uncertainty takes a high toll on Susiya's residents, as Nawaja describes: "Everyone in the village is living on their nerves . . . We're afraid the Israelis might come at any time. We panic every time we hear cars approaching."[37] Yet they are determined to remain and practice *sumud* (steadfastness), as Nawaja makes clear: "This is my land. My mother gave birth to me in Susya. My father is a refugee from 1948, and I am a refugee from 1986. I don't want my children to be refugees . . . This is my place. My life is here; the land, the olive trees, the grapes. If I lose this, I lose my life as well."[38]

Meanwhile, the Jewish settlement of Susya sustains its residents using revenue from the archaeological site by offering guided activities and tours and selling honey, olive oil, and wine produced by local settlements. The settlement also continues to facilitate unprofessional digs, in which students and other untrained private Israeli citizens can actively participate in the excavations, in the service of state narratives and claims to the land.[39] At Susiya, archaeological research serves to transform both the history and the archaeological remnants of a Palestinian village that dates back hundreds of years, thereby facilitating the dispossession of its current Palestinian residents and their replacement with Jewish-Israeli settlers.

The story of Susiya is a familiar one in the landscape of Israeli archaeology. Archaeological inquiry has long constituted an important site of identity formation and nation-building for the Zionist movement. Drawing on extensive fieldwork with Israeli archaeologists across sites of excavation, anthropologist Nadia Abu El-Haj has shown that Israeli archeological practice establishes an "evidentiary terrain" to substantiate the identity of the land as an intrinsically Jewish space and thereby to claim historic Palestine as the Jewish national home.[40] Routinely drawing on the Bible in scientific and historical inquiry and interpreting scientific objects and artifacts through Biblical text, Israeli archeology has emerged as a key site for Israeli assertion of an ancient—and, ostensibly, uninterrupted—Jewish presence in Palestine. Simultaneously, archaeological research was used to efface any Palestinian and Arab claims and evidence of centuries of existence on this very same land.[41]

Through seizing control of archaeological sites, museums, and artifacts, Israel has claimed ownership over the history of the entire territory under its governance. In so doing, the state of Israel not only seeks to erase Palestinian, Arab, Christian, and Muslim history, but to appropriate all Jewish heritage in the region as its own.[42]

Israeli archaeological theft and appropriation through occupation is a longstanding practice. It is also often publicly conducted, and Israel openly displays stolen artifacts in its own museums. Such is the case of the Dead Sea Scrolls seized from the Palestine Archaeological Museum. First opened to the public in 1901, the Palestine Archaeological Museum was reestablished and reopened in its current location in East Jerusalem in 1938. It housed thousands of artifacts uncovered by archaeological excavations or purchased throughout the twentieth century up until

1948.[43] Among the museum's most significant artifacts were collections of scrolls discovered in the Qumran caves in the West Bank, which were put on display beginning in 1960 and declared national heritage artifacts under the jurisdiction of the Jordanian government.[44] With Israel's occupation of East Jerusalem in 1967, Israeli military forces invaded the museum. Soldiers used the Palestinian staff as human shields and looted many of the antiquities.[45] In violation of the Hague Convention, Israel transformed the Palestine Archaeological Museum into the current headquarters of the Israeli Department of Antiquities and renamed it the Rockefeller Museum.[46]

Since bringing the Palestine Archaeological Museum under its military control, Israel has continuously removed artifacts for display at the Israel Museum and international exhibits. The Dead Sea Scrolls were seized from occupied East Jerusalem and transformed into the centerpiece of the Israel Museum's permanent exhibit in West Jerusalem.[47] As the Palestinian Authority and Palestinian and international legal experts have demonstrated, the Dead Sea Scrolls are artifacts discovered and preserved in the Occupied Palestinian Territory (OPT) and, as such, are governed by international law and the 1954 Hague Convention.[48] The scrolls do not constitute Israeli property simply because they are also of Jewish heritage and the Israeli state wishes to claim them. In 2011, Palestine joined as a member of UNESCO with intent to petition for international recognition of sites in the OPT as Palestinian cultural heritage and for the repatriation of artifacts stolen by Israel.[49]

The Israeli government, in collaboration with departments of archaeology from across Israeli universities, has nevertheless continued to display and research the scrolls at the Israel Museum and to showcase and internationally circulate stolen artifacts.[50] Israeli universities have also continued to conduct illegal archeological excavations in and around the Qumran caves in the occupied West Bank, through which they have discovered and seized additional scrolls and other artifacts. Most recently, between 2017 and 2019, Hebrew University archaeologists led an expedition in the Qumran caves and claimed the artifacts for their own research.[51] In 2021, Tel Aviv University and the Weizmann Institute collaborated with the Israeli Antiquity Authority to conduct research on additional scrolls excavated and seized from Wadi Murabba'at near Qumran in the occupied West Bank.[52]

Over decades, the academice discipline of Israeli archaeology has developed in tandem with Israel's military occupation. Archeologists entered the Palestine Archaeological Museum on the heels of the Israeli military in 1967. Just days later, Israel convened an Archaeological Council to take control over ancient sites in the newly occupied Palestinian territory.[53] The Israeli Department of Antiquities conducted its first archaeological "emergency survey" in the occupied Palestinian West Bank and Syrian Golan Heights in 1968, and Israeli archaeologists from across Israeli universities began excavations immediately afterward.[54] The Israeli military body charged with governing the OPT, the Civil Administration, promptly initiated and approved hundreds of digs across the occupied West Bank, adding thousands of sites to Israel's archaeological inventory. Israeli archaeologists formed close professional and scholarly relationships with the Civil Administration, paving the way for research excavations in the occupied West Bank that lay the groundwork for the development of the discipline of archaeology in Israel.[55]

The departments of archaeology across Israeli universities continue to work closely with the Israeli Antiquities Authority, the Israeli military, and the Civil Administration to conduct excavations and research in archeological sites in the OPT.[56] International law strictly regulates the use of archaeological research by occupying powers. Under the Hague Convention for the Protection of Cultural Property, Regulation 43 of the Annex to the Hague Convention, and UNESCO's guidelines, occupying powers are prohibited from carrying out their own routine excavations, and are instructed to support local authorities in preserving cultural treasures and sites.[57] In explicit violation of these regulations outlined in international law, Israel has taken full control over all antiquity sites in the OPT. Over 2,600 ancient sites in the occupied West Bank are currently overseen by the Staff Officer for Archaeology of Israel's Civil Administration, and an advisory council including four elected faculty from Israeli universities.[58] All Israeli universities collaborate with the Staff Officer of Archaeology to conduct archaeological excavations in the OPT, including on privately owned Palestinian lands, lending academic legitimacy to illegal seizure of antiquity sites and artifacts by the Israeli state.[59]

Excavations led by academic departments of archaeology have eliminated and erased Palestinian and Muslim artifacts, compromising scientific standards to advance Israeli claims to land. Their faculty and students continue to collaborate with Jewish-Israeli settlers, using archaeological excavations to illegally displace Palestinian communities and legitimatize or expand settlements on privately owned Palestinian lands, such as the case of Khirbet al-Mazra'a, an excavation supported by Bar-Ilan University. In further violation of international law, the Staff Officer for Archaeology frequently gives private settler entities authority to manage and develop antiquity sites, such as in Tel Shiloh-Khirbet Seilun and the Biyar Aqueduct, and the Israeli Military Commander of the West Bank often places antiquity sites under the jurisdiction of nearby settlements, such as in Khirbet Alamit.[60] All Israeli universities also conduct excavations in antiquity sites administered by Jewish settler organizations or settler regional councils.

These university collaborations with the Civil Administration in the OPT are ongoing. The Institute of Archaeology at Tel Aviv University has participated in and led surveys and digs across the occupied West Bank, including at Shiloh, South Mount Hebron, the Israeli-named mountain range the "Judean Hills," and the city of Hebron.[61] Digs at the archaeological site at Tel Rumeida, a neighborhood in the Palestinian city of Hebron, began with the establishment of a Jewish settlement there in 1984. That same year, Tel Aviv University professor Avi Ofer led excavations at the site, which were continued by the Antiquities Authority and researchers from Ariel University in 2014.[62] The Civil Administration took over the site in 2017 and worked with local Jewish settlers at Tel Rumeida to open an archaeological park, partly on expropriated private Palestinian lands.[63] The park has been visited by thousands of Israeli school children through a Ministry of Education program to legitimize the settlement in Hebron and narrate Jewish-Israeli presence there as a historical right.[64] The Zinman Institute of Archaeology at the University of Haifa led digs in the Jordan Valley and a mountain range near Nablus, both in the OPT.[65] The Department of Land of Israel Studies and Archaeology at Bar-Ilan University conducted excavations in the occupied West Bank in Khirbet Jib'it and Khirbet Marajim in 2020.[66] Most recently in 2022, the department embarked on a new dig in Khirbet Tibnah on the lands of Palestinian residents of the villages of Nabi Saleh, Bayt Rima, and Deir Nidam.[67]

This selective and curated approach to archaeological research to support national aims has also long been a feature of Israeli governance of East Jerusalem. Shortly after occupying East Jerusalem, including the Old City, in 1967, Israel began solidifying claims to it. Just days into the occupation, Israel bulldozed the 700-year-old Maghariba Quarter and evicted its Palestinian inhabitants to clear a large plaza around the Western Wall for Jewish-Israeli visitors.[68] After illegally annexing East Jerusalem and forcibly displacing many of its Palestinian residents, Israel declared the Old City an antiquity site, mandating that all rebuilding require approval from Jerusalem's chief archaeologists.[69] Simultaneously, the government issued a series of expropriation and demolition orders to expand and develop the historic Jewish Quarter for new Jewish-Israeli settlers.

Soon thereafter, the Israeli government supported archaeologists from Hebrew University to conduct excavations on the slopes of al-Haram al-Sharif (the Temple Mount) and later the new Jewish Quarter.[70] Israeli excavations in the occupied Old City of Jerusalem quickly came under criticism by Palestinians and international scholars for their use of bulldozers to dig straight through strata from Arab/ Islamic periods, removing findings from Islamic periods and leveling Islamic monuments. Israeli archeologists were further criticized for inadequate recording of data on remains that were destroyed or ignored, and for showing little interest in early Islamic history of the city. Excavating Jerusalem in this manner thus produced a new archaeological record, in which Jewish history was granted primary visibility in the city's new landscape.[71]

This remains predominant practice in archaeological research in Jerusalem, and Israeli universities continue to participate in these unscientific excavations today. Such is the case at Ir David (City of David), an

Israeli-designated archaeological site just outside the Old City walls, in the occupied East Jerusalem Palestinian neighborhood of Silwan. Inaugural digs there were led by Hebrew University Professor Yigal Shiloh in 1978.[72] Multiple faculty from the institutes and departments of archaeology at Hebrew University, Tel Aviv University, and the University of Haifa have since participated in the digs at Ir David and other archaeological sites in the Old City in Jerusalem and its surrounding Palestinian neighborhoods.[73]

Ir David is currently part of a national park managed by the Israel Nature and Parks Authority, but the antiquity site itself is run by the Jewish settler organization Elad, whose declared mission is to "Judaize" Palestinian East Jerusalem neighborhoods.[74] Elad advances archaeological excavations and tourism in Silwan in particular as part of its work to settle what Israel calls the "Holy Basin" around the Old City and undermine UN-stipulated Palestinian rights in East Jerusalem.[75] Using the antiquity site as its base, Elad has facilitated the gradual Israeli encroachment on the surrounding Palestinian lands and the illegal takeover of Palestinian houses by Jewish settlers in Silwan.[76]

Like the antiquity site itself, the archival research and historical narrative of Ir David have been transferred to Jewish ownership.[77] Freedom of Information Act requests filed by Emek Shaveh, an organization of Israeli human rights advocates and archaeologists outside Israeli universities, revealed significant compromises of professional standards in the digging of the "Path of the Pilgrims," an underground tunnel connecting the antiquity site in Silwan to the Old City in Jerusalem that has been excavated and reopened by Elad.[78] During the excavation, archaeologists uncovered the foundations of a wall identified as part of the Umayyad complex, built at the beginning of the Islamic period (the seventh century CE), which was identified in the al-Haram al-Sharif excavations by Hebrew University. The tunnel digs came under criticism for compromising scientific research by using horizontal digging, which prevented identification of different strata that might have otherwise been uncovered.[79] Several high-ranking officials from the Israeli Antiquities Authority were among the opponents to the dig, sharply criticizing the excavations as "bad archaeology."[80]

The tunnel was also met with strong opposition from the Palestinian community in Silwan, when the poorly regulated digging caused damage to local homes and was used to force residents out of their neighborhood.[81] Structural damage to over thirty-eight Palestinian homes above the tunnel developed over a decade and has led to the collapse of a parking lot and stairs leading to a local mosque.[82] Nevertheless, the tunnel was completed and inaugurated in 2019 by David Friedman, the Trump-appointed US ambassador to Israel, and Sheldon Adelson, major funder of the Netanyahu government and the Republican Party.[83] The event was celebrated by the Israeli government and Elad as another step in the US normalization of Israel's annexation of East Jerusalem, which has long been criticized as a violation of international law and remains unrecognized by the absolute majority of the international community.

As shown by Israeli archaeologists, journalists, and the official website of Ir David itself, the site has been transformed into a physical backdrop for the revival of Jewish Biblical stories, glossing over the gaps between Biblical texts and artifacts on the ground and completely erasing all other civilizations and histories of Silwan.[84] This explicit use of archaeological knowledge production to expand illegal settlement in occupied East Jerusalem has not prevented departments and institutes of archaeology at Hebrew University, Tel Aviv University, and Bar-Ilan University from collaborating with Elad on joint courses, excavations, and research; featuring faculty on the Elad website; or speaking at Elad's conferences and events. These collaborations lend academic legitimacy to an unscientific and illegal settlement project.[85]

Israeli archeologists conducting digs and research in the occupied West Bank, including East Jerusalem, are well aware of the illegality of their excavations. This has led some to obscure their names and details of their excavations, thus explicitly refusing to conduct transparent research. In a 2019 court case, the Jerusalem District Court accepted the request of the Staff Officer of Archaeology to withhold the names of archaeologists who received permits to conduct excavations in the occupied West Bank.[86] The Staff Officer of Archaeology also withheld details of the permits, including the exact locations of the digs and artifacts. The grounds for concealment, which the court upheld, were expressly to protect these archaeologists from the academic boycott and to shield Israel from damage to its foreign relations.[87]

While most international academic journals categorically reject articles based on illegal excavations in the OPT by Israeli researchers, Israeli academic journals edited and peer-reviewed by Israeli scholars do not uphold these international standards.[88] The Israeli discipline of archaeology has thus built its own insulated scholarly ecosystem governed by a shared, and seldom contested, Israeli nationalist agenda. In direct violation of international laws and regulations, Israeli archaeologists and universities continue to participate in excavations across the OPT. Departments lend their archaeological expertise to erase Palestinian, Arab, and Muslim history and buttress Biblical claims to territory that the Israeli government and settler movement are continuously working to appropriate. The discipline of archaeology thus structurally facilitates Israel's illegal theft of Palestinian artifacts and lands and makes possible their continuous appropriation.

Legal Studies

Israel is an innovator in interpreting international humanitarian law, with the Occupied Palestinian Territory as its laboratory.[89] Illegally governing the Palestinian population through military occupation for decades, Israel has developed a corpus of laws and legal interpretations to sanction its permanent military regime. As legal scholar Noura Erakat shows, this development expanded with rising Palestinian resistance throughout the Second Intifada, which began in 2000. As it waged military campaigns to subdue Palestinian protestors and insurgents—and came under international scrutiny—Israel began to advance arguments that its use of force against Palestinians constituted a new form of warfare, which could not be subject to regulation by existing bodies of law.[90]

To sidestep available legal frameworks, Israel argued that it was engaged in what it defined as "armed conflict short of war" against the Palestinians, constituting a *sui generis* situation (one of its own kind) to which existing laws of armed conflict could not be applied.[91] Over the course of its interpretive innovations since, Israel has created the legal infrastructure to justify extrajudicial assassinations, torture, and deployment of what would otherwise be considered disproportionate use of force against civilian populations tantamount to war crimes.[92]

These legal doctrines have not merely been used to shield Israel from accountability in the international arena, they have transformed the arena itself. The United States, and other countries waging what they define as "counterterror campaigns" and "asymmetric wars," have constructed their own legal interpretations based on Israeli theories, rendering new forms of devastating violence permissible and increasingly legitimate.[93]

Over the past two decades, faculties of law across Israeli universities have facilitated this legal innovation in service of the Israeli military and security state. Ethicists from philosophy departments have joined these efforts, theorizing and providing moral justification for Israeli policies and military operations, both in real time and during the international legal probes that followed. One of the philosophers leading this endeavor is Tel Aviv University professor and Israel's distinguished ethicist Asa Kasher. Kasher established himself as an academic in the service of the state in 1994, when he collaborated with the Israeli military to write its code of ethics. Kasher was later joined by philosophers and legal scholars from across Israeli universities and the military to update the code.[94] The revised document, titled *Ruach Tsahal* (the Israeli Defense Forces spirit), was officially adopted by the Israeli military and is conceptualized as an outline of its foundational values and as an ethical guide for its commanders and soldiers with concrete applications.[95]

Building on *Ruach Tsahal*, Asa Kasher began a long-standing collaboration with Major General Amos Yadlin to offer ethical guidance to the military. In 2001, the Israeli military's International Law Department issued a legal opinion governing the nascent Israeli policy of targeted assassinations.[96] Shortly thereafter, in 2002, Kasher and Yadlin joined a committee of military lawyers and academics that came together to formulate Israeli laws of war concerning targeted assassinations. Reportedly, committee members debated what number of Palestinian civilians it would be ethical to kill—in pursuit of a targeted assassination of a Palestinian defined, by Israel, as a militant—all to save a single Israeli. Answers varied between "zero" to "as many as needed"; and the committee average was 3.14 Palestinian civilian lives for 1 Israeli.[97]

Shortly thereafter, Kasher and Yadlin teamed up to write Israel's "Ethical Doctrine for Combating Terror," developed at the National Security College at the University of Haifa with a team of academic and military experts.[98] The final document, supported by three military chiefs of staff who served during the height of the Second Intifada, was broadly considered to be Israel's "counterterror doctrine" and the basis for its military guidelines.[99] The doctrine was developed as part of a broader project of legal innovation led by Israeli military lawyers, with support from Israeli legal scholars and ethicists.

These theorizations and legal interpretations, Noura Erakat and Lisa Hajjar show, sanctioned practices that have been traditionally defined as extralegal in international humanitarian law.[100] Israeli military operations and tactics deployed on the basis of this counterterror doctrine have since been repeatedly deemed war crimes by international human rights organizations.[101] Yet the doctrine is continuously defended by Israeli scholars, who collaborate with Israeli military leadership to elaborate philosophical and legal theses for military commanders on the ground on its basis.

Tel Aviv University has offered itself as a key site for this military strategizing and legal innovation. At its Institute of National Security Studies (INSS), academic experts and senior security state personnel join forces to develop and publish legal guidance for the Israeli government and military. Major General Yadlin himself was appointed as director of the INSS, where he oversaw policy work and published legal guidelines elaborating on the counterterror doctrine for over a decade. In INSS journals, Kasher and Yadlin articulated further justifications for why the point of departure for their doctrine is not international law. They argue that traditional conceptions about the nature of warfare and how to restrict it do not apply to Israel's "war on terror."[102] Kasher even proposed a new category to contravene the legal distinction between combatant and civilian when he coined the term "third population"—persons who appear to be noncombatants but may potentially interfere with Israeli military operations—in reference to Palestinian civilians.[103]

Building on these theorizations, Kasher and Yadlin lay philosophical foundations for the legitimacy of disproportionate killing. They argue that Israel can ethically and legally justify greater "collateral damage" of Palestinian civilian casualties than has been previously allowed under international law. They do so on the basis of an explicit ranking of Israel's ethical obligation to safeguard human life, proposing that Israeli soldiers deployed to the OPT be placed above Palestinian civilians. As a result, they argue that it is in fact immoral for Israel to endanger its own soldiers in order to safeguard the lives of Palestinian civilians.[104] This proposition, Noura Erakat argues, preemptively allows for more Palestinian civilian injuries and deaths in Israel's calculus of proportionality in the advance planning of its military operations.[105]

Kasher and Yadlin's hierarchy of human life was intended to serve as a practical guide for Israeli military commanders facing operational decisions, and its effects were evident in the military operations that followed. In its military offensives on the Gaza Strip in 2008–9, 2012, and 2014, Israel used aerial bombing and artillery shelling that killed thousands of Palestinian civilians, including hundreds of children, and left tens of thousands more severely injured and without homes.[106] Israel waited ten days into its 2014 offensive to send in ground troops, and did so only after massive shelling and aerial bombardment had razed entire neighborhoods.[107] Israeli combat soldiers deployed to the Gaza Strip reported that they were told by commanders that this execution of the offensive was intended to protect their lives in the ground incursion.[108]

Since Kasher and Yadlin, legal interpretations developed by faculty and research fellows at Tel Aviv University continue to shape Israeli military operations and to legitimize their tactics retrospectively.[109] The INSS Law and National Security Program explicitly advances legal scholarship to mitigate international criticism of Israel and support it in evading accountability. Program director Pnina Sharvit Baruch contends that claims about the illegality of Israeli military actions are based on "tendentious interpretations" of the laws of war that greatly limit the freedom of military action.[110] To counter this, Sharvit Baruch advocates that Israeli jurists promote interpretations that offer the military greater flexibility and remake international legal discourse in line with Israel's vision:

> In order to influence the laws of war and their interpretation, it is important that Israel and the Israeli military will be involved in this field. We must strengthen collaborations with legal advisers from other militaries and engage them in a fruitful professional discourse. We must initiate publications by legal scholars who understand the complexity of the battlefield and who will present the practical and applicable interpretation of the laws of war. We must also be active on blogs and online. It is important to attend professional conferences and maintain relationships with the scholars who influence the interpretation of the law.[111]

Sharvit Baruch herself has taken on the mantle. Following the UN Independent Investigation Commission's report on Israel's 2014 offensive on the Gaza Strip, which found Israel to have committed alleged violations of international humanitarian law and laws of war, Sharvit Baruch wrote a rebuttal.[112] Her counterreport argues that the UN commission was ill-equipped to investigate Israel's offensive. She grounds her arguments in opposition to its assessment of Israel's disrespect of the principle of proportionality under international humanitarian law, which is based on the damage caused weighed against the military advantage achieved. Among other arguments, Sharvit Baruch contends that because the UN is not privy to Israel's assessment of the military advantage achieved by its every aerial strike, the UN cannot possibly assess the proportionality of its military actions.[113]

Under Sharvit Baruch's leadership, Israeli scholars continue to construct innovative legal interpretations to shield Israel from accountability, often in direct response to international condemnations or probes, and sometimes even anticipating them during Israeli operations in real time. In May of 2021, for instance, the Law and National Security Program offered a defense of Israel's offensive in the Gaza Strip even as it was still being carried out, claiming that it cleared the threshold of proportionality based on its reading of *excessive damage* in international humanitarian law.[114] More broadly, the program works to undermine the legal arguments and legitimacy of international human rights organizations and regulatory bodies. In 2022, the program published a rebuttal of Amnesty International's report charging Israel with the crime of apartheid, as well as a report that delegitimized the International Criminal Court.[115] The report put forward legal arguments challenging both the ICC's jurisdiction and its definition of war crimes, as well as offering policy recommendations for the Israeli government to thwart investigations into Israeli activity in the OPT on this basis.[116]

Israeli legal studies offer a disciplinary home not only for constructing interpretations that justify Israeli state and military policies in the international arena but also for honing the mechanisms to enforce them. The Israeli discipline of criminology has developed and expanded through the Israeli occupation of Palestinian territory, particularly through collaboration with the Israeli National Police (INP) and the Israeli Security Agency, the Shin Bet. Criminologists serve a critical role in the operation of these policing apparatuses through collaborating on research, formulating policy recommendations, and offering tailored academic training to their personnel.

Governing all the territories under Israeli control requires close cooperation between the military, the INP, and the Shin Bet. As is typical of colonial administration, the Israeli governance of the OPT undermines any traditional jurisdictional distinction between foreign and domestic, military and police. As anthropologist Eilat Maoz shows, the INP is no exception. It serves alongside the Israeli military and Shin Bet as part of the governing apparatuses that establish Israeli sovereignty in the OPT, and the boundaries separating the three agencies are porous; these bodies have overlapping authority as well as shared missions and personnel.[117] One quarter of the INP serve under Magav, the Israeli border police, which began as a military unit and over half of which remains staffed by soldiers during their mandatory military service.[118] Recent INP commissioner Roni Alsheich was appointed to his role after leaving his position as deputy head of the Shin Bet.

As one of the central governing bodies of the OPT, the INP operates a designated police district for the occupied West Bank, and its jurisdiction extends to both Jewish-Israeli settlers and Palestinians. Though ruling both populations in the OPT, the INP governs them differently. Jewish-Israeli settlers arrested by the INP are processed under the Israeli legal system; Palestinians, meanwhile, are interrogated in Israeli police and Shin Bet facilities, and then transferred for trial and incarceration under the Israeli military court system.[119]

Israel's use of the military court system as an apparatus of control over Palestinians has been extensively documented, as has its systematic violations of international law.[120] Since 1967, it is estimated that over 800,000 Palestinians have been tried in the Israeli military court system, which holds a conviction rate of over 99 percent.[121] The trials in Israeli military courts are frequently based upon evidence obtained through Shin Bet interrogations, which have been documented to include serial violations of Palestinian human rights. Palestinians are often denied access to lawyers prior to the interrogations, which can last days or weeks, during which time Palestinians are routinely kept in isolated, windowless cells and subjected to physical abuse and torture.[122] INP investigations are then used to transform the Shin Bet "security investigations" into admissible evidence that can be used in military court system trials. As Israeli attorneys and legal scholars have shown, INP investigations are thereby sanctioning the Shin Bet's illegal practices.[123]

INP officers' role in violating Palestinian rights in the OPT has not stopped Israeli scholars from collaborating with them. In fact, these conditions of Israeli occupation have produced a productive site of study and experimentation for Israeli criminologists, who understand their academic expertise as advancing what they conceptualize as "policing terror," a field that relies upon close cooperation with the Israeli security state and using Palestinians as research subjects.[124] Israel's leading criminologists have established themselves as experts in service of these agencies, and the Israeli security state has responded in kind. Classified data collected on Palestinians by the INP and Shin Bet through illegal interrogation methods and torture serves as the foundation of university-based research, resulting in policy recommendations for these same agencies.[125] Such use of data produced through the violation of human rights and extracted by academics without consent would fail an ethics review in most universities, but it is standard practice among Israeli criminologists.

Former INP commissioner Roni Alsheich personally worked to foster closer collaborations between Israeli academia and the police. In Alsheich's own telling, one of his first moves after beginning his appointment as commissioner in 2015 was to turn to Israeli criminologists for guidance. Israel's leading criminologists at Hebrew University immediately sent him a PowerPoint with hundreds of slides worth of research, which Alsheich claims were instrumental in shaping INP policies under his tenure.[126] Indeed, Alsheich was frequently seen in the halls of the Institute of Criminology at Hebrew University, invited for meetings and seminars and as a speaker at its annual conference. Alsheich himself had been trained at the institute while still serving in the Shin Bet, and continued his studies there as commissioner.[127] Together with criminologists from across academic institutions, Alsheich formed the first advisory academic forum to the police commissioner, with whom he worked closely.[128]

Hebrew University criminology faculty praised Alsheich for opening the INP's doors to academia and working with their institute to continuously assess and refine Israeli police work. Following Alsheich's close cooperation with Israeli criminologists, leading scholars in the field publicly urged the minister of public security to extend his tenure. In making their case for Alsheich, the criminologists cited his collaboration with academia, arguing that he revolutionized the INP and positioned it as one of the world's most advanced "science-based police organizations."[129] When Alsheich completed his tenure as commissioner, the Institute of Criminology held a parting ceremony to honor him. David Weisburd, Israel's preeminent criminologist and Israel Prize laureate in criminology—and a close collaborator of Alsheich—was effusive in his praise: "More than any other commissioner, you promoted the use of police science. Not only did you respect the research, you respected the academy. Not only did you act according to the results of studies, you were open to conducting studies to evaluate your action plan."[130]

Even after Alsheich's departure, these collaborations live on. Israeli criminologists continue to train INP and Shin Bet personnel, as part of what the INP has described as the "academicization" of the police.[131] The Institute of Criminology at Hebrew University was selected to be the "home department" of the INP. It runs an abbreviated BA program in criminology for law enforcement personnel that aims to translate officers' studies into more effective practice "in the field." The institute also runs a designated criminology program for station commanders and officers seeking promotion.[132] At a 2023 cohort graduation, INP commanders highlighted the importance of academic training to honing the capacities of their officers. Hebrew University rector Tamir Sheafer responded in kind, affirming the university's continued commitment to the INP and its pride at "the privilege that fell to us to contribute to your training."[133]

Israeli criminologists understand themselves not only as a research and training arm of Israeli policing apparatuses, but as pioneers in an international field of "counterterror policing." They promote their studies as useful to law enforcement and intelligence and security agencies worldwide, proposing the "ten commandments" for best "counterterrorism practices."[134] These include "field-proven" Israeli strategies and tactics, such as indefinite intelligence gathering from informants and producing a "hostile environment" for insurgents by suspending entire communities in structural uncertainty.[135] Israeli criminologists advocate the export of these Israeli tactics, which have been condemned for violating Palestinian human rights, to countries worldwide.[136] Several key studies at the Institute of Criminology at Hebrew University were funded by the US Department of Homeland Security, while institute faculty serve as experts for international delegations of security agencies— including US police departments—touring Israeli policing apparatuses and infrastructure.[137]

In showcasing Israeli models of counterterror policing, faculty have brought delegates to observe the checkpoints and comprehensive surveillance systems in occupied East Jerusalem.[138] In the context of these trainings and in their publications, institute researchers frame both the policing of occupied Palestinians and the entanglements of the police and the university as a "model for democracies."[139] As Hebrew University criminologists Simon Perry and Tal Jonathan-Zamir put it:

Israel has the potential to serve as a fascinating research laboratory for studying policing . . . whereas police in many Western democracies have begun to see terrorism as an acute problem and as an integral part of their mission only in the recent decade, the INP has almost 40 years of experience in this area.[140]

The occupation of Palestinian Territory has indeed served as a field-defining laboratory for Israeli criminologists and legal scholars. Israeli legal studies has continually expanded to provide the theoretical infra-structure to legitimate and hone Israel's permanent military rule, while its researchers and faculty have become facilitators, authors, and executors of widely condemned Israeli policy.

Middle East Studies

The study of the Middle East has been a national priority in Israel from its inception, a priority extending far beyond the university gates. In Israel, this form of expertise is termed *Mizrahanut* (Orientalism, literally translated).[141] Orientalism, Edward Said argued, is the system of knowledge production about the "Orient" through which the power of the European and US empires operate. It reflects Western ideas and imaginations about the "Orient" articulated through its production as distinct from the "Occident."[142] Building on Said's theorization, Israeli sociologist Gil Eyal argues that *Mizrahanut* is a generic name for the complex of Israelis' encounter with their geographic environment. It is a mechanism that draws and polices boundaries and examines phenomena from what the Israeli state defines as "the other side."[143] *Mizrahanim* (Orientalists) in Israel therefore include not only academics, but government and military officials, journalists, and others engaged in monitoring the Palestinian population and neighboring Arab countries and participating in public debates on Middle Eastern affairs.[144]

Israeli Middle East Studies indeed developed at the intersection of Israeli academia, the military, and the state. *Mizrahanut* was central to the establishment of Israeli academia itself, with the Institute for Orient

Studies developed as one of the first three schools of Hebrew University.[145] In a study of the foundational generations of Israeli Middle East studies scholars, Eyal Clyne shows that many saw no distinction between their scholarly and national commitments.[146] In the 1930s and 1940s, the Institute for Oriental Studies at Hebrew University trained entire cohorts of advisors and officials serving the Zionist movement leadership, who joined the "Arab branch" of the Haganah paramilitary and the departments for Arab affairs and politics of the Jewish Agency. They worked to monitor the Arab press, catalogue and index intelligence data collected on Palestinians, and survey actions, attitudes, and social relations in Palestine and neighboring Arab countries. Having served roles in political intelligence and *hasbara* in the prestate years, roughly half of these *Mizrahanim* returned to Hebrew University after the state's establishment to found the contemporary Department of Islamic and Middle Eastern Studies.[147]

Following the Institute for Oriental Studies, the Dayan Center for Middle Eastern and African Studies was formed as a node of the Israeli state network of intelligence expertise. First called the Shiloah Institute, the center was established by the Israeli military, the Ministries of Defense and Foreign Affairs, and Hebrew University in 1959. It was annexed to Tel Aviv University in 1966 and was renamed after Moshe Dayan, former Israeli chief of staff and minister of defense, in 1983.[148] At its inception, the Dayan Center was founded to serve as a bridge between the Israeli Intelligence Division and academia. It was staffed by both academics and representatives from Israel's Foreign Office, and regularly published articles by military and state officials and hosted them at conferences.[149] At Tel Aviv University, it continued to invite military leaders as guest researchers to publish their own work and to contribute to the institute's publications. Many of its researchers—who formerly or continuously served in the Israeli Intelligence Corps—received classified military information for their studies, while intelligence officers and state officials staffed the institute's committee to select research projects and award research grants.[150] The institute operated within Tel Aviv University as a semi-secret enclave, barring access to Palestinian citizens of Israel and those without state security clearance, including access to master's and doctoral theses that drew on classified data.[151] As such, the center's knowledge production was structured like the Israeli Intelligence Corps and served as the military's auxiliary research arm.

This entanglement of university, military, and state expertise shaped the discipline in its early years. Many of the founding Israeli Middle East studies scholars moved between or held parallel roles in academia and the security establishment or were otherwise bound by loyalty and secrecy commitments to state apparatuses.[152] Prominent examples include Meir Kister, Israel Prize laureate and founder of the Arabic language departments at Hebrew University and the University of Haifa, who also worked for the Haganah's intelligence agency. Also at Hebrew University, Israel Prize laureate for *Mizrahanut* Yaakov Landau supplied research on Palestinian citizens of Israel to the Prime Minister's Office Advisor on Arab Affairs, from which he received materials and proposed research topics. At Tel Aviv University, Yaakov Shimoni contributed his expertise in Arabic and Arab politics to the Israeli military, as well as to Israel's decision to institutionally prevent the return of Palestinian refugees between 1947 and 1949, in direct violation of UN resolution 194.[153]

With Israel's establishment of a military government in the Occupied Palestinian Territory in 1967 came renewed opportunities for academic cooperation with the state. Hebrew University professors Menachem Milson, Amnon Cohen, Moshe Sharon, and Moshe Maoz served as Arab Affairs advisors to the Israeli military and government. Milson also served as the inaugural head of the Civil Administration, Israel's military administration in the OPT, and oversaw the forced closure of the Palestinian Birzeit University beginning in 1981; Cohen, Sharon, and Maoz served as colonels and worked with the military throughout their academic careers. At Tel Aviv University, professor Zvi Elpeleg drew on his expertise as a scholar of Palestinian history while repeatedly serving as military governor over various regions of the OPT, including the Gaza Strip and Nablus.[154]

Leading Middle East studies scholars maintain ties to security apparatuses to this day. Some serve in senior positions in the Intelligence Corps or other elite military units throughout their academic tenure, others secure data or funding from state agencies for their research, and others still are officially or in a classified manner employed by state and military institutions as researchers or instructors.[155] Though they no longer officially operate under the Israeli security state, the leading Middle East studies departments and institutes continue to conduct research and offer expertise in its service.

The Dayan Center declares that it "continues to play a crucial role in safeguarding Israel's future," and its military and security state ties indeed continue to run deep.[156] Prominent current center fellows—most of whom are also faculty at the Department of Middle Eastern and African History at Tel Aviv University—hold parallel roles in the Israeli security state or collaborate on research with the intelligence community.[157] Eyal Zisser, former chair of the department and leading Israeli Middle East studies scholar, has served as an advisor and course director of an elite military unit, the details of which remain mostly classified. Raz Zimmt leads a publication series for the Meir Amit Intelligence and Terrorism Information Center, the primary research institute of the Israeli Intelligence community. Michael Milshtein, who heads the Palestinian Studies Forum at the Dayan Center, also served as the Advisor on Palestinian Affairs in the Israeli Civil Administration governing the OPT and as the head of the Department for Palestinians Affairs in the Intelligence Corps as a retired colonel. Other fellows joined the center after having held senior roles in the Israeli Ministry of Foreign Affairs or in the Intelligence Corps, and many emphasize that they still serve there as reservists.[158]

Accordingly, the Dayan Center's research agenda remains shaped by the needs of the Israeli security state. The center proudly advertises its monthly position papers as an important source of data and analysis—a "toolbox"—for Israel's political and security leadership.[159] Fellows frequently publish their research in cooperation between the Dayan Center press and the Israeli military or Israeli Ministry of Defense presses, often in collaboration with high-ranking military personnel.[160] In the early 2000s, Dayan Center experts worked with the military to guide Israeli policy during the Second Palestinian Intifada.[161] More recently, the center published recommendations for the Israeli government on how to "manage" its permanent military occupation.[162] Lending

academic credence to state and military agendas more broadly, Dayan
Center memos, journals, and books promote racialized tropes about
"jihad" and what they routinely call a "death worship culture" in Arab
and Muslim societies, propagating a view of the Middle East through an
explicitly militarized lens.[163] Written in direct support of Israel's continuing illegal occupation of the OPT, Dayan Center publications are
frequently difficult to distinguish from state documents.

Dayan Center fellows and other Middle East studies scholars directly
leverage their expertise to offer briefings on current affairs and weigh in
with policy prescriptions through major Israeli media outlets. In the wake
of Israel's 2014 offensive in the besieged Gaza Strip and military campaign
across the occupied West Bank, for instance, researchers took to the media
to offer commentary and advice to the Israeli military. Tel Aviv University
professor Asher Susser advocated that Israel embrace "preemptive strikes"
to communicate that "if a red line is crossed, Israel will be the one to strike
first and very forcefully, in the timing, place and method of its choosing."[164]
He was joined by Bar-Ilan University Middle East Studies professor and
former military Lieutenant Colonel Mordechai Keidar, who went on
Israeli radio to argue that deterrence of a Palestinian insurgent can only be
achieved if "his sister or mother will be raped."[165] Drawing on his alleged
expertise on the region, Keidar advocated for a war crime.

Uzi Rabi, current head of the Dayan Center and chair of the
Department of Middle Eastern and African History at Tel Aviv University,
has also become a major news pundit. Rabi has long presented himself as
a military strategist in his interviews and popular writing. In 2018, Rabi
went on Israeli radio to advocate that "those who live in Gaza should
know that if they confront Israel, Israel will strike a blow that will leave
them with a mental and operative disability."[166] As of 2022, Rabi is a
permanent pundit on the Friday night news of the major outlet Channel
13, where he routinely speaks in the first person when referring to military policy and advises on Israeli tactics to counter Palestinian resistance
to Israel's military occupation.

These recurring calls to violate international humanitarian law by
leading Middle East studies scholars are overwhelmingly met with
silence from their colleagues, their departments, and the Middle East

and Islamic Studies Association of Israel (MEISAI).[167] Given the long-standing institutional ties of Middle East studies departments and associations to Israeli security agencies, this tacit support is unsurprising.[168] As the primary association of the Israeli field, MEISAI currently declares itself to be independent of the state but has refrained from condemning Israel's repeated infringements on the academic freedom of Palestinian universities in the OPT. Allegiance to the state remains the broad consensus among Israeli Middle East studies scholars.

Middle East Training for the Security State

As spaces of instruction, Middle East studies departments have consistently offered training in regional expertise in service of the Israeli security state. Language training across universities, particularly in Arabic, is thoroughly militarized. Its pedagogy has long been shaped by commitments to the Israeli state and with little engagement with or reference to academic research conducted in Arabic or by Palestinian and Arab scholars.[169] Like *Mizrahanim,* the vast majority of faculty of Arabic in higher education are Jewish-Israeli.[170] The typical Arabic training of these Jewish experts begins at school, continues through service in the Intelligence Corps and Middle East studies departments, and ends with careers in the military or in language instruction to train another generation of Jewish-Israeli Arabic experts. As Yonatan Mendel shows, this cycle has created a closed system of militarized Arabic expertise, shaping the field to remain devoid of Palestinians and native Arabic speakers.[171]

Arabic studies thus became instruction in a "foreign language," not one that is native to the fabric of life of both indigenous Palestinians and Jewish Arabs. Mendel argues that Arabic became "frozen" in Israel—a language to be decoded and deciphered, to be read but not spoken—and taught mostly in Hebrew and through an Orientalist, militarized lens.[172] Mendel calls this securitized language developed under Zionist governance "Israeli Arabic"; through it, Jewish-Israelis can only come to comprehend or decode "Arabs" but never come to know them.[173] Faculty

interviewed across Middle East studies departments acknowledged that
the majority of their graduates have little to moderate command of
Modern Standard Arabic and overwhelmingly cannot converse. With
less than 3 percent of Jewish-Israelis speaking Arabic today, and few high
schools offering Arabic studies as an elective, Israeli universities play an
important role in the controlled instruction of Arabic and in preserving
its status as a militarized field.[174]

Departments of Middle East studies offer academic programs in
regional expertise for active duty soldiers in elite military units and
tailored courses for security apparatuses. Hebrew University operated
an accelerated BA program in Middle East Studies for the Shin Bet as
part of their personnel training.[175] Four cohorts completed the program,
which ended in 2003. The Department of Islamic and Middle East
Studies willingly ran the program, with then department chair Eli Puda
stating that he considered it "part of the university's obligation to Israeli
society."[176] When a similar sixteen-month tailored BA program for the
agency was scheduled to reopen in the department in 2006, it was ultimately voted down by university administrators and faculty, primarily
due to concerns about the international academic boycott and the
lowering of academic standards to streamline a Shin Bet degree.[177]

But in 2018, the department cooperated when it was once again
commissioned by the Israeli security state. Hebrew University applied
and won the bid to house the Israeli military Havatzalot program.[178]
Havatzalot (lilies, in Hebrew) is an elite degree program offered to
soldiers in the Intelligence Corps as part of their military training.[179]
Soldiers selected by the military undergo basic training and then enroll
in a specialized academic program that the military terms "academic
training." These soldiers complete a joint BA in Middle East studies
and another selected field, alongside military training in intelligence
gathering, all in preparation for a minimum of six years as officers reach-
ing the status of captains or majors in the Intelligence Corps.[180] The
program opened at Hebrew University in October 2019, after the
Weapons and Technology Purchase Unit of the Ministry of Defense
chose to transfer it from the University of Haifa, which had hosted it for
the previous fourteen years.[181]

The selection was celebrated by Hebrew University's administration, despite the military tender's long list of demands, which some faculty argued would compromise the institution's academic freedom.[182] Accompanying the prestige and funding, Hebrew University was required to meet enhanced military demands in preparation to host the program. The bid's terms include far-reaching Israeli military intervention in the program's content, structure, employees, and infrastructure on campus.[183] Unconcerned about these requirements, Hebrew University President Asher Cohen declared: "We are proud of winning [the bid], which is yet another testimony to the high academic level of the Hebrew University, which will henceforth be a partner in the academic and leadership aspects of training Intelligence Corps soldiers."[184] University Rector Barak Medina similarly rejoiced:

> Operating the program will attract high quality students, and it is expected to contribute, directly and indirectly, to strengthening our academic activities and research in the field of Middle East Studies and Political Science. Operating the program is also an expression of the commitment of the Hebrew University, as a public institution, to partake in the training of the future leadership of the State of Israel.[185]

The Hebrew University administration made clear that it understands the institution to be an extension of the Israeli military in so far as it directly utilizes its academic programming to train soldiers for their positions.

As the university administration celebrated Havatzalot's arrival to its campus, few faculty dissented. With the announcement of the program in 2018, a number of faculty members at the Department of Islamic and Middle Eastern Studies and other participating departments responded by organizing a panel to discuss its implications for the university. Following a warning from the Hebrew University administration that holding such a discussion on campus would be nothing less than an "internal terrorist attack," the faculty organizers complied and swiftly moved the event off campus.

What transpired at the only significant dissenting public event reveals the extent to which both the discipline and Israeli academia have been subordinated to the state, and just how marginalized and limited is the critique of this subordination.

The atmosphere was tense as soon as the audience shuffled into the auditorium, a mix of students, faculty, and the general public. It was apparent that any critique of a degree program in support of the military was highly controversial, and the event organizers were on the defensive from the outset. The event took the form of a panel, which was all Jewish-Israeli. As one of the faculty organizers explained, it was important for them to invite an Israeli military representative to the panel, and, as a result, no Palestinian scholar wanted to participate. The panel nevertheless prioritized the military, which ultimately sent no one. Discussing the repercussions of integrating the Intelligence Corps into the Department of Islamic and Middle Eastern Studies, then, was a panel of Jewish-Israeli social scientists. Yet many in the audience were displeased at the very premise of critiquing the program, and the panelists shared measured comments. Some of the panelists themselves served in high-ranking positions in the military, others were scholars of militarism who conducted research in collaboration with the military, and none offered a critique of the university training soldiers to sustain the occupation. At most, they highlighted the militarizing effect of increasing uniformed soldiers on campus and decried the silencing campaign by Hebrew University administrators and faculty against members of the academic community who raised critical questions about the program.

Representing Hebrew University was Reuven Amitai, a professor at the department and head of the Havatzalot program. In the absence of a military representative, Amitai took it upon himself to serve as the program's spokesperson. In this capacity, Amitai asserted that it was the work of the Israeli military that made this very event possible, stating: "It enables us to have this debate, there is nothing to do about it. This is a contradiction that we live with." Amitai dismissed the criticism by his fellow panelists by pointing to Hebrew University's other longstanding elite military degree program, Talpiot, reminding the audience that "those soldiers study how to develop better weapons, we just study the history of Islam."[186] Though later in the panel Amitai himself acknowledged the direct utility of his department's academic training to the military when he reasoned: "To know the history and culture of the Middle East makes people better researchers and probably better soldiers."

The response from Hebrew University clearly demarcated the bounds of acceptable critique and illuminated the institution's identification with the Israeli military. Rector Barak Medina even went as far as to argue that the program would play an important role in "educating" Palestinians on campus and enhancing "integration."[187] He contended that through contin-ual exposure to soldiers, Palestinian students will come to see that "they do not have horns, talk to them at eye level, and everyone will know each other."[188] Turning the criticism about the oppressive effects of the presence of Intelligence Corps soldiers on Palestinian students on its head, Medina represented military interests by suggesting that Palestinian students must learn to become more tolerant of Israeli soldiers, their occupiers.

In the university administration's view, then, it is not Jewish-Israeli and Palestinian citizens who make up its student body and must be "integrated," but Palestinian citizens and Israeli soldiers. Both military and university objectives are served, the administration revealed, in conflating students and soldiers, academic programing and military training, campus and base.

The narrow and short-lived faculty opposition was soon dismissed and the Palestinian student protest ignored. The university administra-tion opened the program in 2019, designating space in one of its few campus dorms to create an official military compound. The military defines the compound as a "closed military base," wherein soldiers are required to train and reside throughout the workweek as they would in other such bases.[189] The compound is demarcated by security guards and cameras and requires identification and military vetting for entry.[190] Within this military compound, in designated floors of the campus dorms, Havatzalot soldiers train, study, and eat together separate from civilian students, but using university infrastructure and services.[191]

Throughout the academic year, the soldiers' training in military and intelligence content takes place in the compound on the Hebrew University campus. Over the course of their degree, soldiers are methodically exposed to the Israeli intelligence community and are trained in its capabilities and research methods, including data collection, processing, and presentation, and intelligence philosophy. Between their semesters, soldiers participate in the "Intelligence Summer" program, where they move between Military Intelligence Directorate units as well as the police, Shin Bet, and Mossad, and conduct a research project for one of the units.[192]

Upon its opening at Hebrew University, Havatzalot was widely celebrated by the military. The former head of the Military Intelligence Directorate called Havatzalot the "flagship project" of the Intelligence Division, while the former head of the Intelligence Corps research division declared: "I cannot imagine the Intelligence Directorate today without the contribution of the graduates of the Havatzalot program, who are found at all the central nodes of the intelligence work."[193] Havatzalot has been heralded as "the habitat for people who were at the center of every operational event in recent years."[194]

Palestinian students in the Department of Islamic and Middle Eastern Studies and across Hebrew University do not partake in these celebrations. Since the opening of Havatzalot, they have witnessed a surge in the number of military uniforms on their already militarized campus. In 2020, Palestinian students organized a campaign and short film contesting this militarization and situating it in the context of ongoing Palestinian dispossession, documenting Havatzalot soldiers in olive-green uniforms overwhelming their classrooms and student spaces. The film sparked outrage among right-wing Israeli student groups, who contended that the film showing the soldiers' faces endangered them and constituted incitement. Knesset members joined in and called for a criminal investigation against the student makers and disseminators of the film.[195] The university response was unequivocal. The administration demanded that the student group take the film offline and released a statement asserting that "the desire to present the university campus as an unsafe environment is completely false."[196]

Yet Palestinian student organizers claim otherwise. Palestinian students at the Department of Islamic and Middle Eastern Studies reported that their learning environment had been compromised by soldiers joining their classes. Palestinian students described feeling unable to speak freely in the presence of Intelligence Corps soldiers training to surveil their families and communities. They reported censoring themselves in the classroom and contended that the only department designed for the exploration of Middle Eastern history, languages, and cultures has now foreclosed this opportunity for its Palestinian students. In training Intelligence Corps soldiers, conducting research in the service of government and security agencies, and reproducing and instructing its expertise under state and military frameworks, Middle East studies has established itself as a central pillar of Israeli military occupation.

Israeli academic knowledge production has long been entangled with the Israeli state. From their inception, Israeli disciplines across the humanities and social sciences were conscripted to sustain Israeli settler colonialism. Archaeology, legal studies, and Middle East studies have developed alongside—and by means of—Israeli military occupation. The Israeli military governance of the Occupied Palestinian Territory made the expansion of these disciplines possible, and these disciplines, in turn, maintain the conditions of Israeli apartheid.

Even in the face of international condemnation outlining Israeli violations of international law, these collaborations are ongoing. These disciplines, among others in the Israeli academy, persist in conducting research that facilitates the Israeli erasure of Palestinian history and ongoing expropriation of Palestinian land and supports repeated Israeli military campaigns that violate international human rights law and the laws of war in the Occupied Palestinian Territory. Across departments and universities, Israeli academic inquiry subordinates itself to the Israeli state, and is therefore accountable for its crimes.

2

Outpost Campus

"Science is one of the most powerful weapons for the realization of Zionism." —Israeli Prime Minister David Ben-Gurion[1]

"If there are institutions whose requirements are to be prioritized, then the university is at the top of the list. Science is the protective wall from Levantine assimilation." —Israel Shuchman, local elected official in the Yeshuv[2]

On June 28, 1967—just two weeks after Israel invaded East Jerusalem and brought the entire city under its rule—Hebrew University held a ceremony at its Mt. Scopus amphitheater, overlooking the newly occupied Palestinian neighborhoods below. State and military leaders joined university administrators for the festive occasion, in which Hebrew University awarded Chief of Staff Yitzhak Rabin an honorary doctorate.[3] Celebrating the reopening of its campus in occupied East Jerusalem, the University Senate thanked Rabin for "returning the entirety of Jerusalem to the state of Israel and returning Mt. Scopus to Hebrew University."[4] Rabin, in turn, commended the university on behalf of the Israeli military for the opportunity to stand at Mt. Scopus with the view of "our eternal capital."[5] In his acceptance speech, Rabin tied the Zionist movement's foremost university to its aspirations to colonize Palestine:

> The question can be asked, what did the university see in giving an honorary doctorate specifically to a soldier, as a sign of appreciation for his activities in the war. What do military personnel have to do with the world of academia, which symbolizes cultural life? What do those who by their profession engage in violence have to do with spiritual values? But I see in this honor, that you share through me with the members of the military, your deep recognition of the uniqueness of the IDF, which is nothing but an expression of the uniqueness of the entire people of Israel.[6]

Not to be outdone, the military bestowed upon the university an honor of its own. At another celebratory ceremony at the campus that shortly followed, the Israeli military commander of Mt. Scopus, Lieutenant Colonel Menachem Sherfman, awarded the university's president the "Six Day War Decoration" for the institution's contribution to the Israeli war effort.[7]

These military-academic entanglements at Hebrew University reveal how crucial a role its campus has played in the Israeli occupation of East Jerusalem. The story of Hebrew University, the first and leading university of the Zionist movement, is the story of how Israeli institutions of higher education were designed to serve Zionist territorial conquest and the expansion of Jewish settlement across historic Palestine.

What early Zionist leaders before 1948 called the "colonization of Palestine," Israeli leaders after the state's founding called "Judaization."[8] A platform shared by both Israel's right and left parties, "Judaization" has always been a national policy publicly pursued by every Israeli government.[9] Since its establishment in 1948 and the mass expulsion of Palestinians in the Nakba, Israel has continuously deployed, across multiple frontiers, the twinned methods of Palestinian land confiscation and strategic Jewish settlement. All Zionist modes of settlement have been based on the logic of Jewish replacement of indigenous Palestinians, and all have sought to establish Jewish-Israeli citizen presence on the

ground to secure effective control of Palestinian land.[10] Following the
1948 war, Israel's targeting of Palestinian lands continued inside the
newly established state borders. After the 1967 military occupation, such
targeting occurred across the Gaza Strip and West Bank, including East
Jerusalem. By the mid-1970s, state "Judaization" programs regained
momentum once again within its 1948 borders, particularly in the
Galilee and Naqab. Across these territories, Israel has worked to maintain Jewish demographic superiority and Jewish population distribution
so as to replace Palestinians and undermine their claims to autonomy or
self-determination.[11]

Since its inception, then, Israel has engineered demographic and
territorial dominance at both the national and regional levels. For over
seven decades, the state has explicitly taken over and shrunk land owned
and inhabited by Palestinians under occupation and by Palestinian citizens of Israel, while it has expanded contiguous territories owned and
inhabited by Jewish-Israelis.[12]

Soon after the 1948 war, and the influx of migration that would triple
the Jewish population size in a decade, Israel began laying the groundwork for national development plans.[13] These centered on Jewish immigrant absorption and "population dispersal": orienting settlement away
from the few large urban centers—where the majority of Israel's Jewish
population already lived—toward both sparsely populated areas and
regions with large Palestinian communities.[14] In implementing national
absorption and settlement plans, the Israeli government collaborated
with and conferred authority on diverse institutions: the World Zionist
Organization, the Jewish National Fund, and Israeli universities. The
first to design a national master plan for the nascent state was Arieh
Sharon, a faculty member at the Technion Institute, Israel's "chief architect," and head of the Prime Minister's Office planning division.[15] In
1951, Sharon commissioned architects, geographers, and economists—
including scholars from Hebrew University—to put forward the national
"population dispersal" plan. Sharon's plan fundamentally altered the
landscape under Israeli governance, initiating dozens of new settlements
and development towns to establish a Jewish presence all across the
country.[16]

In parallel, Israel prohibited the establishment of any new Palestinian villages and towns and further curtailed Palestinian development through land confiscations, zoning and building regulations. It also strategically located Jewish settlements to surround Palestinian villages and prevent their contiguity.[17] Inside state borders, Israel confiscated Palestinian citizens' land through a legally codified and unidirectional transfer of ownership, wherein 93 percent of the land became Israeli state land that now legally and permanently belongs to the collective "entire Jewish people."[18] Palestinian citizens are thus effectively barred from purchasing, leasing, or using the vast majority of the land in Israeli territory.[19] In East Jerusalem, Israel annexed Palestinian territory and curbed development through land confiscation, planning restrictions, and the establishment of Jewish settlements to disrupt Palestinian urban continuity. These policies violate international law, which regards East Jerusalem as Occupied Palestinian Territory.[20]

Israeli universities were designed to serve this national agenda. Across regions, this Israeli program has been codified by laws, written into policies, upheld by the courts, and buttressed by Israeli universities. Their campuses, research, and architectural and planning expertise have been committed toward the state's territorial and demographic project. This is explicitly articulated by the institutions themselves. The Hebrew University charter states that the institution was established "out of the Zionist aspirations of the Jewish people," while the Ben-Gurion University charter explicitly outlines its aim to "develop the Negev."[21] From East Jerusalem through the Galilee to the Naqab, Israeli universities have served as key state institutions in staking Jewish claims to Palestinian land.

Through a study of several representative institutions, this chapter shows that Israeli universities were designed as regionally strategic outposts for the Israeli state's territorial and demographic project. Hebrew University Mt. Scopus in occupied East Jerusalem; University of Haifa in the Galilee; Ben-Gurion University in the Naqab; Ariel University in the occupied West Bank: all these institutions serve as crucial engines of "Judaization" projects in their respective localities.

Hebrew University and the "Judaization" of Jerusalem

"The [Hebrew] University must be the university of all Jewry."
—Samuel Hugo Bergman, first rector of Hebrew University, 1948[22]

"The Hebrew University in Jerusalem is the only university that Israel
established for itself. Therefore, it is not intended to serve the Yeshuv
in the land of Israel alone, but the entire nation of Israel." —Official
Hebrew University document, 1939[23]

Years before the founding of Hebrew University, the World Zionist
Movement purchased land for its campus at the strategic apex of Mt.
Scopus in East Jerusalem. The university cornerstone was laid in 1918,
and it opened in 1925 as a remote enclave amid Palestinian villages, over
two decades before Israel's establishment.[24] Hebrew University was the
first Jewish university established for the Jewish colony in Palestine
under the British Mandate, called the Yeshuv. The idea for Hebrew
University was conceived by leaders and intellectuals of the Zionist
movement, who saw an institution of higher education as crucial to their
mission of building a new collective Jewish identity and nation.
Consequently, the institution was initially called the Jewish University,
befitting the role ascribed by its founders as a central cultural institution
of the Zionist movement and of Jewish communities worldwide.[25]
Moreover, the university's founders, planners, and faculty believed in the
symbolic affinity between the institution and Mt. Scopus, emphasizing
its significance for the Jewish people and referring to the campus as "the
third temple."[26] Together, the mountain and the university became a
symbol imbued with historical mythology and religious meaning, attain-
ing an almost legendary status as the redeemer of the budding nation.[27]

The university was officially recruited by Israel soon after the state's
establishment, and expected to commit its resources, campus, and
research toward building the new state. Prime Minister David
Ben-Gurion called for the university to be conscripted to the emergent
nation, and directed its students to enlist "Jewish science" for the national
industry, agriculture, and military.[28]

While founded as a structurally Jewish institution and established at a strategic location for the Zionist movement to stake symbolic and political claim to Jerusalem, the university's mission remained in debate during its first two decades.[29] Some of the university's founders and its first president, Rabbi Judah Magnes, were critical of the Zionist movement's use of force in pursuing Israeli nation-building. They advocated instead that Hebrew University primarily function as a cultural and scientific center for world Jewry.[30] Magnes and some of the university's leading faculty and administrators were also members of Brit Shalom (Covenant of Peace), which campaigned for equal rights for Palestinians and Jews and a just resolution for all residents of Mandatory Palestine. Yet much of the prestate Zionist leadership was adamant that Hebrew University play an instrumental nation-building role. Opposing the university's trajectory under Magnes's management, Zionist leaders both within and outside the university demanded that administrators and faculty who failed to meet "appropriate" national criteria be dismissed.[31]

The debates about the university's ties to the emergent state of Israel were decisively resolved in the wake of the 1948 War. In the lead-up to and throughout the war, students, faculty, and administrators actively supported the Haganah paramilitary and treated the campus as a base, conducting military trainings and even storing weapons in university buildings.[32] Shortly after Israel's establishment, Magnes was succeeded as university president by Selig Brodetsky, who also advocated preserving relative institutional autonomy from the state. Prime Minister Ben-Gurion responded by facilitating Brodetsky's ousting and, after personally interviewing candidates for the position, appointed the loyalist Benjamin Mazar as the next university president.[33] Mazar responded in kind, encouraging state participation in the university's management and increasing the number of government representatives on the university executive board.[34]

Hebrew University continued to declare its institutional independence. But its state funding significantly increased, and Mazar's administration established close and regular cooperation with the Israeli government. Under Mazar's leadership, ambition for achieving the traditional model of a research institute aspiring to scientific excellence was replaced with a new model: a university in service of the state.[35]

Prime Minister David Ben-Gurion believed that Israeli universities are, first and foremost, subject to government authority and must serve the Jewish state.[36] As such, he personally nominated loyalists as university presidents across institutions. Thus, from the early 1950s through the mid-1960s, the presidents of Israel's first universities were government or military officials—either formerly or simultaneously—and some were not academics at all. At the Technion, Ben-Gurion nominated as president Yaakov Dori, formerly Israel's first chief of staff and later head of the Scientific Council at the Prime Minister's Office. Another Ben-Gurion loyalist, David Bergman, was initially tapped for leadership at the Weizmann Institute;[37] ultimately, chief Israeli diplomat and politician Abba Eban served as president of the institute, while also serving as an elected member of the Israeli parliament, the Knesset.[38]

As the first major academic institution in Israel, Hebrew University played a central role in shaping Israeli academia.[39] Following its lead, Israel's universities were officially enlisted by the state to serve its territorial and demographic project of "Judaization."

The "Judaization" of West Jerusalem

With the inauguration of Hebrew University, the nascent Israeli National Library became the National and University House of Books, and was transferred to the campus on Mt. Scopus. The National Library became embedded in Hebrew University, expanding its collections and operating out of the campus for over two decades.[40] Hebrew University and the library operated on Mt. Scopus until 1947, when violent confrontations adjacent to the campus in the wake of the UN partition plan caused it to close intermittently.[41]

The 1948 Nakba fundamentally altered the trajectory for Hebrew University and the National Library. At first, the university faculties and library were temporarily moved from Mt. Scopus and dispersed among multiple sites in West Jerusalem. But, soon enough, the war offered them opportunities for major expansion.[42]

With the outbreak of the 1948 war and transfer of Hebrew University to provisional sites in West Jerusalem, David Ben-Gurion, prime minister of Israel's provisional government, wrote the administration to urge that the university "must continue to develop its activities within Jerusalem" as a central institution of the state of Israel.[43] To emphasize the national significance of the university, the Israeli government soon allocated land for a new campus in the government precinct in Givat Ram, alongside major state institutions.[44]

According to Hebrew University's official narrative, the campus at Givat Ram was built on a "rocky deserted hilltop."[45] But, in fact, Givat Ram was built on the ruins of the Palestinian village of Sheikh Badr, whose residents were forced out of their homes by the Haganah paramilitary in 1948. The name *Givat Ram* is in fact derived from the Hebrew acronym *Rikuz Mefakdim* (officers' assembly), named for the military base established on the hill where Sheikh Badr once stood.[46]

Sheikh Badr was one of many Palestinian neighborhoods in West Jerusalem depopulated in the first months of the 1948 war. On the heels of the mass expulsion of the city's Palestinians, the head of the National Library and Hebrew University administrators urgently petitioned the Israeli government. They requested official status as custodians of the libraries and public and private collections in Palestinian West Jerusalem neighborhoods, whose residents had been driven out or fled following campaigns by Israeli paramilitaries.[47] After a brief negotiation with the Israeli military governor, the National Library and Hebrew University were granted authority to appropriate books from Palestinian homes, libraries, and educational and religious institutions left behind by Palestinian war refugees. Hebrew University granted funds and official status to this enterprise, and organized teams of librarians to trail Israeli soldiers and collect books from Palestinian buildings. University students and administrators joined them to comb through Palestinian neighborhoods, searching for institutional libraries and troves of private book collections.[48]

Over the course of ten months during the 1948 war, workers of the National Library and Hebrew University appropriated 30,000 books, as well as newspapers and journals, on topics including Islamic law, interpretations of the Quran, literature, science, history, and philosophy. The books were incorporated into the National Library, more than doubling the existing collection of Arabic books at the institution.[49]

In 1948 and into the early 1950s, the Israeli Custodian for Absentee Property collected an additional 40,000 books from Palestinian cities and towns, mostly from academic institutions and schools. After a sorting and vetting process by the Israeli government, over 26,300 books were destroyed as the Custodian deemed them "inappropriate" for containing "material against the state."[50] Of the remaining books, many were resold to Palestinian schools, which were compelled to repurchase their original property, and others were transferred to the National Library.[51] The new Givat Ram campus of Hebrew University was opened in 1958. Today, it still houses the university faculties of natural and exact sciences, as well as the Israeli National Library, with its collections of looted Palestinian books. The Oriental Division of the National Library became the repository of many of the Palestinian books collected from West Jerusalem and around the country, and remains the central research library of Middle East studies at Hebrew University.[52]

The 1948 Universal Declaration of Human Rights and the 1949 Geneva Conventions outline clear protections for intellectual and cultural assets and prohibit looting collective or private property during war.[53] The confiscation of Palestinian books by the Israeli government, National Library, and Hebrew University thus constitutes a clear violation of international law.[54]

Yet this is no accident. In the early 1960s, the National Library erased the names of the Palestinian owners of the books and collections and reclassified many as "Abandoned Property," which remains their classification in the library catalogue to this day.[55] Beginning in the 1960s and into the early 2000s, several Palestinian families have since sought to retrieve their books from the National Library, but were refused by library administrators. The library administration declined to discuss the requests until the Palestinian families provided full lists of books belonging to them, despite having no access to the library records, the only place such a list might be stored.[56] Hebrew University and the National Library have yet to acknowledge or take responsibility for their role in the Nakba and the "Judaization" of West Jerusalem, nor for their ongoing theft of Palestinian books.

The "Judaization" of East Jerusalem

As a result of the 1948 war, East Jerusalem came under Jordanian rule, and Mt. Scopus was declared an officially demilitarized enclave. The terms of the armistice agreement, signed by Israel and Jordan and facilitated by the UN, dictated that Israel could use the campus only for civilian academic purposes.[57] Despite agreeing to these terms, Israel regularly sent Israeli soldiers—disguised as students, faculty, and police officers—to secure "Jewish sovereignty" over the disputed enclave and smuggle in rifles.[58] In further violation of the armistice agreement and UN requirements, a special Israeli military unit was established for the Mt. Scopus enclave that worked between 1955 and 1967 to gather intel, foster collaborators, and smuggle heavy weaponry into university grounds in anticipation of conquering the mountain.[59]

Despite occupying a prestigious, spacious, and more centrally located campus, Hebrew University administrators spent their years at Givat Ram planning a return to Mt. Scopus. With Israel's occupation of East Jerusalem just days into the war in 1967, the university administration immediately lobbied to reopen its original campus. Two days before the ceasefire, Hebrew University officials declaratively raised the university flag atop a high building to demonstrate that the "exile from Mt. Scopus was over" and narrated their "return" to the "liberated summit."[60] Both university administrators and the Israeli government understood the location of the campus to have a functional role, marking the frontier of the "unification" of the new "Jewish capital."[61]

Working with Hebrew University administrators, the Israeli government planned to rebuild the campus on Mt. Scopus as part of its efforts to "Judaize" occupied East Jerusalem after 1967. City planners were instructed to cover the recently occupied lands with "facts on the ground."[62] Rebuilding the Mt. Scopus campus naturalized the development of new Jewish settlements on expropriated Palestinian lands, which linked the university to West Jerusalem's city center. The university's senate-appointed rehabilitation planning committee, created just one day after the ceasefire, similarly argued that—from both a university and a national perspective—expropriating Palestinian lands for the new campus was justified, despite its clear violation of international law. The committee echoed government rhetoric, stating that "empty space in Mt. Scopus and its surroundings must be filled. If we will not fill it, someone else will do it."[63] The committee acknowledged that expanding the campus would entail land expropriation, necessitating "state intervention" to seize the potential "available land" from the neighboring Palestinian village of Issawiyeh.[64]

Hebrew University's administration thus committed itself to its political and territorial role in Israel's project to "unify" Jerusalem, deciding on the isolated Mt. Scopus location. There, they built a fortress-like megastructure with a tall tower that continues to dominate the East Jerusalem skyline and, symbolically, the city's space.[65]

The post-1967 university was planned by architect David Resnick, who envisioned the Mt. Scopus campus as a "beacon of the resurrection of the Jewish people."[66] Its massive megastructure was designed to create a wall-like sequence to mirror the Old City walls, highlighting the Jewish people's longstanding ties to Jerusalem. But Resnick also clarified that the megastructure design was intended to solidify Israeli control of East Jerusalem by creating "a strong presence" and signifying "I am here, and you cannot remove me."[67] Reserve Major General Joseph Harpaz, Hebrew University's executive director, joined the university architect team in the plan for an expanded campus on Mt. Scopus, likewise advocating for monumental construction to strengthen Jewish hegemony in Jerusalem.[68]

Tall walls distinctly separate the Mt. Scopus campus from its neighboring East Jerusalem Palestinian communities. The campus architecture, as Diana Dolev shows, limits accessibility from the outside and obstructs the visibility of East Jerusalem, with few windows, balconies, or courtyards opening out to the landscape. Entry to the campus requires permission from guards at all points of entry. Entrances to the underground parking lots for private vehicles are difficult to find, while entry through the underground tunnel used by public transportation leads directly into the general campus corridor, whose openings are directed toward inner courtyards.[69] The university's iconic water tower, one of the tallest in the Jerusalem skyline, served as a military lookout on East Jerusalem until 2006; today, it remains inaccessible due to military use.[70]

In its location, architecture, and structure, Hebrew University operates as a besieged-yet-hegemonic fortress serving a select part of the city's population, and as a militarized base for the "Judaization" of Palestinian East Jerusalem.

The Occupation and "Judaization" of Al-Issawiyeh

The Palestinian community most directly encroached upon by Hebrew University is the neighborhood of Al-Issawiyeh, located on the slopes of Mt. Scopus and right beneath the campus. Following the 1948 war, when Mt. Scopus and its surrounding Palestinian villages were included in the territories under Jordanian rule, the UN facilitated the creation of a demilitarized enclave that included the Hebrew University campus and part of the adjacent Palestinian village of Issawiyeh. But even as its residents remained officially governed by the UN, the enclave and lands of Issawiyeh included in its territory came under de facto Israeli control. Initially, Hebrew University and the Israeli government committed, in UN-facilitated negotiations, to allowing Issawiyeh residents displaced during the war to return. Yet soon thereafter, Israel tried to limit the number of residents allowed to return.[71]

During the nineteen years of the enclave's existence, Israel demonstrated its control with routine military "sovereignty patrols" on the Mt. Scopus campus and interfered in the lives of Issawiyeh residents using various alleged "security justifications."[72] This included invading and conducting searches in residents' homes, preventing farmers from cultivating their lands, and restricting entry to and exit from the village. Israel strictly limited the use of the main paved road to the village by Palestinian residents, constructing checkpoints and demolishing

independent renovation attempts to improve access to it. It also barred
residents from accessing the main road between Ramallah and Jerusalem
that passed by their village, forcing them to use an alternate dirt path.
Issawiyeh's residents, who had neither Israeli nor Jordanian citizenship,
were left without legal protections to object to Israel's abuse of their
rights.[73]

With Israel's occupation and annexation of East Jerusalem and the
reopening of the Mt. Scopus campus in 1967, Issawiyeh came entirely
under Israeli rule. But Israel included only one-quarter of Issawiyeh's
original lands within what became the annexed neighborhood's borders,
confiscating its lands, first to expand Hebrew University and later to
build adjacent Jewish settlements. Over the five decades since annexation, Israel has incrementally expropriated over 90 percent of Issawiyeh's
lands. Today, the neighborhood is encroached on all sides by the Hebrew
University Campus, Hadassah Hospital, a Jewish settlement, major high-
ways, and two military bases.[74]

As part of the Jerusalem municipality's "Judaization" program in the
city, it has strictly limited the development of Issawiyeh. For years the
municipality refused to update the neighborhood's 1991 master plan or
accept the one prepared by Issawiyeh's residents. Only in 2015 did the
municipality commission a new plan, though without consulting residents; it has yet to be approved.[75] The decades-long absence of a plan has
created a major housing shortage and compelled residents to live in
overcrowded conditions and to build without permits. As of 2020, residents of at least 136 homes have pending Israeli demolition orders
against them, face tens and up to hundreds of thousands of dollars in
fines and fees, and live in permanent uncertainty. Others live in cramped
and improvised housing conditions, as one Issawiyeh resident and father
of three described:

> Living in these crowded conditions is very difficult. I have three chil-
> dren. My 18-year-old daughter is studying medical administration.
> She's in her first year. She has a separate bedroom, but it's tiny and it's
> hard for her to study there. All three kids used to sleep there, but once
> she grew up it became hers . . . The boys now sleep in the living room,

without any privacy and with no space for personal matters or to sit and study quietly.[76]

The mother of the household added: "In the morning it's a terrible mess, with blankets and pillows everywhere. That's no way to live in the 21st century. My daughter studied for her matriculation exams in our other room, because her bedroom is underground and doesn't have enough light."[77]

But even under conditions of underdevelopment by design, the residents of Issawiyeh have never accepted their status as occupied subjects. Issawiyeh has long been known as a center of Palestinian resistance and organizing, with residents regularly holding demonstrations against the illegal annexation of their neighborhood and their governance by Israeli occupation. This sustained mobilization has caused the Israeli National Police (INP) to label it an "extremist village" and to target the neighborhood with physical closures and violent repression.[78] Since the Second Palestinian Intifada, the Israeli police have regularly closed the neighborhood's exit toward the university with checkpoints and placed large cement blocks to bar access to Jerusalem through the road adjacent to the campus and Hadassah, one of only three entrances to the neighborhood.[79] In their streets and homes, Issawiyeh residents have faced regular invasion of Israeli security forces; mass and arbitrary arrests of residents, including children; and a particularly heavy use of tear gas and other weapons to disperse demonstrations, which has caused several Palestinian deaths and dozens of severe injuries.[80]

Yet in April 2019, Israel's targeting of Issawiyeh significantly escalated, with the launch of a new police operation in the neighborhood. Israeli police officers, special patrol unit officers, and border police forces began to routinely raid the neighborhood and disrupt everyday life, imposing a permanent regime of collective punishment. Israeli forces set up checkpoints, ambushes, and roadblocks, randomly closing off main streets during the day and setting off patrol car loudspeakers at night. Forces began conducting drone surveillance and patrols in full riot gear and with weapons drawn as well as enforcing a policy of stopping and searching vehicles and issuing tickets with hefty fines for minor infractions as a means to discipline residents.[81] The campaign included routinely sweeping up dozens of residents, with most released afterward with no charges. Israeli forces repeatedly and violently targeted the neighborhood's leading activists in particular, arresting and threatening local leaders with punitive house demolitions. Raids by fully armed units with dogs were conducted in residents' homes, often in the middle of the night.[82]

As residents soon learned, the neighborhood had also become the set for a new Israeli reality television series about the Jerusalem police, which began airing in May 2019. For years, Issawiyeh served as a training ground for Israeli police and border patrol forces, but the filming of the show was further cause for escalation. In at least one documented case, police planted a weapon in the home of an Issawiyeh resident so that it could be "discovered" by the INP in a night raid shown on Israeli prime television. Residents reported that staging for the show orchestrated other police raids and arrests throughout the neighborhood.[83]

One month after the show's airing, in June 2019, Israeli forces shot and killed Muhammad 'Abeid, a twenty-one-year-old resident, during a police raid.[84] After the killing, police repressed commemoration of 'Abeid, recurrently tearing down signs, posters, and Palestinian flags hung in his memory.[85]

It is no coincidence that the most targeted Palestinian neighborhood in Jerusalem is the one right beneath Mt. Scopus and the Hebrew University campus. The Hebrew University administration has long collaborated with the repression of Issawiyeh, carried out with the overwhelming support of its Jewish-Israeli students. Over the last decade, student union chairpersons and leaders of student groups have demanded increased policing of the neighborhood. Some even deployed racialized tropes to allege that Palestinian men pose a danger to Jewish-Israeli women as a basis to call for further segregation and for the university to build an additional separation wall between the campus and Issawiyeh.[86]

In the face of the recent escalated campaign to repress Issawiyeh, the Hebrew University administration again supported the work of Israeli forces in the neighborhood. In December 2019, the INP was documented conducting surveillance of Issawiyeh atop one of the Hebrew University campus buildings. Palestinian and progressive joint

Palestinian and Jewish-Israeli student and faculty groups demanded that Hebrew University push to reopen the entrance to Issawiyeh adjacent to campus and prohibit the INP from using its campus as a lookout.[87] In response, Rector Barak Medina refused to acknowledge the institution's role in the occupation of Issawiyeh, stating: "The responsibility for protecting human life and property lies with the police. The university plays no role in determining the police's modes of action, in Issawiyeh or anywhere else."[88] Yet Medina himself affirmed that the police outpost was conducted in coordination with campus security.[89] Members of the Issawiyeh popular committee were further informed by the police that their neighborhood entrance was in fact closed at the request of the university, and that it would be reopened were the university to inform the police that it no longer had a "security need" for the closure.[90]

While Issawiyeh residents have consistently called for solidarity from Hebrew University's students, faculty, and staff, and have renewed those calls since 2019, they have been overwhelmingly met with silence. Building on occasional solidarity tours and a handful of protests and letters from marginalized Palestinian and progressive Jewish-Israeli student and faculty groups, several Hebrew University faculty joined Issawiyeh residents in a petition to the Supreme Court in 2021 to demand reopening the main road leading from the neighborhood to Jerusalem's center, the Old City and the Al-Aqa Mosque, as well as the campus.[91] The road, one of only two leading directly to the city, was closed intermittently for some twenty years and permanently since 2014. Neighborhood residents report that the closure causes serious disruption to their daily lives and argue that it constitutes discrimination and a form of collective punishment by the police.[92] The INP responded by reiterating its long-standing claim that the roadblock is necessary to protect the university.[93] In exchange for a commitment that the INP will reassess the need for the roadblock every few months, the suit was dropped in 2022, yet the road-block still stands.[94]

The intensified policing campaign against Issawiyeh continues unabated, as does the crackdown on neighborhood activists. Most recently, in January 2023, police dispersed the neighborhood parents' committee meeting, convened to address the shortage of classrooms for their children as a result of discriminatory Israeli planning and budgetary policy.[95] The "Judaization" of Jerusalem, Israel makes clear, requires the continued shrinking of Palestinian lands, as well as limiting opportunities for Palestinian education. Ignoring Issawiyeh resident mobilization and the dissent among its faculty and students, Hebrew University institutionally supports ongoing escalation tactics by the INP and the violent occupation of the Palestinian neighborhood right below its campus.

University of Haifa and the "Judaization" of the Galilee

Hebrew University was only the first institution of higher education designed to advance "Judaization" in its region. As Ron Rubin, president of the University of Haifa, explains, Israeli universities are defined by and tied "by the umbilical cord" to their geographical locations, and his institution is no exception.[96] Founded under the auspices of Hebrew University in 1963, the University of Haifa received full accreditation as an independent institution in 1972 as the first multidisciplinary university in the Galilee. Established in the largest city of the only region within Israeli borders where Palestinians constitute a majority, the University of Haifa was designed to further Israel's regional demographic project. While claiming the title of Israel's "most pluralistic" institution for serving the greatest number of Palestinian students (with Israeli citizenship) and touting "an atmosphere of tolerance and multiculturalism," the University of Haifa has long worked to advance Palestinian dispossession.[97]

According to senior government planner and professor emeritus at Tel Aviv University Elisha Efrat, Israel has always considered the Galilee's Palestinians an acute "demographic problem," whose absorption as citizens was an "undesirable inevitability."[98] The city of Haifa in particular was defined, according to Baruch Kipnis, senior planner and professor of geography at University of Haifa, as a "very problematic area, in the sense of creating a 'demographic balance' between Jews and Arabs," due to its sizable Palestinian population.[99] Israel has long conditioned its sovereignty over the Galilee on engineering a Jewish majority living there. To address the threat of a regional Palestinian majority that might fuel a national movement for independence, the Israeli government has officially endorsed and promoted a policy to "Judaize the Galilee."[100]

Like Hebrew University at Mt. Scopus, the University of Haifa campus is positioned atop Mt. Carmel, overlooking the city and somewhat removed from it. The campus architecture, Ilan Gur-Zeev shows, was designed to symbolically dominate the apex of Mt. Carmel, following the mountain's conquest by Israel.[101] The Carmel mountain range was populated by Palestinian villages before the Nakba, whose residents were expelled by Zionist militias and the Israeli military in 1948.[102] Remains of the Palestinian villages were demolished, covered in forests of pine trees planted by the Jewish National Fund, and replaced with Jewish-Israeli towns and Israel's largest national park. Part of the campus itself was built on lands of one of these Palestinian villages, al-Khureiba.[103]

The university's signature thirty-one-story tower dominates the city skyline and overlooks the remains of destroyed and depopulated Palestinian villages on the slopes of the mountain below.[104] The tower itself served a dual academic-military use until at least the early 2000s, with communication and relay antennas on the roof staffed by Israeli soldiers, giving the university campus additional characteristics of a military base.[105] With its roof in the service of the Israeli military, above the top floors housing university executives, the tower—Gur-Zeev argues—symbolically hierarchizes the institution's chain of command and solidifies Israel's domination over the mountain range.[106]

The University of Haifa has long worked with the Israeli government to advance its regional "Judaization" program.[107] The departments of urban planning and geography have contributed their expertise to assess, improve, and design "Judaization" policies. Faculty and graduate students have researched and published studies on these policies with the Ministry of Defense and the University's Society for Applied Scientific Research. These policy-oriented publications construct scholarly justifications for the expulsion, containment, and discrimination of Palestinian citizens, alongside exclusive and increased investment in Jewish settlements in the Galilee. This research fully embraces Israeli state terminology, labeling low percentages of Jews in the Galilee as a severe demographic "negative balance" and defining state lands subject to "Arab infiltration" as "infected areas."[108] Constructing classic colonial narratives to justify Palestinian expulsion, University of Haifa research frames Palestinian presence as antithetical to the "natural landscape" and to Israeli efforts at regional environmental preservation.[109]

Crucially, the University of Haifa anchored research and planning for what would become one of the key "Judaization" programs in the Galilee: the *mitspim* project. Mitspim (lookouts) were nuclei of Jewish settlement built on strategically selected hilltops throughout the Galilee. They were designed to create "facts on the ground" and solidify control over Palestinian lands, while also serving new sites of surveillance for Jewish residents to monitor Palestinian land use and potential expansion.[110]

Mitspim were initiated to address Israeli government concerns about potential calls for Palestinian autonomy in the Galilee in the wake of "Land Day" in 1976, which featured nationwide Palestinian strikes and protests over Israeli land expropriation. Land Day became a watershed event for Palestinian citizens of Israel, with Israeli forces killing six Palestinian citizens and injuring dozens, and later conducting mass arrests throughout the country.[111] Shortly thereafter, the settlement division of the Jewish Agency initiated a new plan to strategically expand the Jewish population in the Galilee through the rapid establishment of thirty new Jewish mitspim within six to eight months.[112]

As a "deterritorializing device" for the Galilee's Palestinians, the locations of the mitspim were specifically selected to form "wedges" between Palestinian village blocs that might otherwise form a territorial continuum, as well as to help preserve state land in Jewish hands.[113] As explained by Baruch Kipnis, a regional planner and University of Haifa professor, the mitspim project sidestepped standard procedures: Israel's statutory planning authorities were not initially consulted, and there was no period for public comment, so as to maximize the plan's secrecy and prevent Palestinian protest.[114] Between 1979 and 1980, dozens of mitspim were established, each with a small nucleus of Jewish citizens settling in temporary edifices with minimal infrastructure.[115] The locations of the mitspim were not marked on the original outline plan that the national planning board preliminarily approved. While unauthorized construction by Palestinians in state-defined agricultural zones routinely results in demolition orders, the mitspim were granted approval for construction in agricultural zones. The project expanded through 1986, with Israel building a total of sixty mitspim, which became permanent Jewish settlements.[116]

Forty years later and much developed and expanded, the mitspim remain exclusively Jewish settlements and maintain "admission committees" to vet all potential new residents. These committees across mitspim and other Jewish settlements in the Galilee were set up to exclude Palestinian applicants, but they have also routinely rejected Mizrahi and Ethiopian Jewish-Israelis, and have been legally challenged due to their explicitly racialized selection criteria.[117] Following the latest legal challenge to the admission committees filed with the Supreme Court in 2011, the Israeli government legally codified them in settlements in the Galilee, Naqab, and the West Bank. The new law permitted admission committees to reject residents who may "harm the social and cultural fabric of the community," so long as the settlements are no larger than 400 families.[118] New legislation in 2022 expanded criteria for settlements to maintain admission committees to include those with as many as 700 families, citing the mitspim project as precedent.[119]

Legislation attempting to curb such admissions committees has been repeatedly decried by University of Haifa publications, which outline "unequivocal justifications" for them as a "sorting and control mechanism" to protect the "Israeli Zionist minority" in the Galilee.[120] These publications even claim a "human right" to preserve the "character and culture" of the mitspim and "Jewish sovereignty" in the region.[121]

No one has been a more vocal advocate and respected authority on the "Judaization of the Galilee" than Arnon Sofer, Israel's preeminent demographer and one of the most celebrated faculty emeritus at the University of Haifa. He served multiple senior positions, including the chair of the Institute for Middle East Research, dean of the Faculty of Social Sciences, and deputy chair of the Center for Defense Research. For years, Sofer headed the prestigious Chaikin Chair of Geostrategy at the university, which has self-published dozens of books and articles about how Israel can win its "demographic battle" against the Palestinians.[122] Sofer's relentless public campaign on the subject of

Palestinian demographics and dozens of policy recommendations submitted to the Israeli government over his career earned him the title "Arnon Sofer Aravim," meaning "Arnon the Arab counter" (a play on *sofer*, "to count" in Hebrew).[123]

Sofer claims credit for the idea of transferring the concentration of Palestinian towns known as the "triangle" from Israel to the West Bank, a proposal repeatedly debated in the halls of the Knesset and decried by Palestinian citizens and civil rights attorneys as a racist policy of forced transfer.[124] Yet Sofer characterized his idea to unilaterally eject tens of thousands of Palestinian citizens "not as expulsion, but as an irredenta."[125] Sofer also claims credit for promoting Israeli policies of territorial segregation in the Occupied Palestinian Territory, including the removal of Jewish settlers from the Gaza Strip, as a policy of demographic containment. He contends that he wrote Prime Minister Ariel Sharon in 2002 suggesting the idea of "separating" from Palestinian territory, arguing that "on the same day that the Israeli military invests efforts and manages to eliminate one terrorist or another, on the same day, as every day of the year, about 400 children are born in the territories of western Israel, some of whom will become new suicide bombers."[126] Sofer has long been and remains one of the most explicit articulators of the elimination of Palestinians as national policy.

Like Sofer, University of Haifa faculty and researchers have been continually hired as consultants for state "Judaization" programs. In 1982, Professor Baruch Kipnis was commissioned by the settlement division of the Jewish Agency to survey the mitspim and recommend a municipal structure to serve the new settlements. Kipnis worked with city planners and proposed establishing new Jewish-only regional councils and jurisdiction for mitspim and other settlements in the region.[127] In 1985, Arnon Sofer and Racheli Finkel were contracted to assess if the mitspim were meeting their goals, whether their model could be applied in other areas of the country, and in what ways the program needed to be adjusted or improved. Based on institutional data, field tours, maps and aerial photographs, and interviews with mitspim planners and residents, the team concluded that the mitspim were effective as a land-seizing enterprise.[128] In 1986, the national planning and building council commissioned Baruch Kipnis and a team of researchers to assess the results of the Galilee settlement policy. Using maps and statistics, the team achieved a precise accounting of the efficacy of "Judaization" programs and showed that they were successful in increasing Jewish presence, numbers, and percentages in the Galilee.[129] Subsequently, in 2003, Arnon Sofer supervised an assessment of the mitspim that deemed them highly effective at land takeover and at breaking up contiguous Palestinian territory, serving as a catalyst for the massive transfer of private Palestinian land to the Israeli state.[130]

Over the decades of Israeli programs of demographic engineering in the Galilee, University of Haifa experts have been recruited by the state to research, assess, and improve them. Anchoring the mitspim project and other regional programs of Palestinian dispossession, the University of Haifa remains a pillar of the Galilee's "Judaization."

Ben-Gurion University and "Judaization" of the Naqab

"If we don't settle the land, someone else will." —former prime minister Ariel Sharon[131]

"How does one maintain a border from the Zionist perspective? Through activist communities that live on the border. Not armored vehicles and tanks but human power, absorption, young people—a security belt in the deep sense of the word." —Tirael Cohen, founder and executive director of Kedma Student Villages[132]

Just as Hebrew University and University of Haifa served to establish Israeli sovereignty over occupied East Jerusalem and the Galilee, Ben-Gurion University has constituted a central force for Israel's "Judaization" of the Naqab region.[133] Ben-Gurion University was established in 1969 with the explicit goal to "develop the Negev" and, as the Zionist adage puts it, "make the desert bloom."[134]

The Naqab, called the Negev by Israel, has long constituted a difficult field for the state's "Judaization" project. The region makes up 60 percent of Israeli state territory but is currently home to only 8 percent of its citizen population.[135] During the 1948 war, approximately 80 percent of the Naqab's Palestinian (majority Bedouin) inhabitants were expelled, but few Jewish-Israelis were willing to settle in the region's desert conditions.[136] Sparse Jewish settlement was understood to be a threat to Israeli sovereignty and signaled the potential for Palestinian territorial contiguity.[137] Founded to incentivize Jewish settlement in the Naqab, Ben-Gurion University has played a major role in offering education, employment, and economic opportunity to the region's Jewish residents.[138]

As in the Galilee, Israel simultaneously worked to concentrate the Naqab's Indigenous Bedouin Palestinian population and appropriate their lands, while strategically settling Jewish-Israelis across the region. Though Palestinian citizens currently constitute 35 percent of the Naqab's population, they live in only 3.5 percent of its territory.[139] The process of re-engineering Bedouin settlement in the Naqab began in the 1950s, shortly after the Nakba. The historic Palestinian town of Beersheba became a military administrative center to govern the 11,000 Bedouins who remained in the region and who were ultimately granted Israeli citizenship. Still, most were concentrated in a military-controlled zone known as "the *siyag*" (fence), and—like all Palestinian citizens of Israel—were governed by military rule until 1966.[140] Israeli planning and legal policy implemented since the end of military rule has consistently moved to concentrate Palestinian Bedouin communities in increasingly shrinking territories while expanding Jewish settlement in their place.

All regional and national plans from the state's founding to the present have consistently advanced the Naqab's "Judaization" and the takeover of Palestinian Bedouin ancestral lands. This has been the case from the 1951 Sharon Plan (which worked to settle Jews on Bedouin lands) to the 1982 District Plan 4 (which aimed to move all Bedouins to Israeli-constructed dormitory towns) to the 2012–17 Prawer-Begin Plan (which intended to incentivize Bedouin relocation to larger towns and urban centers).[141] Following a sustained policy of concentrating the Bedouin population, the Israeli government criminalized their original villages and towns. Today, roughly half of the Naqab's Bedouins reside in seven Israeli-designed urban centers, and the rest live in forty-six villages that are either unrecognized or only semi-recognized by the Israeli state.[142] In an effort to force residents to relocate, these villages have been denied planning and civil services, including roads, electricity, and clinics, and have eviction and demolition orders pending against them.[143] Israeli policies of home demolitions and land and housing discrimination against Palestinian Bedouins have been repeatedly condemned by international human rights organizations as violations of international human rights law.[144]

At the same time as containing Palestinian Bedouins, Israel has been advancing Jewish settlement expansion for decades. As part of Israel's population dispersal plan starting in the 1950s, Israel developed the city of Beersheba into a regional metropolis, building nine development towns and more than a hundred rural settlements for Jewish residents.[145] Similar to the Galilee's mitspim project, beginning in the 1990s the government allocated plots of land to Jewish families to establish twenty-four "individual farms" across the Naqab, which currently offer boutique guesthouses and homemade wines.[146] These individual farms received state lands for free or at heavily subsidized prices, due to an official policy of "ensuring state control of strategic locations" and purporting to "safeguard" state lands from Bedouin villages.[147] The government has also continuously directed new Jewish immigrants to settle in the city of Beersheba; from North Africa and the Middle East in the 1950s, the former Soviet Union in the 1970s and 1990s, and, finally, Ethiopia in the 1990s.[148]

Today, Beersheba is Israel's fourth largest metropolis, but it remains sprawling, underdeveloped, and lacking sufficient economic prospects for its residents. Ben-Gurion University generates vital education, employment, and economic opportunities for Beersheba and the Naqab—but designed for its Jewish residents.[149]

These opportunities are explicitly not extended to Palestinian Bedouins. Instead, they continue to face barriers to education, such as inadequate conditions in primary and secondary schools in unrecognized villages, and insufficient means of transportation to institutions of higher education. Many villages still do not have paved access roads or access to public transportation. Students in unrecognized villages must travel to recognized villages for high school, and their primary schools are inadequately built and equipped, often with insufficient classrooms and no connection to running water or electricity.[150] Ben-Gurion University plays a central role in facilitating the very state policies that dispossess and deny education to the region's Bedouin Palestinian population.

The university has gradually expanded and opened satellite campuses, becoming a major stakeholder in regional development plans. Propelling both city and regional growth, the university works closely with the municipal government and the Israeli military to attract young Jewish-Israelis from central Israel to Beersheba and the Naqab.[151] As part of these efforts, the university collaborated with the Israeli state to relocate military bases to the Beersheba metropolis, and did so by incentivizing thousands of career soldiers and their families with tailored degree programs. The university also joined the municipality in opening a new high-tech park adjacent to the campus housing military industries, which offer veterans prestigious jobs in their fields and the opportunity to stay in Beersheba after their service. Its sciences and engineering departments have made plans for institutional collaboration with the Israeli military units of information and communications technology and air force technology, also slated to be located in the high-tech park.[152] Ben-Gurion University is scheduled to receive at least NIS 55 million (over USD 16 million) from the government to expand the campus and enable the absorption of thousands of new soldier-students. As the brigadier-general at the Ministry of Defense overseeing the project explained, the Israeli military will encourage locally based soldiers and their spouses to pursue studies at Ben-Gurion University to "strengthen the ecosystem between the security apparatuses, academia, and the population in the Negev."[153]

Facilitated by Ben-Gurion University, the development of the Naqab as the new regional home of Israeli military bases constitutes another vehicle of "Judaization." The move of a large campus of intelligence bases to the Naqab will require seizing additional Bedouin Palestinian lands and evicting thousands of Indigenous residents from towns included in the bases' zones.[154]

This territorial project is explicitly advanced by Ben-Gurion University's Jewish-Israeli student population itself. With government and institutional university support, students founded exclusively Jewish settlements across the Naqab, which provide student housing with the explicit goal of facilitating permanent residence on state lands previously inhabited by Palestinian Bedouins. Ayalim is one such initiative by Israeli military veterans to "revive Israel's settlement model" in the Naqab.[155] Ayalim has facilitated the establishment of twenty-two university "student villages," which work to facilitate permanent migration by developing university-centered Jewish communities.[156] Soliciting all Jewish university students at Ben-Gurion University, Ayalim offers highly subsidized housing and an additional scholarship for regional volunteer work.[157] The student villages are run in collaboration with the local government, the Jewish Agency, and the World Zionist Organization settlement division.[158] They are also promoted by Ben-Gurion University and student union websites and operate an information center on campus.[159]

What began as a Ben-Gurion University and Naqab-based initiative has since expanded to other universities and regions. Ayalim and Kedma—another demographic-engineering organization—are currently working to extend student-led "Judaization" efforts to the Galilee, the occupied West Bank, along the Gaza border, and "mixed" Jewish-Palestinian cities across Israel.[160] With support from the Ministries of Education, Agriculture, and Defense, these organizations are anchoring Jewish settlement growth in the student life of Ben-Gurion University and all Israeli universities.[161]

Ariel University and the "Judaization" of the West Bank

"To support Ariel University is to support Zionism." —Avraham Zion, professor at Ariel University[162]

The latest academic-territorial frontier is being advanced by Ariel University, founded with the explicit goal of expanding Israel's settlement project and promoting the "Judaization" of the occupied West Bank.[163] One of the earliest Israeli academic institutions in the OPT,

Ariel University was first established as "Judea and Samaria Academic College," under the auspices of Bar-Ilan University in 1982. The academic college was named after the settlement of Ariel, which hosts the institution, and was planned as a vehicle for the settlement's development and growth.[164] Ariel's founders sought to develop it into an Israeli urban center in the West Bank, which would, in turn, provide services and facilitate the establishment of other smaller Jewish settlements and outposts.[165] Like the mitspim in the Galilee and the "single farms" in the Naqab, the settlement of Ariel was strategically built as a partition along a mountain ridge to break up Palestinian territorial contiguity and curtail development of the Palestinian district of Salfit.[166]

Ariel was established in 1978 in the central West Bank by a "settlement core" led by employees of Israeli Military Industries and their families.[167] In 1973, they proposed that a settlement be founded at the heart of the West Bank yet a short commute from the Israeli Military Industries headquarters just north of Tel Aviv.[168] The founders planned to establish a secular urban center in the OPT, which would reduce the "psychological distance" for Israelis between the West Bank and the Tel Aviv Metropolitan Area and encourage further settlement expansion.[169] At the suggestion of the Planning Directorate of the Israeli military General Headquarters, the settlement core selected a hilltop on the farm and grazing lands of the Palestinian village Haris.[170] In violation of international law, Israel forcibly seized the territory from the Palestinians of Haris and declared it state land.[171]

Though the founders of Ariel described the location as a "rocky deserted hilltop," they initially named their town "Timnat Haris" for the Palestinian village on whose lands they built.[172] A few months later, the settlement name was officially changed to Ariel, one of the biblical names for Jerusalem, which the founding settlers believed would solidify its status as "the center of Israel."[173]

Central to Ariel's claims to Palestinian land and to its development plans was the aspiration to establish a university. Just one year after Ariel's founding, Ron Nachman, founder and then head of the Ariel local council, wrote a 1979 memorandum to Prime Minister Begin outlining his vision for establishing a city in the West Bank. In the memorandum,

Nachman defined the needs of the future city as including access to a freeway, connection to a seaport or airport, and, most crucially, a university. He contended that the contribution of a university to branding the city is "enormous," as it would increase demand for housing and serve as a strong pull for visitors and future residents.[174] "Anyone who comes to study here becomes our supporter," Nachman argued. "Instead of Ariel being a sleepy city, cafes and restaurants are opening here and it is becoming a university city. Success brings more success."[175]

Ariel became a city within a decade, with the college fueling its population growth. Ads to solicit new settlers centrally featured the college, and the city's real estate has been tied to its development.[176] With the institution's recognition as a university in 2012, real estate investment and rental prices shot up as both developers and students flooded the settlement.[177] The university is considered the engine of Ariel's growth, producing a demand for housing that spurred increases in rent and property prices as well as a flurry of new real estate development designated as student housing. Ariel is now marketed as a "student city" and has even been dubbed a "university with a city."[178] It is through the university, then, that Ariel has been transformed in Israeli public perception from an illegal and heavily militarized settlement into a suburb of Tel Aviv.[179]

Like Ben-Gurion University in the Naqab, Ariel University directly facilitates the engagement of its students in regional "Judaization" programs. The student-led organization Kedma established "student villages" in Ariel and in nearby settlements across the West Bank catering to Ariel University.[180] The university promotes the villages and collaborates with a government subsidized nonprofit to offer its student residents affordable housing and a scholarship, in exchange for their contribution to immigrant absorption and service provision in the settlement.[181] The university also grants academic credits to students volunteering for night shifts as guards and day shifts in farming in twenty-eight illegal outposts across the occupied West Bank, including on private Palestinian lands.[182]

Since its establishment in the OPT, the settlement of Ariel has continuously encroached on the lands of neighboring Palestinian villages in violation of their rights and international law.[183] A network of roads and a checkpoint serving Ariel—and the illegal separation barrier intended to surround the settlement and annex it to Israeli territory—serve to confiscate additional lands from indigenous Palestinian villages and violate the right to movement of tens of thousands of Palestinian residents.[184] The municipal area of Ariel contains enclaves of privately owned Palestinian cultivated farmland and grazing territory whose owners are prohibited from accessing them. Israel progressively declared most of the territory under the municipality as state land, gradually expropriating and annexing Palestinian enclaves to Ariel as the city expands. Ariel's untreated wastewater pollutes the water sources of neighboring Palestinian villages, causing disease among residents and damage to livestock and crops.[185]

The university itself seized private Palestinian land. Adjacent to the campus, the expropriated land is used by the university as a parking lot and space for outdoor student events, as well as a site to dump several tons of waste generated by construction for new student dorms.[186]

In the face of repeated condemnation by the UN, international human rights organizations, and the governments of the United States and European Union, Israel continues to establish facts-on-the-ground and expand the settlement of Ariel and its university.[187] Prime Minister Benjamin Netanyahu vowed that Ariel would continue to develop around its academic institution. "Anyone who understands geography knows how important Ariel is," Netanyahu asserted, declaring it to be an "integral and inseparable" part of the state of Israel.[188] Indeed, Israel has designated Ariel as an immovable "settlement bloc," whose annexation to Israel is not subject to negotiation. Despite statements from both Palestinian leadership and international experts that such an annexation would be detrimental to Palestinian sovereignty in the West Bank, Israel insisted on it during the 2000 Camp David negotiations as well as at the 2007 Annapolis Conference.[189]

The administrators of Ariel University waged a coordinated campaign with the Israeli government and the Council of Higher Education (CHE) to develop the academic institution. Initially designated as a college under the auspices of Bar-Ilan University, the institution's administration requested that the CHE recognize its bachelor's degree–granting programs as independent from Bar-Ilan. Unable to officially extend its jurisdiction to Ariel as an institution in Occupied Territory, the CHE collaborated with the Israeli government to extend the scope of its authority to the West Bank through an order from the governing military commander in 1992. The CHE further created a subordinate body called CHE Judea and Samaria that same year.[190] Funded by the same Planning and Budgeting Committee and later consisting of the same governing committee members, the CHE and CHE Judea and Samaria worked in coordination to extend recognition to bachelor's degrees granted by the college at Ariel.[191]

As it grew its degree-granting programs, the college also expanded the reach of Israeli legal jurisdiction in the West Bank. Ariel's institutional independence from Bar-Ilan University was further extended in 2005, when CHE Judea and Samaria granted recognition to the institution to begin operation as a "university center," while it was being evaluated for full university status. The institution changed its name to the Ariel University Center in Samaria and opened new master's degrees programs to meet CHE guidelines.[192] Full accreditation came soon thereafter in 2012, authorized by the Israeli military. The CHE Judea and Samaria officially recognized the institution at Ariel as a university, a move that was finalized with the approval of the major general of the Israeli military Central Command, the official regional sovereign authority in the occupied West Bank.[193] The CHE then extended formal recognition and support for the accreditation of Ariel as Israel's eighth university in 2013.[194]

As soon as it achieved university status, both Ariel and CHE Judea and Samaria unilaterally stopped requesting ratification from the CHE, as required for all doctoral degrees from institutions outside of Israel, declaring that the CHE's regulations already apply to it.[195] This created irregularities in the adjudication of degrees that Ariel University administrators and annexation proponents in the Israeli government both orchestrated and used to advance Israeli sovereignty in the OPT, leading to the final step toward official annexation facilitated by Ariel University. In 2018, the Knesset voted to amend the CHE statute to disband CHE

Judea and Samaria and apply CHE authority to Ariel University and all Israeli institutions of higher education in the West Bank.[196] The Minister of Higher Education and head of the CHE as well as Knesset members of far-right parties immediately celebrated the move as "making history" and "another step of establishing sovereignty" in the OPT.[197] They openly dismissed the denunciations by Palestinian Knesset Members for this blatant violation of international law, explicitly asserting that "we came to govern."[198]

As the final move before its dissolution in 2018, CHE Judea and Samaria voted to approve the establishment of a faculty of medicine at Ariel University.[199] The faculty's inaugural ceremony at Ariel that same year included Israeli government officials and Sheldon and Miriam Adelson, major funders of Prime Minister Netanyahu and the Israeli right and, now, a new medical school that bears their name. President Reuven Rivlin and Minister of Education Naftali Bennett praised the expansion of Ariel University, commendations echoed at the ceremony by Miriam Adelson when she declared: "True Zionism is knowing what belongs to us by right."[200]

The normalization and development of Ariel University and the Israeli settlement of the West Bank have thus been intertwined. The institution confers degrees as a means of expanding Israeli sovereignty and advancing the annexation of the OPT.

In the face of the overtly articulated use of academia to serve Israeli territorial expansion internationally condemned as illegal, the Israeli academic community has used Ariel University to whitewash their own participation in the national "Judaization" project. The recognition of Ariel University in such flagrant violation of international law threatened to undermine Israel's other universities, which share its state funding and are governed by the same accreditation process. This led to a short-lived opposition campaign waged by Israeli university administrations against Ariel University's accreditation. Most of the opposition staged by Israeli universities centered on the technical and financial implications of accreditation. Following the 2012 recognition of Ariel as a university by the CHE Judea and Samaria and the Israeli military Central Command, a committee of university presidents sent letters of objection to Prime Minister

Netanyahu and the minister of finance. They primarily cited funding and budgetary constraints that would be exacerbated were research funds to be directed to an additional university.[201]

Seven Israeli universities then petitioned the Israeli Supreme Court to block the certification. In their petition, the universities objected to the accreditation decision on account of its bias and lack of procedural transparency, its failure to consider recommendations made by the Planning and Budgeting Committee, and its negative financial implications for all existing universities.[202] This petition was rejected by the Supreme Court in 2013, which deemed the accreditation procedure appropriate and consistent with the CHE laws and regulations governing all other Israeli universities.[203] Once the accreditation was upheld by the Supreme Court, institutional opposition by Israeli universities was effectively dispelled.

The primary concern for Israeli academics throughout Ariel University's accreditation process has been their own self-preservation. In response to the 2018 legislation extending CHE jurisdiction to the occupied West Bank, some Israeli academic associations and individual faculty warned that this move constituted a breach of the scientific cooperation agreement that Israel had signed with the European Union, mandating a separation between the academic institutions in Israel and in the OPT.[204] The committee of university presidents further cautioned that by including Ariel University under the CHE, all Israeli universities have become implicated in scientific inquiry in the OPT: a move with potentially significant repercussions for international cooperation and funding.[205]

Even so, in 2021 the committee of university presidents announced a decision to accept Ariel University into the committee. Explaining this reversal, sources from the committee reasoned that once the CHE Judea and Samaria was disbanded, Ariel had already formally become an Israeli university. Another source conceded that the committee's opposition was muted after the significant international repercussions it anticipated in response to the accreditation of Ariel University did not transpire.[206]

~

Israeli universities tried, for a time, to frame Ariel University as exceptional. Yet it is but the latest frontier in a well-established tradition of demographic and territorial programming promoted by Israeli institutions of higher education. Despite initially distancing itself from Ariel, Hebrew University has served as a model for all the universities that followed it to become state outposts and pillars of regional "Judaization" efforts. The Hebrew University's charter states that the institution was established "out of the Zionist aspirations of the Jewish people," and, in direct continuity, Ariel University's charter proclaims its aim to be a "Zionist university."[207]

For over a century, Israeli universities have been expanding national borders and advancing "Jewish sovereignty" across all historic Palestine. Israeli universities continue to serve as settlement outposts on confiscated Palestinian lands, warehouses of looted Palestinian books, and militarized bases for the Israeli state to further Palestinian dispossession.

3

The Scholarly Security State

"Unlike in the United States where research is conducted at national labs, Israel has no such equivalent institutions ... Military R&D in Israel would not exist without the universities. They carry out all the basic scientific investigation, which is then developed either by defense industries or the army." —Former Major General Professor Isaac Ben-Israel, former head of the Yuval Ne'eman Workshop at Tel Aviv University[1]

"Without us there would be no industry ... the Israeli knowledge industry relies almost entirely on public-funded infrastructure and investment, which is funded by taxes, such as the military technological units, primarily Unit 8200, the defense industries such as IMI and Rafael, academic research at universities and budgets of the Chief Scientist." —Professor Isaiah Arkin, vice president of research and development at Hebrew University[2]

The development of Israeli universities is imbricated with the rise of Israeli military industries. Designed as state-building institutions, they were recruited to support its apparatuses of violence soon after their founding. Following the establishment of Hebrew University in

Jerusalem in 1918, the Zionist movement founded two additional institutions of higher education in Palestine: the Technion opened in Haifa in
1925, and the Weizmann Institute of Science in Rehovot in 1934. Hebrew
University was the Zionist movement's first comprehensive university
dedicated to research and teaching across disciplines; the Technion was
designed as the center of engineering; and the Weizmann Institute was
committed to scientific research for state-building.[3] During the intensifying military campaigns leading up to the founding of Israel in 1948,
the Zionist movement officially enlisted its three universities.

In 1946, the Haganah Zionist militia established HEMED, the Science
Corps, which opened bases on all three campuses. Universities soon
became central to the development and manufacture of weapons.[4] In
February 1948, a Hebrew University doctoral student in microbiology
initiated and headed the biological department at HEMED. By April
1948, the department prepared typhoid-dysentery bacteria to be used as
a biological weapon.[5]

Throughout the spring of 1948, the Haganah and other Zionist militias led military campaigns to expel Palestinians and claim their lands.
HEMED supported these efforts through departments that focused on
chemical, biological, and nuclear research and warfare capabilities, aided
by university students and researchers.[6]

HEMED's biological department typhoid-dysentery bacteria was
used in the Haganah's Cast Thy Bread operation to poison Palestinian
water sources.[7] This operation was personally overseen by Prime Minister
David Ben-Gurion and planned as a mechanism to prevent Palestinian
return to the villages from which they were expelled by Zionist militias.
On May 13, 1948, just before the war, Cast Thy Bread was implemented
in the recently depopulated Palestinian village of Bayt Mahsir.[8]

As part of the Haganah campaigns to depopulate major Palestinian
cities in the weeks leading up to the 1948 war, typhoid-dysentery was
used to poison Palestinian communities where they were still living. In
early May, the Haganah poisoned water sources in Palestinian neighborhoods in Jerusalem and the Kabri aqueduct that fed Acre. The poisoning
caused a disease outbreak in the targeted Palestinian communities but
did not have the debilitating effect its proponents had hoped for.[9]

Moreover, when the operation was expanded to target Egyptian and other Arab forces, Zionist operatives were caught and Arab states brought reports of the poisoning to the UN Security Council.[10] The representative of the Jewish Agency for Palestine, Abba Eban, vehemently denied the operation and worked to prevent further probes into the poisoning by accusing the Arab states of peddling in "antisemitic incitement."[11] A few months later, by December of 1948, Cast Thy Bread was discontinued by the Zionist leadership and military establishment in Palestine.[12] Despite this, the operation proved to be only the beginning for the Science Corps.

Throughout the remainder of the 1948 war, all HEMED departments were activated, and the faculty and students of the three universities were recruited to conduct military research and experimentation. The Weizmann Institute officially put its equipment and campus buildings at the disposal of the Haganah and, later, the newly formed Israeli military. For its part, the nascent Israeli government's central recruitment committee released all institute researchers and employees from their military duties and designated them as soldiers by virtue of their work. Senior researchers, employees, and students sustained the institute's activities 24/7 in rotating shifts. Faculty and students across the three institutions began developing and manufacturing diverse weaponry, including plastic explosives, rockets based on synthetic propellant compounds, shells for mortars and cannons, and ignition mechanisms for Napalm, tear gasses, and mines.[13]

By the end of the war, the Weizmann Institute had come to anchor the Military Science Corps and, together with the Technion, became the military-scientific center of the Israeli state.[14] The 1948 war marked the beginning, not the end, of university militarization.

Senior administrators and faculty at the Weizmann Institute and the Technion later led the development of Israeli military industries. They advocated establishing Israeli science as the basis of Israeli military power by developing and manufacturing Israeli advanced weaponry. In so doing, these scientists even went against the Israeli military leadership, which often espoused a more conservative approach to military research and development and favored purchasing weaponry from other states.[15] Ultimately, the scientists won. As Israeli research and development of weapons became institutionalized, the Science Corps was detached from the military. In 1952, HEMED was brought under the Ministry of Defense, where university scientists wielded more influence. It became the Research and Design Directorate, led by David Bergman, one of the founders and senior administrators of the Weizmann Institute. In 1958, the directorate became the Authority for the Development of Armaments (Harashut Haleumit Lepituach Emtzaei Lehima), best known by its Hebrew acronym, Rafael.[16]

One of Israel's leading state-owned weapons corporations, Rafael is now a major supplier to the Israeli military.[17] It is particularly known for its development and production of missiles, and armor and weapon systems for tanks, jet aircraft, and naval forces. Rafael technology and weapons are deployed in the Occupied Palestinian Territory and, on this basis, exported internationally. True to its origins at the facilities of the Weizmann Institute and the Technion, Rafael still calls itself "the national laboratory of Israel."[18]

Rafael was not the only weapons company birthed by Israeli academia. With support from the state, the Technion opened a Department of Aeronautical Engineering in 1954. The department tailored specialized courses based on Israeli military needs, and its faculty and students spearheaded the development of Israeli Aerospace Industries (IAI), transforming it into a company that produced Israeli-designed and manufactured fighter jets and missiles.[19] Today, IAI is one of Israel's leading weapons corporations, supplying the Israeli military with jets, drones, and weapons systems, and exporting them worldwide as "battle proven."[20]

Since the establishment of these military industries, they have remained embedded in the Technion and are often difficult to distinguish from the university. Scientists and engineers regularly moved back and forth between the university and the weapons companies and have sent their students to join them as employees. The companies, for their part, have funded the establishment of major Technion laboratories, and a network of Technion faculty dedicated to military research and development have functioned as their shadow employees. Technion researchers have developed a wide range of technologies—including new missiles and drones—which have gone into production by Rafael, IAI, and other Israeli weapons corporations, and then gone on to be used by the Israeli military.[21]

Though an industry leader, the Technion is not alone. This chapter reveals how Israeli universities support and advance the work of the Israeli military, security state, and weapons corporations. Universities run tailored academic programs to train Israeli soldiers and security forces personnel to enhance their operations. University institutes and academic courses serve the state through research and policy recommendations, which are designed not only to maintain Israeli military rule but also to undermine the movement for Palestinian rights in the international arena. Departments and faculty collaborate with the Israeli military, government, and Israeli and international weapons corporations to research and develop technology for Israeli military use and for international export. By collaborating with state apparatuses and private entities that enforce Israel's military occupation and apartheid, Israeli universities function as an academic arm of the Israeli security state.

Academic *Hasbara*

On March 30, 2018, tens of thousands of unarmed Palestinians began marching in the Gaza Strip toward the Israeli walls and barriers that enclosed them.[22] For the next fifty-one weeks, Palestinian men, women, and children marched every Friday, tens of thousands of people gathering at the wall.[23] Kept under a debilitating and illegal Israeli siege that has been deemed collective punishment, the Gaza Strip suffers from a critical shortage of clean drinking water, food and raw materials, and medicine and medical services.[24] The Israeli blockade suffocates Palestinians in the Gaza Strip in overcrowded refugee camps and in severe poverty, without avenues to leave, including for medical treatment.[25] In what became known as the "Great March of Return," Palestinians demanded their freedom, an end to the blockade, and the right to return to the homes and lands from which they were displaced in the 1948 Nakba or by Israel's 1967 military occupation.[26]

The Israeli military met these demonstrations by positioning snipers along the wall, who used high-velocity rifles to shoot directly at protestors. The snipers shot and killed at least 195 protestors, including medical personnel and journalists.[27] Over 35,600 protestors were injured, including 533 children.[28] Thousands of Palestinians were severely wounded or maimed by Israeli live ammunition, with at least 76 demonstrators requiring amputation of upper or lower limbs as a result of their injuries.[29]

The UN Commission of Inquiry found that Israel's deliberate use of live ammunition against civilian protestors violated international humanitarian law and may constitute crimes against humanity.[30] What the UN deemed a war crime, the Institute for National Security Studies (INSS) at Tel Aviv University considered a public relations crisis.

As early as June 2018, the INSS collaborated with the Israeli Military Spokesperson Unit to host a conference titled "The Battle for Public Opinion: Gaza as a Case Study."[31] The conference brought together military experts, officials from the Ministry of Foreign Affairs, journalists, and INSS fellows to discuss how Israel could best spin reports of Israeli military snipers shooting unarmed Palestinian protestors. The conference conceptualized the Great March of Return as an Israeli public relations problem, with panelists lamenting the inferiority of the Israeli narrative in the international arena. Israeli correspondents explained that the state's public relations failure was caused by the photographs and videos of Palestinian civilians maimed and killed at protests, images they claimed were "better" and more memorable for international audiences. Ron Ben-Yishai, a senior journalist at *Yedioth Ahronoth* put it bluntly: "When [an Israeli] sniper fires a bullet at someone's leg, it's a kinetic aspect of a public opinion battle."[32] Ben-Yishai explained the challenges of narrating the Israeli perspective when the international community is exposed to images from the March of Return: "Israel is from the outset at a disadvantage. We are Goliath and they are David."[33]

Concurring, government representatives discussed their tactics of establishing "shared messaging" and credible public relations, as well as their close coordination with international media to influence coverage of Israeli operations. State representatives stressed the importance of a coherent and unified system of military intelligence and government offices that could coordinate "shared messages." They discussed their strategy of maintaining a narrow pool of Israeli spokespeople, who become known to the international community and can be trusted to stay on message, alongside tours for international media to introduce them to Israeli messaging. Finally, government officials explained their strategies of demanding corrections to what they considered "distorted headlines" in international media, as well as lobbying major American media outlets to cover the marches as a "Hamas ploy" rather than civilian protests. Together with INSS fellows, journalists and military and government officials explicitly strategized about countering criticisms of Israel's military occupation and facilitating international identification with Israel.[34]

The use of academic spaces and fora to build state propaganda strategy, called *hasbara*, is common practice across Israeli universities. Housed at Tel Aviv University, the INSS is Israel's leading and most prestigious university-based think tank in the service of the state. The stated mission of the INSS is to conduct research on—and offer the Israeli government analyses and recommendations about—issues central to the state's "national security agenda."[35] The institute maintains close ties with the Israeli government, military, and security state forces; the executive staff, and the majority of its fellows, have previously occupied high-ranking positions in the Israeli military.[36] The institute's annual conference brings together senior policy-makers, influential Knesset members, and government and military leaders to debate Israel's major strategic issues.[37] Its flagship publication, the annual *Strategic Assessment for Israel*, is received by the Israeli president at an official ceremony each year. The INSS publication offers the state key policy recommendations on issues of "national security," including groundwork for military operations in the OPT and strategies for thwarting measures to hold Israel accountable for its violations of international law.[38]

The INSS plays an important role in shaping Israeli public policy in other aspects of Israeli foreign relations, particularly with research

projects for maintaining Israel's international status and legitimacy in
the United States and with American Jewry. This includes the institute's
research programs "Delegitimization and BDS" and "The American
Jewish Community and Israel's National Security," which regularly put
together conferences and roundtables and publish scholarly reports
including policy recommendations. These programs aim to create timely
opportunities for the Israeli state to draw lessons from past experience
and improve Israeli *hasbara* efforts, often in response to current events.[39]

INSS researchers regularly formulate policy for the Israeli state to
combat the BDS movement and other campaigns critical of Israel,
including the recommendation to employ Israeli intelligence agencies to
"incriminate," "undermine," and "sabotage" activists working for
Palestinian rights.[40] To address what they call the "delegitimization" of
Israel, the INSS offers policy recommendations for disrupting BDS
organizing, including through covert action by Israel's intelligence
community. Assembled by an INSS group of Tel Aviv University faculty,
former Israeli diplomats, and military personnel, the recommendations
include "maligning and incriminating" BDS activists for connections
with organizations construed by Israel as "terrorist" or human rights
violators, disclosing personal histories of activists "contravening Western
norms," and exposing the "dubious validity of their resources," as well as
"actively sabotaging" social movement activities.[41] On American university campuses, the recommendations include Israeli intelligence forces'
collaboration with civilian bodies and "to 'launder' classified intelligence
products" so that partner organizations can effectively work against criticism of Israel.[42]

At the University of Haifa, the Comper Interdisciplinary Center for
the Study of Anti-Semitism and Racism plays another role in Israeli
hasbara, primarily by mobilizing students. "Ambassadors Online," a
program initiated and led by center head and media studies professor Eli
Avraham, offers academic and "practical training" to cultivate student
capabilities to become "unofficial ambassadors" and leaders in Israel
hasbara.[43] As shown by previous syllabi, the course content includes
lectures by University of Haifa faculty and deans, alongside members of
the Israeli state *hasbara* apparatuses, including from the Prime Minister's

Office and the Ministry of Foreign Affairs. The course final assignment was to create content for Israeli public diplomacy.[44]

When initially launched in 2012, "Ambassadors Online" was offered as an extracurricular activity. Today, it is an accredited course at the University of Haifa, which even offers select scholarships for participating students.[45]

The Comper Center offers research scholarships for the study of what it calls the "delegitimization of Israel and the new anti-Semitism." Sharing resources for Israeli advocacy, the Center's website links to the Israeli military, Ministry of Foreign Affairs, and a range of Israeli and international Zionist advocacy organizations, as well as a report, entitled "Strategies to Combat the Academic Boycott of Israel."[46] Co-authored by Eli Avraham, the report is intended for "Israeli scholars going on Sabbatical, attending conferences overseas or studying abroad" and proposes *hasbara* talking points to respond to or spin some of the main arguments of the Palestinian BDS movement.[47] The report's many claims are broad and often overtly colonial, backed by examples that are anecdotal and inaccurate or completely unsubstantiated; these include statements such as, "there is no discrimination between Jewish and Arab students on Israeli campuses," and "the situation and living conditions of the Palestinians have improved under Israeli rule."[48]

The University of Haifa markets itself as especially well positioned to make claims about Palestinian life. Located in the Palestinian-majority Galilee and servicing the highest number of Palestinian students than any Israeli university, the university likes to showcase its own campus as modeling Israel's alleged multicultural pluralism. As such, the "Ambassadors Online" program has been particularly eager to employ Palestinians to do the work of Israeli *hasbara*. In 2017, the program gave honorary awards exclusively to Druze Palestinians—who are also the only Palestinian citizens drafted to the Israeli military—at a ceremony honoring their contribution to state propaganda.[49] Eli Avraham was explicit that the awards were intended to deploy Palestinians and other minorities in showcasing a different image of Israel to the world:

This time we wanted to give only to the men and women of the Druze community; the idea was showing respect and appreciation and thanking those people in order to encourage and strengthen them. Our institution works on the relationship between academia and the government and the relationship with civil society. I believe that soon it will also be given to members of other ethnic groups who are engaged in Israeli *hasbara*.[50]

This mobilization has already proven effective. Just two months after the awards ceremony, the University of Haifa hosted a delegation of the Ohio House of Representatives, in which Palestinian students selected by the Comper Center were deployed to aid in portraying their campus as a beacon of pluralism. The message was received. As representative Tim Ginter proclaimed to the press: "When you look at the Israeli academy, you realize how much the BDS lie to the whole world. The Israeli Academy treats all students equally, regardless of religion, race or gender. We are here to encourage more and more collaborations with this great university and to denounce this [BDS] phenomenon."[51] President Ron Rubin returned in kind:

We were proud to host our friends from the US parliament in Ohio, who these days are passing another important legislation against the BDS movement. The University of Haifa operates a unique platform to fight against these entities; through the project "Ambassadors Online" Jewish, Arab, and foreign students receive unique training in digital diplomacy and spread the truth about life in Israel in general and academia in particular. We will continue to develop intellectual and other means, in order to strike the industry of lies.[52]

At a ceremony in 2019 celebrating the new academic track crediting students for the study of methodologies in Israeli *hasbara,* Rubin proudly declared: "The University of Haifa is at the forefront of the fight against anti-Semitism and the boycott movement."[53]

Indeed, "Ambassadors Online" is designed to repress the BDS movement, in Israel and globally. The university has been mobilizing its students and resources to develop communication tools to counter the BDS movement and, where state-led propaganda is no longer sufficient, to criminalize it. Through centers such as the INSS and Comper, Israeli academia offers resources to the Israeli state in its campaign to evade accountability for its illegal military occupation and regime of apartheid. They produce scholarly work to justify its military operations in the international arena, fortifying the state against the anticipated scrutiny yet to come.

But Israeli universities' support for the military does not stop there. Their academic programs train Israeli soldiers before they are deployed to the Occupied Palestinian Territory, in military offensives that violate international laws of war.

Academic Bases: Training Israeli Security Forces

"The combination of military and academic training requires close and deep cooperation between the university and the air force flight academy. Each side brings to this joint program tradition, principles and values that at first glance seem very different, but upon deeper examination it is evident that their similarities are greater than their differences." —Professor Michael Codish, former head of the air force program at Ben-Gurion University[54]

"The University of Haifa is responsible for the academic training of the IDF's command core for years to come, and we are proud to open our door to IDF forces and to be the academic home of the security forces. These dear people are working day and night for the security of the State of Israel and we will provide them with the highest level of educational content." —Professor Ron Rubin, former president of the University of Haifa[55]

Israeli universities run programs that conceptualize academic and military training as one and the same. All public universities offer their facilities, faculty, and expertise for Israeli military training, advancing the career development of soldiers and security state personnel through specialized degree-granting programs.[56] Atuda (academic reserve) is a specialized academic program for soldiers—run by the Israeli military and Ministry of Defense, in collaboration with weapons manufacturers and the Administration for the Development of Weapons and Technological Infrastructure—that is administered through the Israeli university system. The Atuda program was developed to offer the Israeli military a cadre of highly educated and specialized soldiers, amid a national draft of high school seniors.[57]

Through Atuda, the Israeli military offers fifty degree programs across all public Israeli universities, covering soldiers' tuition and granting needs-based stipends in exchange for extended military service as commanders and officers.[58] The wide-ranging disciplines include languages, humanities, law, life sciences, data sciences, and engineering. Through Atuda, soldiers are drafted and then sent to complete academic degrees and basic training, followed by a minimum six years of military service. This elite academic-military track has long operated as a pipeline to both military leadership and academia, as well as to Israel's military and tech industries.[59]

By the accounts of senior military personnel and academics, the program outputs are consequential. They claim that Atuda is central to Israel's technological capabilities and competitive edge in the global market. Knowledge and ideas developed through Atuda are not patented by the military, allowing for a "knowledge spillover" into the Israeli private sector.[60] Graduates of Atuda degree programs in physics, math, and computer science have frequently assumed key positions in Israeli military research and development; some later established their own security sector companies worth millions of dollars.[61]

Complementing Atuda degree programs, Israeli universities run specialized degrees for high-ranking military personnel. The University of Haifa houses flagship programs of this kind through three Israeli military academies: the National Security College, the Tactical Command College, and the Alon Command and Control College. Through the National Security College, the University of Haifa offers a tailored master's degree in security theory for Israeli colonels and high-ranking members of Israeli security agencies.[62] Though under the auspices of a public university, the National Security College is headed by an Israeli major-general, and all students are enrolled in the master's program by the military and their respective security agencies, and cannot independently apply.[63] As explained by the Israeli military, these academic programs are designed to ensure uniformity and continuity in the training of Israeli commanders. Through the Alon Command and Control College, the University of Haifa offers tailored master's degrees in political science to army battalion commanders and air force squadron commanders, with a specialization in "military security."[64]

The boundaries are blurred between military training bases and Israeli university campuses. In some elite programs, soldiers complete specialized degree programs throughout their active military service, such as with Ben-Gurion University's accelerated BA for fighter pilots designed to complement their professional training.[65] In others, military and academic training are intertwined and carried out across both university campuses and military bases, such as with Hebrew University's Talpiot combined BSc in physics, computer science, and math. Under the auspices of the Administration for the Development of Weapons and Technological Infrastructure and the Israeli Air Force, the program fosters leadership in "technological research" for the maintenance and development of weapon systems for the Israeli military and the security establishment.[66] Most of the training takes place at the Air Force Command and Leadership School at Hebrew University's Giv'at Ram Campus, but soldiers are also trained in military bases and security state facilities. Following their graduation and training, Talpiot soldiers are integrated into units of the Israeli military and security state in leadership positions in areas of technological innovation and development.[67] After their mandatory nine years of service, an average of one-third of Talpiot graduates stay in the military, another third enter academia, and the rest move into the private sector.[68] Across these three spheres, Talpiot soldiers play pivotal roles in the research and development sustaining Israeli military capabilities and in the sales of weapons in the global security market.

Though Talpiot is by far the Israeli military's most elite Atuda program, Hebrew University does not hold a monopoly on military research and development.[69] The Technion runs Alonim, an accelerated BSc to MSc program in data science for soldiers, after which they are incorporated into R&D projects in technological military units and the security state.[70] Alongside Ben-Gurion University, the Technion offers the Brakim BSc to MSc program in engineering, training soldiers for R&D in Israel's military and military industries.[71] The accompanying Bareket master's program in data engineering, run with Bar-Ilan University, trains soldiers in data science, coding, and programming for military application.[72] Tel Aviv University's School of Electrical Engineering runs the Galim MSc program, where soldiers receive academic guidance from the Intelligence Corps to prepare for placement in technological units of the Israeli military and in the security forces.[73] Elite programs such as these offer directed academic training to soldiers to integrate them into R&D for the Israeli military and military industries. As head of the School of Electrical Engineering Mark Shtaif explained: "The Galim program is another important step in strengthening the relationship between academia and industry, and in this case the IDF. It is about utilizing the potential that exists in the connection between exceptionally high-quality youth, and the needs of the IDF's intelligence units."[74]

Tel Aviv University professor Evyatar Matnia, himself a Talpiot graduate, pushed the Israeli Intelligence Corps to utilize academic training to advance their capabilities. While serving as lieutenant colonel in the reserves of the Israeli Intelligence Directorate in 2003, Matnia walked unannounced into the office of the Chief Intelligence Officer and placed a twelve-page proposal on his desk. This document lay the foundation for what became the flagship Intelligence Corps Atuda program, the result of what Matnia called "thinking about the right way to build the future officers of the Intelligence Directorate."[75] The intent was to develop tailored degree programs that were "adapted for the needs of the intelligence community in the modern era."[76] Hebrew University runs two such elite programs: Havatzalot, which offers soldiers regional and linguistic expertise in Middle East studies, and Gamla, a BA program for Intelligence Corps officers preparing for extended service at the rank of major.[77]

This daily labor of Israeli Intelligence Corps soldiers violates Palestinian human rights, as stipulated in international law and the Fourth Geneva Convention.[78] Many of the soldiers graduating from Hebrew University's tailored degree programs serve in Unit 8200, the largest and most central Intelligence Corps unit. Unit 8200 is the military's central collection unit, responsible for amassing all intelligence transmissions, including phone calls, text messages, and emails.[79] As Palestinians have long reported—and as Israeli whistleblowers from the unit have corroborated—soldiers from Unit 8200 use their routine surveillance of Palestinians in the OPT to extort or try them, based on their most personal information. Soldiers reported that their daily work included gathering data used to try Palestinians in military courts without ever seeing the evidence against them and documenting a wide variety of personal information that can be used to extort Palestinians into serving as informants or otherwise collaborating with the Israeli military and Shin Bet: including financial difficulties, sexual orientation, serious illness, or medical treatments needed by a loved one.[80]

In a 2014 protest letter to the Israeli government, forty-three soldiers and reservists from Unit 8200 revealed that "information that is collected and stored harms innocent people and is used for political persecution and creating division in Palestinian society by recruiting collaborators and turning parts of Palestinian society against itself . . . the Intelligence Corps enables continuous control over millions of people, in-depth and intrusive supervision and invasion of most areas of life."[81] These Intelligence Corps soldiers exposed the wide latitude they had in making highly consequential decisions over Palestinian life. As one of the letter writers explained: "Junior soldiers can decide that someone is a target for information gathering. There is no procedure in which they consider whether the violation of a person's rights is justified. The idea of Palestinian rights does not exist at all."[82] Unit 8200 soldiers reported firsthand knowledge of Israeli security personnel extorting and recruiting Palestinians based on their loved ones needing cancer treatments. As one soldier testified: "If you need urgent medical treatment in Israel, the West Bank or abroad—we were looking for you. The state of Israel will let you die before it will let you go for medical treatment without giving information about your wanted cousin."[83]

Palestinians across the OPT have been reporting these forms of Israeli coercion for years, including interrogations and extortion of Palestinians seeking care for serious illnesses. A thirty-eight-year-old Palestinian father of two living in the Gaza Strip was one of many to report this experience in 2007. Diagnosed with Hodgkin's lymphoma, he petitioned to obtain entry to seek treatment at an Israeli hospital but was questioned and extorted as he tried to cross the Erez checkpoint. Interrogated for hours, he was asked to inform on his brother and other relatives, after which the Israeli interrogator threatened to withhold his access to treatment, telling him: "You have cancer, and it will soon spread to your brain, as long as you don't help us."[84] After being forced to wait for over ten hours, he missed his appointment and returned home.[85] Al Mezan Center for Human Rights reports that Israeli practices of extorting and arresting Palestinian cancer patients as they travel to and from the Gaza Strip are ongoing and have documented such cases up to 2023.[86] Al Mezan and Physicians for Human Rights–Israel have documented these Israeli practices, which they argue may constitute a war crime for violating international humanitarian law, and violate Article 31 of the Fourth Geneva Convention and the UN Convention against Torture and Other Cruel, Inhuman or Degrading Treatment or Punishment.[87]

Intelligence Corps soldiers whose daily work violates Palestinian human rights and international law are trained yearly at Israeli universities. So, too, are Israeli Air Force pilots and military engineers, as Israeli campuses have taken on many functions of military training bases. In tailoring courses and degrees to soldiers and offering soldiers exclusive training under their auspices, Israeli universities have become integral to honing Israel's military capabilities and reproducing its labor power.

Meanwhile, at labs on other corners of their campuses, faculty and students busily work to supply the Israeli military and military industries with research to develop the technologies with which Israeli soldiers sustain the occupation of Palestinian Territory.

The University-Military-Industrial Complex

"The Technion is woven into Elbit's DNA." —Michael Federmann, chairman of Elbit Systems[88]

"Elbit Systems is proud to be an active partner in advancing the research being carried out at the Technion ... the investment in research and development is one of the key factors for Elbit Systems' success so far and it is a vital condition for our continued leadership in the global defense industry." —Yossi Ackerman, Elbit Systems president[89]

"The new program that we are launching and the annual contribution that Elbit Systems will give each year to research ... is an example of fruitful cooperation between the Technion and the industry. I have no doubt that our students and Elbit Systems will enjoy and reap the fruit of this cooperation soon." —Yitzhak Apeloig, Technion's president[90]

Developed through collaborations with Israeli universities, Rafael, IAI, and Elbit are Israel's leading military corporations and global exporters of technologies of war. Elbit is a world leader in the design and manufacture of drones, while Rafael and IAI are known for their missile systems. Initiated as nationally owned industries designed to supply domestically produced technologies to the Israeli state, their main client remains the Israeli military. As such, their products are routinely adopted by Israeli combat brigades and the Israeli air force and deployed against occupied Palestinians.

Elbit and IAI drones carrying Rafael missiles were used in Israeli offensives on the besieged Gaza Strip in 2008–9, 2012, and 2014.[91] Elbit military aircraft display systems are integrated into F-16 fighter jets and Apache helicopters, including their helmet-mounted displays, enabling fighter pilots to fire weapons by pointing their head.[92] These aircraft were used to fire missiles on Palestinians in all Israeli offensives on the Gaza Strip between 2008 and 2021.[93] Israeli Merkava tanks were also used in these offensives, equipped with technology and weaponry designed and manufactured by the same corporations. Merkava tanks are produced by a designated directorate at the Ministry of Defense, in collaboration with the Israeli military and Elbit, and fitted with a Rafael Trophy radar system that provides Israeli soldiers with coordinates and shortens the "sensor-to-shooter cycle" to improve artillery effectiveness.[94]

Due to its disregard for and inadequate protection of Palestinian civilians, Israel was found by the UN Human Rights Council and international human rights organizations to have committed war crimes in all its major offensives on the Gaza Strip in 2008–9, 2012, 2014, and 2021.[95] Weapons and technologies designed and manufactured by IAI, Elbit, and Rafael were deployed to commit these crimes. Yet the use of Israeli military industries' technology against Palestinian civilians has not interrupted their collaborations and partnerships with Israeli universities.

The Technion remains instrumental to the expansion of Israeli military industries and continues to fuel them with new ideas and new employees.[96] The Technion has created a university-to-military-industry pipeline, bringing Israeli weapons corporations onto campus and building programming so as to integrate their students into the industry while they are still enrolled. Rafael routinely arrives on campus to solicit students as employees, guiding them in choosing academic concentrations to meet the future needs of the company. Rafael has even tailored positions for Technion students, including transportation between campus and its facilities and offers select students guaranteed tenure at the company.[97] Elbit has granted hundreds of thousands of dollars to fund directed research grants and scholarship programs and also trains students at the advanced laboratory it installed on campus and, through funding, directed that research and supporting instruction in electro-optics and other fields with military industry application.[98]

The Technion also operates long-standing joint R&D projects with Rafael and Elbit. With the launch of the Global War on Terror, the Technion opened its Center for Security Science and Technology, with the aim of enhancing collaboration with the Israeli security state and private industry abroad. Its annual conference features military industry leaders and Ministry of Defense representatives alongside Technion faculty and students presenting their recent technological innovations with military applications.[99] The Technion's Department of Aerospace Engineering was developed alongside and continues to run a wide range of collaborations with Israeli military industries.[100] These include faculty and student projects funded by the Israeli Ministry of Defense and Rafael to develop research and technology for drones and missiles, among other weapons.[101] The biannual Conference on Aerospace Science—put on by the Technion together with the Israeli Air Force, Rafael, and IAI—facilitates collaboration between students and faculty with the Israeli military and military industries and directed toward global export.[102] In one of its most recent contracts in 2021, the Technion committed to developing new software for Rafael, Elbit, and Lockheed Martin.[103]

Though leading the development of weapons, the Technion is not alone. All Israeli universities work closely with the Israeli government to develop the state's military industries and technologies for the military. Israel's Administration for the Development of Weapons and Technological Infrastructure (MAFAT), the R&D directorate of Israel's Ministry of Defense, maintains close ties with university administrations. MAFAT's stated aim is to "ensure Israel's ability to develop weapons to build its strength and to continue to maintain its qualitative advantage."[104] MAFAT is therefore responsible for weapons and technology infrastructure, cultivating technological research personnel, soliciting and funding research from Israeli universities, and collaborating with academic institutions and military industries on development for the Israeli military.[105]

The close cooperation between MAFAT and Israeli universities is often facilitated by their shared personnel. Isaac Ben-Israel, now a retired major general, held a variety of senior roles in the Israeli military, the last of which was head of MAFAT. With his retirement from the military in 2002, Ben-Israel immediately joined the faculty at Tel Aviv University. At the university, Ben-Israel founded and continues to head the Yuval Ne'eman Workshop for Science, Technology, and Security, which leads academic research with concrete applications for the security state, including cybersecurity, robotics, missiles, and guided weapons. The workshop also holds a conference series at Tel Aviv University that includes members of the Israeli military and security agencies as well as Israeli and international military industries.[106] Its annual cybersecurity conference on campus is organized with the Israeli government and Israeli weapon expos and is intended to showcase technological innovations from Tel Aviv University and Israeli military corporations.[107]

The Yuval Ne'eman Workshop is not alone in openly showcasing university-facilitated academic research in service of the state and military industries. Many of MAFAT's collaborations with academic departments and faculty are openly advertised. These include the programs, conferences, and expos of nanotechnology centers operated by six universities in collaboration with Israeli government agencies and military industries.[108] Tel Aviv University's Center for Nanoscience and Nanotechnology, for example, collaborates on R&D with Israeli weapons companies, including IAI and Elbit.[109]

Other initiatives are classified, with funding from MAFAT or other Israeli government agencies to support research projects announced only indirectly or without key details about the technological innovations that emerge from them.[110] Some of these technologies are developed through collaborations with Israeli agencies and advertised only when they are brought to the private market. TAU Ventures, Tel Aviv University's venture capital fund, for instance, worked with the Shin Bet to establish the Xcelerator program for start-ups.[111] Selected student projects received a $50,000 grant from the Shin Bet and participated in a mentoring and consultation program run by the agency.[112] Talamoos and Cyabra, two start-ups that emerged from the program, developed algorithms and systems for predicting user behaviors and inducing them to consume content, install software, or open links that enable state surveillance.[113] These types of cooperation between universities, the security state, and military industries further transform campuses into facilities to develop technologies both for Israeli military use and for international export.

Alongside their campuses, Israeli universities often operate technological "parks," where the application of their research can be translated into innovation for the Israeli security industry. The Weizmann Institute operates Kiryat Weizmann, a high-tech science park adjacent to its campus that facilitates joint research and product development between the institute and private corporations. It houses facilities of Israel's weapons companies Rafael and Elbit and Elbit's subsidiary El-Op, among others.[114] The National Laboratory for the Development of Space Cameras, inaugurated by the Ministry of Defense at El-Op's facilities at the park, works on technology for detecting targets illicitly photographed by drones, developed by the Weizmann Institute and Ben-Gurion University.[115]

Another such facility is Gav-Yam Negev, the advanced technologies park at the edge of the Ben-Gurion University campus. Launched in cooperation with the Be'er-Sheva Municipality, the Israeli military, and private investors, Gav-Yam Negev is slated to be Israel's chief research and development center.[116] Rafael's research and development branch at the park serves to anchor technological innovation in advanced autonomous systems.[117] President of Ben-Gurion University Rivka Carmi called Rafael's facilities at the advanced technologies park a "realization of our vision."[118] Ran Gozali, senior vice president at Rafael, similarly rejoiced at the partnership: "This collaboration will help support our autonomous systems by working with leading experts in the field, such as the researchers at Ben-Gurion University. We are confident that this collaboration will help maintain the quality advantage and innovative solutions that Rafael offers its customers."[119]

All seven of the major public universities in Israel have also established subsidiary commercialization companies to streamline this foreign export.[120] These companies patent intellectual property for profit and market student and faculty innovations through collaboration with Israeli and international corporations.[121] Expectedly, most of the university commercialization companies have formed long-term partnerships with Israeli and international military industries. Hebrew University's commercialization company, Yissum ("application" in Hebrew), currently claims status as a global leader in technologies used for "homeland security."[122] The US government invests millions of dollars annually in supporting Hebrew University's "counter-terrorism" research and Yissum's technologies acquisition.[123] Yissum also holds an agreement with Lockheed-Martin granting it the opportunity to acquire exclusive licenses for any invention or product resulting from joint applied research.[124]

Ben-Gurion University's commercialization company, BGN Technologies, operates joint research and cooperation with Rafael, Elbit, IAI, and Lockheed-Martin.[125] Bar-Ilan University's commercialization company—BIRAD—operates a long-term partnership with Rafael and has facilitated a research collaboration with Elbit's technological incubator.[126] Meetings between the technology team at Elbit and university researchers are intended to expose weapon developers to academic research "on the verge of implementation."[127] This collaboration is critical to Israeli military industries, as Elbit's chief scientist made clear: "These meetings are one of the tools that Elbit uses in order to maintain technological leadership, monitor emerging and breakthrough technologies, and provide feedback to academia on the needs of industry."[128] Israeli universities are critical nodes in the state's military-industrial complex, sustaining Israel's apartheid regime and the occupation of Palestinian Territory that serves as its laboratory.

The Technion not only facilitated the birth of the Israeli military industry but also continues to support the international sales of its weaponry, even going so far as to explicitly offer courses on arms and security marketing and export.[129] Offered through 2015, the course was taught by Technion faculty and Israeli security industry experts and designed in close collaboration with the Ministry of Defense. The course covered applied topics such as security exports and its supervision, payment terms, communication marketing, and the interrelationships between security exports and the foreign relations of the Israeli state.[130] Meir Shalit, the program's academic advisor at the Technion, is also former head of the Department of Export Supervision at the Ministry of Defense. He lauded the program as an engine of Israeli growth in the security sector and as particularly useful for budding Israeli weapons corporations; Shalit stated, "The potential for growth in the field is found among small and medium-sized manufacturers, so it is desirable for them to professionalize," and emphasized that the program "provides all the elements that are important to know."[131] The course is designed, Shalit explained, for "people who are actually engaged in security exports," including company managers, board members, senior officers, legal advisors, accountants, and internal auditors.[132] Eyal Bar Or, who served in various research and development positions in the Israeli Air Force and the Ministry of Defense before moving into private industry, is one of the course lecturers and put it bluntly: "People are not aware of how much money can be made in the field of defense exports."[133] This course, then, is also for them.

The Israeli state's military industries and its universities have always been co-constituted. Universities have birthed, funded, and advanced their scientific research through the Israeli security state and Israeli weapons corporations. Israeli universities train soldiers and security state personnel as students, so that they can hone their capabilities to maintain the military governance of the Occupied Palestinian Territory, while producing policy recommendations to thwart Palestinian mobilization and growing international scrutiny. They offer their campuses, resources, students, and faculty to aid in the development of technology and weaponry deployed against Palestinians and then sold worldwide as "battle-proven."[134] Far from fighting to become civilian institutions, university campuses are continually expanding their operations not only as military training bases, but as weapons laboratories for the Israeli state.

PART 2
Repression

4

Epistemic Occupation

In February 2019, the Center for Palestine Studies at Columbia University invited Nadera Shalhoub-Kevorkian to give a talk. A Palestinian professor of law, criminology, and social work at Hebrew University, Shalhoub-Kevorkian shared insights, from her decades of research, about the daily violence that Palestinian families and children in occupied East Jerusalem endure at the hands of Israeli police and military forces. This oppression is not only lethal but also profitable, she argued, since Israel uses occupied Palestinian neighborhoods to test its policing methods, surveillance technologies, and weapons before marketing and exporting them abroad as "combat proven."

Segments of Shalhoub-Kevorkian's talk were edited and played on "Good Morning Israel," a primetime program on Israel's most popular radio station, run by the military. The coverage sparked outrage among some Israeli students and academics and raised the ire of Minister of Education Naftali Bennett. In an interview on the same radio show, Bennett called for her firing, exclaiming that "it is not possible for a university to employ a person who slanders IDF soldiers."[1]

The military radio requested a response from Hebrew University, demanding to know why Shalhoub-Kevorkian presented her claims as academic research conducted under its aegis. The university immediately distanced itself from Shalhoub-Kevorkian, calling her research "personal opinions" that "do not represent or express the Hebrew University in any way."[2] Multiple mainstream media outlets picked up the story, condemning her and echoing the minister of education's accusation of slander. An outpour of vitriol soon followed, including death threats and a barrage of racialized and sexualized verbal violence.

With her institution failing to defend her, Shalhoub-Kevorkian was left alone to face this intimidation campaign. She returned to work amid students and colleagues who treated her with open contempt, with many calling for her dismissal and some echoing threats against her. For Shalhoub-Kevorkian, this was a familiar story. As an outspoken scholar of Palestinian life and resistance under Israeli state violence, who is uncompromising in her research and analysis, she had been subjected to frequent harassment. But the attacks against her had escalated in recent years, and have continued since. Time and again, mainstream media and the Israeli right have sought to silence Shalhoub-Kevorkian, and multiple Israeli ministers of education have personally intervened to suppress her work. In each instance, Hebrew University has disavowed her research and refused to commit to her safety in the face of widespread threats within and outside the university.[3]

The claims that have angered much of the Jewish-Israeli public are based on Shalhoub-Kevorkian's scholarly research, published in leading international peer-reviewed journals.[4] The data underlying her analysis is based on ethnographic observations and interviews with Palestinians living under occupation. A resident of East Jerusalem, Shalhoub-Kevorkian lives and witnesses this oppression on her way to work at Hebrew University's Mt. Scopus campus, which towers over the city's occupied Palestinian neighborhoods.[5] Israeli violence in East Jerusalem has also long been documented by leading human rights organizations, including Israeli groups.[6] Israel's use of technologies and weapons in the Occupied Palestinian Territory (OPT) and their subsequent international export as "field-tested" is, likewise, public knowledge and, indeed, a key marketing strategy for Israeli military industries themselves.[7]

Yet Shalhoub-Kevorkian's decolonial scholarship—on what she calls "state criminality"—challenges the hegemonic frameworks of Israeli academia. For the Israeli government and for many of her colleagues, such critique is illegitimate and grounds for her banishment from the university.

Shalhoub-Kevorkian is not alone in this experience. Palestinian citizens of Israel across Israeli universities face attacks on their critical research and writing. This is particularly the case for those who wish to explore the history and present conditions of Palestinians under Israeli rule, both within the Israeli state and in the OPT. Israeli universities have long constrained the right of Palestinian faculty and scholars to investigate the subjects and events most central to the Palestinian experience: the founding of the state of Israel in 1948 and, with it, the mass expulsion, dispossession, and fragmentation of the Palestinian people, thereafter divided into refugees living in the diaspora, those living under Israeli military rule in the OPT, and those living as citizens within Israel's pre-1967 borders.

Israel was established through the forcible displacing of over two-thirds of the Palestinian population, in what is called the Nakba. The Palestinians remaining in the territory controlled then by Israel became a minority placed under Israeli military rule until 1966, with most later granted suffrage and then citizenship.[8] Israeli citizenship, however, did not offer Palestinians full rights or equality under the Israeli state. As Nadim Rouhana, Lana Tatour, and Areej Sabbagh-Khoury show, Israeli citizenship—like Israeli military rule—served as a governing apparatus to dispossess Palestinians and as a mechanism to prevent them from returning to their lands. Instead of the right to return to their original communities and homes, the Israeli state offered citizenship to Palestinians as a contingent protection from future expulsion, thereby enshrining their domination and exclusion.[9]

This continues to be the main function of Israeli citizenship for Palestinians, who were and remain, as Nimer Sultany argues, "occupied citizens" in the Israeli state.[10] As such, Palestinian scholars entering Israeli universities have long been treated with suspicion, their investigation of the foundational questions for Palestinian society curtailed, and their critical research and teaching routinely made untenable.

This chapter explores how Israeli universities systematically disallow critical academic research, teaching, and discussion of Israeli settler colonialism, military occupation, and apartheid. In Israel's first decades, academic disciplines subordinated their knowledge production to the state and foreclosed Palestinian and critical scholarship. In the 1980s, new openings emerged for exploration of the Zionist movement and the 1948 war in Israeli academia, principally in history and sociology.[11] As of the late 1990s, Palestinian scholars have increasingly studied the Israeli state through the analytic of settler colonialism, with a few even forging paths into Israeli universities.[12] In the years since, Palestinian—and some critical Jewish-Israeli—scholars across humanities and social science departments have expanded investigation of the historical violence of the Zionist movement and the founding of the state of Israel, as well as of the ongoing dispossession and oppression of Palestinians living under Israeli rule.[13]

The backlash to this scholarship has been fierce. Beginning in the 1980s and intensifying since the early 2000s, critical debates concerning the most foundational questions from the Palestinian perspective have been excluded from the Israeli academy. Wherever critical research and discourse have begun to emerge—as this chapter shows—they have been continuously stifled. This is particularly the case at Israeli departments and programs of history, sociology and anthropology, politics and government, and cultural studies.[14] Beginning with research into the establishment of Israel and the Nakba, Israeli academia has limited opportunities to critically explore Palestinian history and, with it, the Palestinian present. These constraints were extended—albeit in different forms—to the work of critical Mizrahi Jewish-Israeli scholars who investigated state violence directed at their communities and the identity of the "Arab-Jew" as part of a broader political and intellectual project that might have fostered Mizrahi anticolonial alliances with Palestinians within the Israeli academy.

The list of untouchable subjects in Israeli universities has only expanded with rising far-right influence and political power over the past two decades. Most recently, almost any critique of the military or of Israeli soldiers has become taboo on Israeli campuses.

Rather than make room for critical scholarship, Israeli university administrations and many of their faculty members have aligned with the Israeli state and far-right Israeli groups to move in the opposite direction: expelling scholarly debates that might challenge Zionist hegemony. The widespread—and increasingly enforced—consensus in Israel excludes foundational critiques and conversations from the university. University administrations, and the majority of Jewish-Israeli faculty, repeatedly refuse to defend the right to conduct research or express views that stray too far from this consensus.

Rising harassment has driven many Palestinian scholars, and some of the most critical Jewish-Israelis, out of the Israeli academy. Those who remain frequently face silencing campaigns or intimidation from administrators and colleagues. The result has been further erosion of fundamental academic freedoms in Israeli universities, which were always already structurally limited and contingent for Palestinian scholars.

Defining the Permissible: Israeli Academia and the Palestinian Nakba

"There are circumstances in history that justify ethnic cleansing . . . If [David Ben-Gurion] was already engaged in the expulsion, maybe he should have completed the job. I know that this stuns the Arabs and the liberals and the politically correct types. But my feeling is that this place would be quieter and know less suffering if the matter had been resolved once and for all. If Ben-Gurion had conducted a big expulsion and cleansed the entire country. All of the land of Israel, to the Jordan River."
—Benny Morris, professor emeritus, Ben-Gurion University[15]

Beginning in the 1980s, the contemporary boundaries around critical scholarship of the 1948 war were redrawn and reified in Israeli academia. In 1978, thirty years after the war, materials were declassified in Israeli, American, and British archives that shed new light on the establishment of the Israeli state. Though still largely inaccessible to Palestinian scholars, the declassified documents in Israeli archives enabled Jewish-Israeli historians to reexamine the state's national historiography and foundational narratives.[16] Pioneered by Benny Morris, Ilan Pappé, and Avi Shlaim, among others, the Israeli scholars who explored these archives came to be known as Israel's "new historians."[17] They called into question many widely accepted facts that were the bedrock of the Israeli national ethos, reexamining Zionist ideology and practice in the late nineteenth century, the 1948 war, and Israeli state policies toward its Palestinian and Mizrahi Jewish citizens.[18]

Through exposing previously classified data, the new historians particularly challenged the dominant narrative about the establishment of Israel. They presented a very different account of the power asymmetry between Zionist militias and Arab forces on the eve of the 1948 war and showed that the Jewish community in Mandatory Palestine was not under existential threat of annihilation.[19] Drawing on documents produced by members of Zionist militias and the Israeli military and government themselves, the new historians corroborated long-standing Palestinian accounts of the mass expulsion and systematic dispossession of Palestinians throughout the war, as well as of massacres of Palestinian civilians.[20] In Israeli archives, they found evidence that the expulsions— and some of the massacres—were premeditated and well planned and revealed how the new Israeli state immediately prevented Palestinians from returning to their homes and lands by demolishing their villages and establishing a military rule over those who survived and remained.[21] In so doing, Ilan Pappé argues, the new historians attempted to contextualize and integrate the historiography of Zionism and Israel into world historiography. This was a radical departure from the predominant historiography in Israel, which has long argued for the singularity and exceptionality of Zionist historiography.[22]

With the publication of their first books, the new historians came under fire from Israeli academics and the media, were labeled "antisemitic," and were even likened to Holocaust deniers.[23] For years afterward, a controversy over their scholarship ensued. This had serious repercussions for themselves and created a chilling effect for younger scholars considering any critical examination of Israeli national myths. Of the leading new historians, only Benny Morris ultimately remained in Israeli academia. He eventually managed to obtain an appointment as a professor at Ben-Gurion University, though David Ben-Gurion's son personally tried to have him dismissed.[24]

Morris then surprised the nation by fully realigning with Israeli national ideology, announcing that his mere documentation of the violence inflicted upon Palestinians in 1948 had been mistaken for criticism. In an interview to mark the publication of updated editions of his books, Morris reported new archival findings further revealing the scale of massacres committed in 1948, as well as at least a dozen cases of Zionist forces raping and killing Palestinian women. These documented cases from his research, Morris contended, constituted "just the tip of the iceberg."[25] And yet, Morris clarified that both his original and updated research were written in an "ethically neutral" tone, which was misread as condemnation by much of his Israeli readership.[26] Indeed, he went as far as to contend that "in certain conditions, expulsion is not a war crime. I don't think that the expulsions of 1948 were war crimes. You can't make an omelet without breaking eggs."[27] Having disavowed any leftist affiliations attributed to him, Morris was rehabilitated and embraced by Israeli academia. He went on to become a full professor at Ben-Gurion University until his retirement.

Meanwhile, to prevent the kinds of research conducted by the new historians, the government reclassified hundreds of important documents.[28] The reclassified documents joined millions of other papers that have never been accessible to researchers. A little under 3 percent of the files in Israeli governmental archives, and under half a percent of files in the Israeli Defense Forces and Defense Establishment Archive, are currently available to the public.[29] Moreover, Israeli Ministry of Defense representatives acknowledged that, since 2002, they have methodically concealed and reclassified documents about the Nakba and 1948 war in state archives, including many of the documents used by the new historians.[30] Aligning with the state and broad public opposition, university administrators and many Israeli historians signaled that anyone critically using such state documents in the future would suffer great professional cost. Nevertheless, the new historians helped to open the way for other Jewish-Israeli scholars to investigate the state's foundational narratives and myths.[31]

The next test for Israeli academia's tolerance of critical research into the 1948 war came in the form of a master's thesis submitted in 1998.

Theodore Katz, a University of Haifa student of history who had taken a course with Ilan Pappé, investigated the 1948 expulsion of Palestinians from the villages Umm Zaynat and Tantura at the southern foot of Mt. Carmel near his university. Based on archival research and oral history interviews with Palestinian village residents and survivors, as well as with former Israeli soldiers who participated in the expulsion, Katz's work brought the story of Tantura into Israeli academia for the first time. In a thesis that corroborated previously collected testimonies from village residents and studies by Palestinian researchers, Katz showed that the Israeli military's Alexandroni Brigade invaded the village on the night of May 22, 1948, with the objective of expelling its people.[32] In the course of the invasion, Israeli soldiers massacred dozens of Palestinians, most of them unarmed and after having surrendered. Katz estimated that as many as 225 Tantura residents were killed.[33] Today it is known that Israeli soldiers killed at least 200 and as many as 250 Palestinians of Tantura.[34]

In May 1948, Tantura was one of several Palestinian villages whose residents were expelled as part of an Israeli campaign of "coastal clearing" of Palestinian communities south of Haifa. The expulsion and massacre in Tantura took place after the establishment of Israel. Though its Palestinian residents later became citizens of the state, Israeli state policy designated Tantura and other Palestinian villages as "enemy bases," labeled entire Palestinian communities as enemy combatants, and treated any Palestinians captured as prisoners of war. Palestinians of Tantura who survived the massacre, including over 1,000 women and children, were transferred to Israeli internment camps, under conditions that a visiting Red Cross delegation deemed "inhumane."[35] Interned men and teenaged boys from Tantura were abused by camp guards and forced into labor for the Israeli state, including picking fruit from expropriated Palestinian orchards, removing stones from demolished Palestinian villages, and digging Israeli military trenches and fortifications.[36]

Documented for decades and continually investigated by Palestinian researchers, the story of Tantura was obscured to most Jewish-Israelis until Katz's work appeared.[37] Katz's thesis drew on 135 interviews with both former residents of Tantura and Israeli soldiers of the Alexandroni

Brigade who invaded the village.[38] It was the first graduate thesis submitted to an Israeli university that called into question Israel's narrative about the 1948 war. The thesis was read by two of Katz's supervising faculty and received high marks. It was then accepted by the university and filed away, until it was read by Amir Gilat, an Israeli investigative journalist.[39] Gilat independently corroborated many of the thesis's findings and published a story about the massacre in Tantura in the mainstream Israeli paper *Ma'ariv* in January of 2000.[40] Just three months after the article's publication, the organization of Alexandroni Brigade veterans filed a lawsuit against Katz for NIS 1 million in libel charges, accusing him of misinterpreting interview data and erroneously presenting the brigade soldiers as war criminals. It was only then that the massacre began to create waves in Israeli higher education and among the Israeli public. The massacre in Tantura, historian Rana Barakat illuminates, "broke into Israeli public and academic discourse, not as its own story but rather as a libel case within Israeli courts."[41]

The University of Haifa quickly withdrew legal support and responsibility for Katz's research, leaving Katz to assemble his own legal counsel, including family members and Adalah, the leading Palestinian human rights organization in Israel. Two days into the trial, Katz was pressured by the university's legal team and his family to settle the lawsuit, and—without his own legal counsel present—signed a statement withdrawing allegations of a massacre in Tantura. Just hours later, Katz tried to withdraw from the settlement, but the court would not allow it. The prosecutor then demanded that Katz's master's thesis be rescinded.[42]

Though Ilan Pappé was Katz's former professor, he had not overseen his thesis. But as a historian at the university and expert on the subject, Pappé opted to conduct his own reexamination of Katz's interviews as well as other archival data and testimonies collected by Palestinian researchers. Pappé then published the most revealing accounts on the university website and urged a debate about the facts themselves. Yossi Ben Artzi, dean of the Faculty of Humanities, and Yoav Gelber, chair of the history department, led a counter-campaign and called on the university to take disciplinary action against both Katz and Pappé. A University of Haifa–appointed committee then inspected the interview transcripts and claimed to find serious errors in some of the interview translations that called Katz's analysis into question.

Pappé's investigation showed otherwise. Pappé found that the university's accusations of systemic or egregious errors in translation were grossly exaggerated, selectively highlighting four misquotations out of hundreds of accurate ones, two of which were acceptable procedure for oral history compilation. Pappé concluded that a massacre had in fact occurred, and that the available data could substantiate even further-reaching conclusions than those advanced in Katz's thesis. Pappé contends that senior faculty and administrators led the charges for rescinding the thesis on grounds that were neither scientific nor academic. Nevertheless, without addressing the question of the massacre, the university committee rescinded Katz's degree and purged the thesis from the university library.[43] Throughout the trial and for years after, Katz was subject to a public smear campaign that framed him as a liar and a traitor. He was the target of recurring intimidating phone calls and death threats, including against his family.[44]

In what became known as the "Tantura affair," Pappé expressed serious criticism of the University of Haifa and its adjudication of the case. He decried the insularity of Israeli academic publications on the state's history, edited by a small group of gatekeeping scholars who refused to publish any critical pieces. Pappé's criticisms triggered his isolation at the university, as he was informally punished by administrators and shunned by most of his colleagues. He was later summoned to a disciplinary proceeding in which the prosecution demanded his dismissal from the university on the grounds of "violation of duties" and "slander," a case which the university ultimately closed only amid international academic outcry and campaigns.[45] But in the wake of the disciplinary proceedings, threats, and attacks by the media and academic colleagues that ensued, Pappé left the university in 2006 and moved to the UK to teach at the University of Exeter.[46]

The Israeli debate concerning the massacre in Tantura resurfaced in 2021, when a documentary by Israeli filmmaker Alon Schwarz presented evidence in a new accessible format. For his film *Tantura*, Schwarz interviewed Katz and Pappé about the research and integrated audio recordings from Katz's oral history interviews. Crucially, Schwarz also conducted his own original interviews with Palestinian survivors, as well as members of the Alexandroni Brigade, some of whom openly admitted to participating in the killing of Palestinian residents after Tantura was conquered.[47] The documentary forced open yet another public discussion about Tantura in Israel and offered an opportunity for the University of Haifa to affirm its commitments to academic freedom and to scholarly investigation of atrocities committed in the vicinity of its campus.

The university did the opposite. A 2022 statement circulated to university faculty from the rector dismissively described the "Tantura affair" as resurfacing once every few years "like a phoenix," which has come to serve as a symbol "for those who wished to point to the ethnic cleansing that took place in 1948 and the Israeli public's denial of the Nakba."[48] The rector's statement not only stood by the university's decision to rescind Katz's thesis but continued to deny the expulsion and massacre that took place near its campus, insisting on terming the events "alleged."

In its most recent response, the University of Haifa has continued two long-standing traditions in Israeli academia: erasing Palestinian academic knowledge production and undermining verifiable, evidence-based research that exposes the crimes of the Israeli state. As Rana Barakat argues, to insist that Palestinian testimonies be corroborated with those of Israeli soldiers constitutes another form of settler-colonial elimination of Indigenous people.[49] In fact, Palestinian scholarship on the Nakba offers a wealth of research through the deconstruction of massacres, including in Tantura, far beyond what was produced by Katz and other Israeli scholars.[50] Yet the University of Haifa persists in holding an insular internal Israeli discussion about Israeli state violence, overlooking the vast research on the topic by Palestinian, Arab, and international scholars.

In so doing, the university administration continues to corroborate the state narrative and shield Israel from accountability for its violations of international law. It does so instead of upholding free academic research and debate, which seeks to expose and to reckon with historical events.

Expanding the Illegitimate: Israeli Military
Occupation and the New McCarthyism

Since the Tantura debate surfaced some two decades ago, censorship in Israeli universities has only intensified. In the wake of the Second Palestinian Intifada that broke out in 2000, and the growing international criticism of Israel's military occupation that followed, increasing political mobilization of Palestinian citizens of Israel has been met with forceful state repression. The Israeli government worked in tandem with right-wing organizations and student groups to prevent Palestinian organizing and critical discussions from spreading on university campuses. To this infringement on campus affairs, university administrations have overwhelmingly responded by aligning with the Israeli state. They allied with forces outside the university to ensure that certain discussions—critiques of Israel's military occupation and violations of Palestinian human rights, to say nothing of analyses of Israeli apartheid and settler colonialism—are formally out of bounds.

The boundaries of what is acceptable to research, teach, and discuss became even more pronounced as the right-wing organization Im Tirtzu teamed up with government bodies to further encroach on and regulate institutions of higher education and escalate silencing campaigns.[51] Founded in 2006 by Likud party activists and students, Im Tirtzu ("If you will it," in Hebrew),[52] is an organization whose declared mission is to "reinvigorate" the Zionist ideology in Israel.[53] It currently runs branches at all Israeli universities, where representatives monitor "leftist" Jewish faculty and intimidate Palestinian student groups.[54] As Im Tirtzu campaigns gained traction and official state backing, university administrators have repeatedly capitulated to their demands and prioritized their lobbying, at the expense of protecting the academic freedom of Palestinians and dissenting Jewish-Israelis.

In 2010, Im Tirtzu was commissioned by the Knesset Education Committee to prepare a report on "anti-Zionist bias" in Israeli academia, to be submitted to the Israeli Council for Higher Education (CHE).[55] The report argued that leftist and anti-Zionist faculty were imposing their political views upon their students, jeopardizing Israeli academia and

Israel's international standing. In particular, the report accused the Department of Politics and Government at Ben-Gurion University of "leftist bias" among faculty, with syllabi assigning too many scholars representing "one-dimensional liberalism" and theories of nationalism as a modern construct.[56] Gideon Sa'ar, minister of education and chair of the CHE at that time, praised the report and committed to examining its findings.[57] Emboldened, Im Tirtzu followed the report with a letter to the president of Ben-Gurion University, Rivka Carmi, demanding that she put an end to "anti-Zionist bias" on campus and threatening to complain to university donors in Israel and abroad if she failed to take action.[58] Im Tirtzu later published another report in which it explicitly named faculty with "leftist" affiliations and called for their termination. Much of the criticism was focused on Neve Gordon, a scholar and outspoken critic of Israel's military rule in the OPT, with the minister of education joining Im Tirtzu in calling for his firing.[59]

The response from Ben-Gurion University in defense of academic freedom was politically selective. A senior university administrator assured the press that the university was "Zionist," reminding the public that the Department of Politics and Government trains active-duty Israeli Air Force personnel.[60] Meanwhile, the university senate passed a directive that faculty must refrain from mentioning their university by name if expressing their own "political opinions."[61] The institutional message was clear: critical analyses of the Israeli occupation could in no way be associated with the university. Faculty at Ben-Gurion University and at other institutions took notice and began taking new precautions. They reported excluding critical scholarship on their syllabi, making explicit requests not to record their classes, and censoring their own commentary in the classroom.[62] The Israeli consensus on the boundaries of acceptable critique was becoming more strictly enforced.

Meanwhile, the campaign targeting the Department of Politics and Government at Ben-Gurion University escalated when an evaluation committee was commissioned by the CHE to assess Israeli political science departments. The committee's 2011 report determined that the department's scientific rigor was "impeded" by its stated commitment "to combine academic excellence with social activism."[63] The report advocated that the department expose students to more "balanced views," defined as an increase in Zionist material. The report further recommended that the university close the department if its alleged "academic weaknesses" were not addressed.[64] Shortly thereafter in 2012, the CHE determined that the department had insufficiently implemented the required changes and was therefore prohibited from enrolling new students, in effect instigating its closure.[65] The university administration appealed the CHE decision but also affirmed that it would work with the council to "ensure the high academic level" of the department.[66]

Ultimately, in the face of international outcry from multiple academic associations, including the American Political Science Association, the department was left open.[67] But its faculty faced extended public and media campaigns that framed them as traitors, as well as consistent harassment, including death threats. Of the nine department faculty, two of those most targeted for their critical scholarship on the Israeli occupation and advocacy for Palestinian rights—Neve Gordon and Haim Yacobi—have since left the university to teach in the UK.

The campaign to curb discussion of Palestinian rights in the Israeli academy continues unabated. What began as repression of academic research on the Nakba and Israel's founding has since expanded into public scrutiny of syllabi addressing Israel's military occupation and apartheid and, most recently, into a broader purge of any critical discourse on the military and the racial violence of the Israeli state.

Acceptable academic debate further narrowed with an Im Tirtzu campaign targeting Hebrew University cultural studies professor Carola Hilfrich in 2018. Like many classes at Hebrew University and across institutions, Hilfrich's courses included both Palestinians and active-duty Israeli soldiers as students. During one class discussion, a Palestinian student drew on an assigned text to comment on Israel's occupation. After class, when the Palestinian student was approached by an active-duty military officer taking the class, she replied that she did not wish to engage with a soldier in uniform.[68] Outraged, the officer—an active member of Im Tirtzu—turned to Hilfrich, who responded by stating that the classroom should facilitate tolerance of the diverse reactions which a military uniform may elicit among students.[69] As it turned out, the event was a setup by Im Tirtzu. The exchange was caught on film and immediately made national headlines.[70] The very next day Im Tirtzu staged a protest on campus calling for Hilfrich to be fired, and the media and right-wing parties framed the event as an attack on the Israeli military.[71]

The Hebrew University response was swift and decisive. The administration immediately issued an apology and published a statement welcoming all soldiers who are students to its campus, reiterating its institutional commitment to supporting the military.[72] With Hebrew University refusing to publicly back her, Hilfrich became the target of an intensified popular media campaign and received a barrage of vitriol and threats, leading her to leave midsemester for a hiatus.[73]

In its response, the Hebrew University administration signaled that it valued loyalty to the military above the right of faculty to facilitate critical discussion about it in their classrooms.[74] In the wake of the affair, Hebrew University added Im Tirtzu in 2019 to the list of recognized entities whose volunteer work can earn university credit.[75]

Following years of sustained campaigning against critical expression on campuses—including protests, reports, and secret recordings—Im Tirtzu formalized its tracking apparatuses in 2019: it published a list of faculty members who expressed support for Palestinian equality and human rights and established an online platform for students to report critical Palestinian and Jewish "leftist" faculty.[76] The list was initially condemned by the committee of university presidents as an act of intimidation. Even so, university administrations have refused to take any sustained action to safeguard the free expression of those targeted by this silencing campaign.[77] The Israeli government has, in turn, codified such increasingly repressive norms in academia into formal regulations.

These efforts bore new fruit when head of the far-right party HaBayit HaYehudi (The Jewish Home) Naftali Bennett became minister of education. In 2017, Bennett asked Asa Kasher, a professor of philosophy at Tel Aviv University who wrote the military "ethical code" for Israeli soldiers, to articulate such a code for faculty conduct.[78] Kasher's proposed guidelines for the "depoliticization" of universities contained instructions for campus activities, classroom lectures, publications, and faculty promotion.[79] The code included guidelines prohibiting faculty from "deviating from their syllabi and disciplines" in ways that might be interpreted by students as political speech. It proposed offering students the opportunity to demand clarification from faculty they deemed to be engaging in "political activity" in the classroom, followed by institutional disciplinary action when needed.[80] Im Tirtzu praised the code as a necessary first step and urged that it include sanctions for noncompliant universities.[81]

The proposed "academic ethical code" posed a conundrum for Israeli university administrators and some of the faculty. The state's long-standing power over universities threatened to directly affect many of them for the first time and was, suddenly, construed as an overreach. A petition by faculty members across universities called on the CHE to reject the code as an infringement on freedom of research, pedagogy, and expression, which would curb what they construed as "the independence" of Israel's academic institutions.[82] The committee of university presidents likewise declared that the code's political censorship undermined the most basic principles of academic freedom and research, calling it a "'big brother' of government who aims to transform higher education into a tool of politicians."[83]

And yet even in their opposition to the code, university administrators and the majority of faculty fundamentally accepted the code's definition of the "political." In so doing, they reinforced the notion that their own universities' decades-long imbrication with the Israeli state was apolitical and naturalized the repression of Palestinian and critical scholars as legitimate.

But even this limited opposition was short-lived. Soon thereafter, the CHE subcommittee adopted an abbreviated version of the ethical code in 2018. This time, university administrations did not dispute the decision.[84]

The CHE termed the abbreviated code as "ethical principles" and called on the universities to integrate them into their disciplinary bylaws. The principles outline five prohibitions, including calling for a boycott of Israel or of Israeli institutions (including those that illegally operate in the OPT), promoting "partisan propaganda" during class time, and

discriminating against students based on their political views.[85] No
university administration publicly pledged to disobey the decision. Left
unopposed by university administrations, the "ethical principles"
currently serve as the official state-mandated regulations governing
faculty expression. Further left uncontested by faculty and administrators alike are their universities' institutional ties to the state and to its
military-security establishment. Once the dust from the public controversy had settled, universities returned—emboldened—to their routine
policing of the minority of faculty who work to keep academic debates
about Israeli settler colonialism and military occupation alive: namely,
Palestinians and a handful of Jewish-Israelis construed as "far-left."

In the face of the academic ethical code and escalated right-wing
campaigns on their campuses, faculty across disciplines and institutions now report practicing increased cautionary measures. In interviews, faculty describe a fear of uttering opinions critical of the occupation or of including critical texts on the subject in their syllabi that
could come under scrutiny. Some admit that they go out of their way to
avoid any topics that could be deemed "political" under the CHE code
in classroom discussions, and dozens detail altering their research and
publication agendas and pedagogical practices. Yoram, a Jewish-Israeli
professor in the social sciences, described in an interview one of the
new protocols he has instituted in his classes: "I used to integrate a
variety of texts and mediums into my syllabi. I don't do that anymore.
I am very careful to only assign academic texts, because anything else
might get me accused of being 'political' and have students complain
about me to the department." Those few Jewish-Israeli faculty whose
scholarship critically explores Israeli occupation and apartheid
describe inhabiting the university like a besieged and marginal minority, among colleagues who overwhelmingly identify with the state.
They practice self-censorship in their writing and in the classroom,
unsure of who they can trust in their departments, or if they might be
"turned in" to administrations that are increasingly unlikely to defend
their rights.

Research Under Siege: Settler Colonialism and the Policing of Palestinian Scholarship

The limits placed on the study of the Israeli occupation and apartheid, as well as the 1948 war, have different consequences for Palestinian scholars at Israeli universities. The Nakba is the foundational event that led to the very creation of Israeli citizenship for some Palestinians. Most Palestinians who survived the expulsion and massacres and remained in the territory that became the Israeli state were later granted Israeli citizenship. But most of those forcibly displaced were forbidden from returning after the 1948 war to their original homes and lands and were severed by Israeli borders from the rest of the Palestinian nation and often members of their own families.[86] To study the Nakba is, therefore, essential to the study of Palestinian citizens of Israel.

The rising interest of Palestinian citizens in their history has been met with growing limits imposed on its study, as well as on events commemorating it. These restrictions intensified as Palestinian citizens began mobilizing around May 15, coinciding with Israeli celebrations of its independence day. On May 15, 1998, Palestinian civil society organizations in Israel organized a march alongside Palestinians in the OPT to commemorate the fiftieth anniversary of the Nakba.[87] Thereafter, the annual marches organized by Palestinian citizens of Israel have sought to highlight that they, too, were displaced and likewise denied the right of return. This mobilization, argue Nadim Rouhana and Areej Sabbagh–Khoury, gained momentum in the wake of the Second Palestinian Intifada. Then, Palestinian citizens of Israel began to move away from the paradigm of nominal equality under the Zionist Jewish state and toward a politics that understands their citizenship to be "rooted in the historic events of the Nakba," what Rouhana and Sabbagh-Khoury call the "return of history."[88]

As the commemoration of the Nakba became a fulcrum of Palestinian citizen discourse, the Israeli state has moved to criminalize it. In 2011, Israel passed the "Nakba Law," limiting state funding for organizations that commemorate the Nakba.[89] That same year, Im Tirtzu published *Nakba-Nonsense*, a booklet that denies the Nakba and seeks to provide

Israeli students with "ammunition" to eradicate its discussion and study on Israeli campuses.[90] No Israeli university administration publicly came out against the Nakba Law, and Nakba commemoration events across Israeli campuses have since been routinely met with permit denials and sometimes violent arrests.[91]

In spite of this growing repression, Palestinian scholars and students are bringing the study of the Nakba into Israeli universities, as well as exploring its contemporary effects for Palestinian citizens of Israel and for the Palestinian people at large. Several Palestinian scholars have been investigating the Nakba and the establishment of the Israeli state through the analytic of settler colonialism as early as the 1960s.[92] But, for decades, this research was not cited by Israeli academics, nor were its Palestinian theorists permitted to enter the Israeli academy.[93] This has begun to change with the rise of the contemporary generation of Palestinian scholars, Areej Sabbagh-Khoury argues, who study settler colonialism as an enduring structure of Israeli governance and who study Palestinians "not only as victims but also as agents of history."[94] Rejecting the confines of the Israeli state, Palestinians are asserting their national identity and mobilizing their citizenship as a mechanism for development of an anti-colonial politics.[95]

Yet on their arrival at Israeli universities, Palestinian scholars encounter structural barriers to their exploration of Palestinian history and identity. Palestinian students come to Israeli universities from the Israeli educational system, which, as Khaled Furani argues, "seeks to create 'Israeli Arabs' closed in a box and reconciled with Zionism and with its state," and through the denial of Palestine.[96] Palestinian students hope to find that universities are different from their state education. But they, too, are embedded in Israeli society, "whose existence is based on the negation of the Palestinian existence."[97]

Palestinian junior researchers find that their place at an Israeli university is contingent on their staying within confines of acceptable critique that these institutions are willing to tolerate.[98] Many graduate students, therefore, discover that their scholarly exploration, their thinking, and their writing are strictly restrained and disciplined from the outset. When engaging in research on Palestinian citizens of Israel, Palestinian scholars must constantly field accusations of exaggeration or bias, particularly as they pertain to the effects of Israeli policy.[99] As scholar of education Ayman Agbaria argues, the very identity of Palestinian students is broadly considered a hindrance to their "neutrality" and "objectivity" as researchers by their Israeli supervisors and institutions. He contends that Palestinian scholars face a tension between "the writing of representation, acceptance and assimilation," and "the writing of rejection, liberation and renewal," in which they can go beyond established knowledge and truly innovate.[100]

This policing of Palestinian knowledge production is central to the experience of Palestinian researchers at Israeli universities. One of the mechanisms by which this disciplining occurs is through the consistent accusation that Palestinian epistemology and critique are "political," therefore undermining their scholarly validity. Based on research with Palestinian faculty across Israeli universities, Sarab Abu-Rabia-Queder shows that knowledge production is considered "political" when it deploys terms that challenge Israeli colonial power relations. "Apolitical"—and therefore acceptable—knowledge in Israeli academia is devoid of critical decolonial language and any trace of the colonized. This binary fundamentally undermines Palestinian scholarship, delegitimizing it as nonacademic.[101] This routinely forces Palestinian academics, as Agbaria shows, to study their own reality "with artificial abstraction and with false objectivity."[102]

Such Israeli gatekeeping, according to Abu-Rabia-Queder, not only maintains the racial hierarchy between Israeli and Palestinian researchers but also seeks to "eliminate" an Indigenous epistemology.[103] Some of this gatekeeping is overt and punitive, as in the case of one junior Palestinian faculty member who was told by her dean that she "will pay dearly" if she writes on her proposed research topics.[104] Other forms of gatekeeping are framed as benevolent mentoring by senior scholars, who pepper junior Palestinian faculty with ostensibly generous advice. Palestinian junior scholars are routinely told not to publish in Arabic—which is, by definition, suspect—but also not to publish critical work in Hebrew. They are advised to refrain from publishing any pieces that might be read as "political" and to avoid writing for public-facing publications that might invite scrutiny of their work.[105] Striving to produce knowledge and write under these restrictions, one scholar told Abu-Rabia-Queder, is to operate in "a mentality of checkpoints."[106] Palestinian researchers described struggling not to internalize this policing and impose self-discipline on their own scholarship, or to erase their own identities in the face of the permanent demand to prove to their Israeli colleagues and institutions that their knowledge production is not undermining the Israeli state. Abu-Rabia-Queder calls these mechanisms "unmarked forms of discipline and punishment."[107]

These demands, as Shalhoub-Kevorkian and Abu-Rabia-Queder show, are not only racialized but also gendered. Critical knowledge production about Palestinian women is particularly scrutinized in Israeli academia. A Palestinian Bedouin feminist scholar, Abu-Rabia-Queder describes entering Israeli academia in the 1990s, when research on Palestinian Bedouin women was entirely subject to an Israeli theoretical framework that was dominated by Orientalist tropes about Israeli "modernization" of Bedouin communities.[108] Despite a gradual increase in Palestinian feminist scholars at Israeli universities since that time, research on gender under these institutional auspices cannot overcome this Israeli epistemological barrier. Palestinian feminists continue to face an overwhelming campaign by colleagues and administrators that redirects and reincorporates them into the Israeli framework and stifles their critique.[109]

Palestinian feminist scholars have been discouraged by their departments from writing about gendered oppression of Palestinian women, that is, unless such women were identified as "Arab-Israelis" and not as Palestinian, and so long as they did not analyze the colonial structures of violence imposed by Israel on Palestinian women.[110] This erasure produces what Abu-Rabia-Queder calls "research injustice" toward Palestinian women and constitutes a colonial epistemology that de-indigenizes Palestinians.[111] It poses significant challenges for Palestinian feminist scholars, who seek to attend to the "invisible and invisibilized."[112] To indigenize critical knowledge and create "resistance-based knowledge," Shalhoub-Kevorkian argues, Palestinian feminist scholars must insist on contending with the ongoing effects of the Nakba on the lives of Palestinian women, precisely in the face of their continued erasure by Israeli institutions.[113]

These limits on knowledge production follow Palestinian faculty into their classrooms. Regardless of their expertise or course topics, Palestinian professors report being treated as suspect by both their colleagues and students and routinely accused of "bias" against Israel and Israelis in their scholarship, lectures, and syllabi. In the face of this relentless hostility, many describe navigating their campuses with daily trepidation. They report receiving vitriolic or explicitly racist comments in their classrooms and at faculty meetings, or having to take on their own administrative labor at the department because staff overtly refuse to assist them. Palestinian women faculty are particularly harassed and sidelined by their Jewish-Israeli students and colleagues, their scholarship and pedagogy subject to heightened—gendered and racialized—scrutiny.[114] Ibtisam, a tenured faculty member, described in an interview being routinely undermined by her Jewish students with frivolous claims that she was unqualified to teach her courses' subject matter: "Year after year I am accused of bias, the students complain to the department that I can't teach the topics of my courses. I always have to reestablish my legitimacy as the professor in front of the students."

The language that Palestinian faculty use in their teaching is itself policed by Jewish-Israeli students. "Every time I use 'Palestinian' to refer to Palestinian citizens of Israel it is itself a whole conversation," Nisreen, an assistant professor, explained in an interview. "Students always demand and ask why I define myself this way and why I use this term in my courses. Even using the word 'occupation' is light-years away in the discourse." Calling Palestinians "Indigenous," as well as including texts that apply the analytic of settler colonialism to the state of Israel, are entirely beyond the pale. To do so requires paying a high price, according to Palestinian faculty members, in the form of protracted battles with their colleagues and university administrations and refuting student complaints. Mona, a faculty member in the social sciences, summarized in an interview her daily experience of over a decade in Israeli academia: "It is a constant war. It is exhausting." Having long faced a work environment hostile to their teaching, scholarship, and very identities, many

Palestinian faculty have responded to the escalation in repression of critical expression by intentionally laboring to fortify Palestinian voices of opposition. "We have to be strong for our students," Rim, a professor in the sciences, insisted at an off-campus organizing event. "Our Palestinian students are coming to us now and tell us they feel afraid. They are afraid to speak, to do anything, because of the violence they see on campus."

The experience of Palestinian scholars at Israeli universities is marked by isolation. Though constituting over 20 percent of the Israeli citizen population, only 3.5 percent of faculty at Israeli universities are Palestinian.[115] They therefore often find themselves in the position of being the sole Palestinian scholar in a department, faculty, or even a research domain.[116] This isolation is also political. Every day Palestinian faculty must take on the struggle—for themselves and for their Palestinian students—to make space for Palestinian identity, scholarship, and politics in Israeli higher education. Yet this struggle has yielded limited results. For years Palestinian academics and students have lobbied the Council for Higher Education to establish a Palestinian university in the Galilee, only to be persistently ignored.[117] Meanwhile, not a single Israeli university has offered itself as a space for unencumbered critical Palestinian knowledge production and debate.

Palestinian scholars have therefore been compelled to carve out their own academic spaces outside the Israeli system of higher education, forming Mada al-Carmel, the Arab Center for Applied Social Research in Haifa. Funded by international foundations, Mada al-Carmel was founded by Palestinian scholars and civil society leaders to "further the human, civil and political rights of Palestinian citizens of Israel through applied social research," and to "offer a much-needed home for Palestinian academics in the social sciences and humanities, both locally and in exile, where they can discuss ideas, receive support, mentor junior scholars, and advance their scholarship."[118]

Mada al-Carmel also seeks to guide the next generation of Palestinian scholars, and is the central institution to offer support for Palestinian graduate students.[119] Other major initiatives for Palestinian junior scholars also take place outside Israeli universities. In these groups, Khaled

Furani explains, Palestinian scholars create space to critically examine the conditions that both shape and impede their research and knowledge production.[120] They consider ways to advance Palestinian knowledge, as well as how to safeguard and strengthen critical Palestinian work in the face of the Israeli state project "to erase all that is Palestinian."[121] In so doing, Palestinian scholars seek to liberate themselves from the intellectual control of the Israeli university and the censorial "regimes of ignorance" and mechanisms of self-denial that they impose.[122] Mada al-Carmel and other Palestinian scholarly initiatives outside of Israeli universities, as Furani and Agbaria argue, create essential spaces of refusal and resistance.[123] These are spaces to study "what is lived, what is neglected and marginalized, and what is not thought about and unspoken at the Israeli university."[124]

Against these erasures of their history and identity, Palestinian scholars, political representatives, and civil society leaders came together at Mada al-Carmel to write the "Haifa Declaration" in 2007. This foundational document articulates scholarly and political commitments of Palestinian citizens of Israel and puts forth a vision of the Palestinian "collective future."[125] As the document insists, such a future for Palestinian citizens not only relies on achieving "a dignified life in our homeland and building a democratic society founded upon justice, freedom, equality,"[126] but also requires reclaiming the Palestinian national narrative and identity. As the writers of the declaration affirm: "Our close affinities with the rest of the Palestinian people and with the Arab nation are in fact a form of connection to ourselves. They are our natural space, of which we were deprived following the Nakba, and this connection is the embodiment of the complete Self."[127]

Academia's Other Exclusions: On Anticolonial Critique and the Question of the "Arab Jew"

An extension of limits imposed on research on the Nakba and the events most foundational to the Palestinian identity and experience, Israeli academia has also limited other lines of inquiry into race and racialization under Zionism. Israeli universities continue to serve as gatekeepers of critical conversations about the violence endured by Middle Eastern and Arab Jews at the hands of the Zionist movement and the Israeli state, as well as their continued discrimination within and outside Israeli academia. In this way, scholarly exploration that might have opened up space for a broader anticolonial critique has been overwhelmingly ejected from Israeli universities and, with it, potential avenues for building alliances with Palestinian scholars to expand scientific research and promote academic freedom.

Palestinian scholars, for their part, have consistently challenged the foundational myths of the state of Israel, despite long-standing—and increasingly escalating—restrictions. They have forced open the conversation about Zionism as a settler-colonial project and demanded that Israel contend with—in the words of Edward Said—"the standpoint of its victims."[128] In a response to Said's seminal essay, cultural studies scholar Ella Shohat wrote a piece subtitled "Zionism from the Standpoint of Its Jewish Victims," which illuminated the erasure of a topic no less controversial for the Israeli state: Zionism's complex and contested relationship with Jews from the Middle East and North Africa.[129] Because the idea of the "ingathering of Jews" constitutes Zionism's raison d'être, critical scholarship about the Zionist construction of the Mizrahim—"the Eastern ones"—as an identity category was overwhelmingly excluded from Israeli academic space in the state's first four decades. So, too, was Zionism's violent erasure of Arab-Jewish identities, cultures, and histories.[130]

Led by Shohat and other critical scholars, the 1980s and 1990s saw the emergence of a new intellectual and political project concerned with the term and identity of "Arab-Jews" in the context of the Israeli state. But this project was never permitted to flourish within the Israeli academy. Mizrahi intellectuals who wished to identify as Arab-Jews were not permitted to do so as Israeli academics. Other phrases, such as "Moroccan-Jew" or "Iraqi-Jew," were deemed neutral, merely indicating Mizrahi Israelis' countries of origin. But the term "Arab-Jew" was understood as harboring the "explosive material of identification with what most Israelis consider the enemy."[131] And, indeed, the research and

discourse that some of the critical Mizrahi scholars began to develop
harbored the potential for political and intellectual anticolonial alliances
with Palestinians. It was, therefore, stymied in Israeli academia.

Israeli universities foreclosed epistemologies, research questions, and
critiques that foundationally called into question the Israeli state narrative of "inevitable" or "perpetual" conflict between Arabs and Jews. In so
doing, universities relegated the Arab-Jewish or Jewish-Arab identity as
out of bounds and, with it, the budding decolonial scholarship of Mizrahi
academics.[132] Mizrahi scholars who defied the scholarly severing of
Middle Eastern Jewry's history and culture with their arrival to Israel
and who critically investigated identity formation under Zionism and
the Israeli state, Ella Shohat shows, could not integrate this work into
their academic settings. Critical Mizrahi scholarship on these subjects
was met with verbal attacks and delegitimization by the Israeli state and
Israeli universities, and a number of leading Mizrahi scholars were
forced to find academic homes abroad.[133] It took years of sustained
organizing and perseverance, on the part of those Mizrahi researchers
who did manage to make their way into the Israeli academy, to carve out
some space for exploration of the "Arab-Jew."

Having lived only under Israeli governance and Zionist hegemony,
younger generations of Mizrahim have overwhelmingly been "de-Arabi-
zed": severed from their Arab cultural ties and from the Arabic
language.[134] Currently, leading critical sociologist at Tel Aviv University
Yehouda Shenhav argues, the concept of the "Arab-Jew" mostly functions as a "counterfactual category" that seeks to challenge what he calls
"methodological Zionism," an epistemology "where all social processes
are reduced to national Zionist categories."[135] Lital Levy similarly
contends that the "Jewish-Arab" identity today is a declaration of its
impossibility.[136]

The critical Mizrahi scholars who wished to explore concepts and
ideas that challenged Zionist hegemony and who did find paths into
Israeli universities mostly did so by setting aside these questions until
they were tenured. Reflecting on his own journey into Israeli academia,
Yehouda Shenhav explained:

If I came to the university with what I work on today, I would have never been accepted. With good Mizrahim, in the sense of being obedient and not making waves, there is no problem. There are very few of them anyway, but the "good" Mizrahim are not a problem. There are excellent researchers who come into the system and progress very well on the condition that they ignore these issues. But anyone who comes with a Mizrahi dowry has no chance.[137]

The hindered entry of Mizrahim into academia is itself a subject relegated to the margins of Israeli universities. Throughout the 1950s, Mizrahi immigrants were forcibly settled in transient camps and peripheral development towns, and universities almost exclusively served Ashkenazi Jews. Israeli schools were largely segregated, with Mizrahi children offered subpar education and continually steered toward vocational training.[138] Institutionalized marginalization, discrimination, and disinvestment in schools in Mizrahi communities formed significant barriers to higher education.[139] Tuition subsidies, scholarships, adjustments in admissions, and government assistance in student employment were disproportionately directed to Ashkenazi students, while university administrations repeatedly blocked initiatives to increase Mizrahi enrollment.[140]

The 1959 police shooting of a Mizrahi resident of Haifa ignited the Wadi Salib riots and instigated nationwide Mizrahi demonstrations against state racial discrimination and violence. This watershed event in the Mizrahi movement for Jewish civil rights was met with campaigns of police violence, as well as other pacification measures to quiet the "civil unrest."[141] Chief among them was a Ministry of Education proposal to help "dull the discrimination" by establishing preparatory academies to increase Mizrahi university enrollment, which in 1959 was under 5 percent, though Mizrahim constituted the majority of the Jewish-Israeli population at the time.[142]

Research on the academic exclusion of Mizrahim remains institutionally unacknowledged if not outright denied by Israeli universities and the CHE.[143] While the Israeli government openly and methodically tracks demographic trends among Jewish and Palestinian citizens of

Israel, the state census through 2022 refrained from recording the ethnicity of Jews whose parents were born in Israel.[144] A lack of systemic data obscures the persistent racial disparities in universities and stymies critical research.[145] Piecing together existing government data and generating their own, researchers nonetheless consistently reveal wide gaps in access to higher education between Ashkenazim and Mizrahim—gaps that are not shrinking between generations.[146] Though currently constituting roughly half of Israel's Jewish population, Mizrahim are still underrepresented among students, faculty, and senior administrators in higher education.[147] The delegitimization of research on the racialization of Mizrahim in academia, Mizrahi scholars argue, serves as a form of Ashkenazi gatekeeping of acceptable research topics and as a mechanism to eject critical Mizrahim from the university.[148]

Mizrahi feminist scholars in particular argue that Israeli academia has persistently delegitimized Mizrahi feminist theory and has denied Mizrahi racialized and gendered exclusions in Israeli universities.[149] As Yali Hashash shows, numerous Mizrahi feminist graduate students and junior scholars have been denied opportunities to advance in Israeli academia despite their awards or publications, their scholarship devalued and undermined. These exclusions persist even in departments and programs where such critical work is expected to flourish, including gender studies, cultural studies, sociology, and anthropology.[150] From its research topics to its terminology, critical feminist Mizrahi scholarship remains overwhelmingly illegible and sidelined across universities.[151]

Mizrahi scholars show that Israeli university curricula and research agendas continue to sideline the study of Middle Eastern and Arab Jewry.[152] Across universities, there are still no designated departments or academic programs dedicated to the study of Mizrahim or the Jewry of the Middle East and North Africa. Only in 2022, after years of advocacy and a comprehensive research report, did the CHE finally approve a proposal to recognize the field of Sephardi and Middle Eastern Jewish studies as its own discipline in Israeli academia.[153]

But the commissioned CHE report itself indicates just how removed this soon-to-be official field is from the intellectual and political project advanced by critical Mizrahi scholars in the 1980s and 1990s. Though the report recommendations include expanding historical education on complex and controversial issues for the Israeli state—such as the relationship of Middle Eastern Jewish communities to European colonial rule and the diversity of Middle Eastern Jewish thought, including anti-Zionism—nowhere does it mention the role of Mizrahi communities in Israeli settler colonialism.[154]

This exemplifies a larger trend in current critical Mizrahi scholarship in Israeli universities. With notable exceptions, this scholarship overwhelmingly excludes investigation of the role of Mizrahim as perpetrators and colonizers vis-à-vis the indigenous Palestinians.[155] In this way, as Lana Tatour argues, even critical Mizrahi thought ultimately reproduces Zionist hegemony and its racialized, Orientalist epistemologies upholding Jewish superiority.[156] Rather than advancing anticolonial theorization, contemporary Mizrahi scholarship in Israeli academia has largely been contained within the confines of Zionism.[157]

Most critical Mizrahi scholars have failed to join their Palestinian colleagues in calling for expanding academic investigation of the Nakba and foundational Israeli state violence. This despite the fact that the data needed for much of their own research remains classified in the same state archives. An extension of their enforcing silence on the Nakba, Israeli universities institutionally fail to challenge the state in its limiting access to data it has classified.

Such is the case with the disappearance of babies and toddlers from Yemeni and other Mizrahi families, known as the "Yemenite, Mizrahi and Balkan children affair."[158] While subjected to forced residence in transient camps as part of Israeli state "modernization" efforts during the 1950s, some Mizrahi immigrants were also subject to the disappearance of their children following encounters with the Israeli state medical and welfare systems. While frequently told their children had died, families report having been denied the opportunity to see the body or an identifiable burial site, and many still consider their children unaccounted for.[159]

The affair has roiled Israel in controversy for decades and has been the subject of social movement mobilization among Mizrahi—particularly Yemeni—communities, as well as a number of lawsuits that triggered state commissions of inquiry.[160] For years, Mizrahi scholars researching the disappeared children were forced to seek academic training, funding, and a career abroad.[161] After decades of sustained campaigning by families and civil society advocates, in 2021 the Israeli Ministry of Health commissioned a report about the role of Israeli medical professionals in the disappearance of the children.[162] The report compiled findings of previous state commissions of inquiry, media publications, and oral testimonies, and was designated as a starting point for renewed public discussion of the affair.[163]

But following a critical assessment of the report by Shifra Shvarts—a historian and professor emeritus at Ben-Gurion University who dismissed the validity of the report's use of oral testimonies—it was never adopted or officially released by the Ministry of Health.[164] Some Israeli academics—including historians, anthropologists and sociologists of science and medicine, and scholars of bioethics and the law—have since pointed to methodological and conceptual weaknesses in Shvarts's assessment and independently published their own research showing serious methodological and data inconsistencies in previous state commissions of inquiry reports. They have joined the families and their advocates in renewing the call for the Ministry of Health to officially release its report, highlighting the need for more research.[165] Ignoring these calls, Israeli academics, departments, and institutions overwhelmingly continue to stand by as the Israeli state limits what constitutes permissible topics of investigation.[166]

The recent debate concerning the use of oral testimony in the case of the Yemenite, Mizrahi, and Balkan children affair surfaced anew the question of access to Israeli archives in the Jewish-Israeli public. Palestinian member of the Knesset and chair of its Science and Technology Committee Ayman Odeh used this opening to challenge the Israeli state on its censorial policies. On May 15, 2023, the Palestinian commemoration day of the Nakba, Odeh initiated a meeting at the Science and Technology Committee to discuss academic and public access to Israeli state archives.[167] Some Palestinian and Jewish-Israeli faculty—scholars researching Israeli state violence, from the Nakba to the disappeared children affair—independently attended the meeting to testify to the impossibility of conducting any meaningful research in

Israeli state archives. They spoke of months- to years-long delays in receiving data, rejections of requests for files without cause, and the vast trove of important documents included in the 97 percent of files that remain inaccessible in Israeli governmental archives.[168]

No university sent representation to implore the state to open its archives to the academic community and enable scientific investigation of the most central questions to entire communities living under its rule.

As an extension of the restrictions it upholds on research on the Nakba and Israeli settler colonialism, Israeli academia has disallowed exploration of the racialization of Middle Eastern Jews that might have lent itself to a broader anticolonial critique or to generate solidarity with Palestinian scholars. In so doing, it has foreclosed yet another avenue for Jewish-Israelis to investigate and reflect on their role as perpetrators of violence against Palestinians and as settlers in a colonial state.

The increasingly strict limits set on acceptable subject matters across Israeli universities are acutely felt by faculty and researchers. Every day, scholars face university administrators who not only fail to challenge the escalating state-led repression of academic freedoms but also proactively uphold that repression. The right to conduct research into topics the Israeli state considers unacceptable has long been contingent and is increasingly being eroded. Yet whatever protections remain afforded to critical Jewish-Israeli academics have never applied to Palestinian scholars, who continue to face conditions of academic siege.

Rather than distinguishing themselves from the state and marking themselves as spaces for scientific study of the conditions of the state's founding, Israeli universities have aligned with far-right groups and the Israeli government to limit and police research and discourse on the Nakba. By extension, the critical study of Israeli occupation, apartheid, and settler colonialism has been defined as out of bounds. Foundational critical conversations, then, have been excluded from the Israeli academy.

Israeli universities define research and discussion of historical and ongoing Israeli state violence as illegitimate. In so doing, they deny their faculty and students not just academic freedom but also the opportunity to debate and intervene in present and future injustice.

5

Students Under Siege

"Were there no Arab students perhaps it would be better. If they would remain hewers of wood perhaps it would be easier to control them." —Uri Lubrani, advisor to the Israeli Prime Minister on Arab affairs, 1961[1]

"The state invests large sums of money in Arab education. If we don't find a way according to which the content and the method of education is directed by the in charge [Jewish] persons, we would be investing money in raising snakes." —Abba Hushi, co-founder of the University of Haifa, 1964[2]

In July of 1965, a classified meeting was held on Israel's policy toward the state's Palestinian citizens. High-ranking members of the Israeli government attended—including representatives from the Ministries of Education and Foreign Affairs, officers of the Israeli National Police, and the heads of the Mossad and Shin Bet—all to discuss a document prepared by Shmouel Tolidano, the prime minister's advisor on Arab affairs. Tolidano's document contended that "loyalty in the full sense of the word cannot be demanded of the Arab minority, to the extent of identifying with the goals of a Jewish state." It therefore recommended, instead, that Israel simply strive to direct Palestinians "to accept the state's existence and mold them into law abiding citizens."[3]

Keeping the Palestinian citizen population uneducated was deemed central to this task. Tolidano stressed the importance of "preventing as much as possible the formation of a wide educated stratum that naturally strives for radical leadership."[4] This could be achieved, Tolidano advised, through discouraging Palestinians from entering institutions of higher education and, instead, directing them toward vocational training and industries with secure employment.[5]

In Israel, it has never been broadly agreed that Palestinian citizens had a right to an education. Nor, in fact, was it consensus that they had a right to citizenship. The 1948 war and the establishment of Israel displaced over two-thirds of the Palestinian population, turning them into refugees. The minority of Palestinians who remained in the territory that became the state of Israel were placed under an Israeli military government, which ruled over them until 1966. While still under military governance and after extensive deliberation among Israeli leaders, many of these Palestinians were granted suffrage and then citizenship.[6]

But Israeli citizenship, far from guaranteeing Palestinians equal rights, actually enshrined their subjugation. Israel's decision to extend citizenship to the Palestinians who remained, as Lana Tatour shows, was intended to "solidify the demographic outcomes of the Nakba" and prevent Palestinian return to their lands.[7] Israeli citizenship, then, functioned as an "institution of domination" that ingrained Palestinian inferiority and facilitated their dispossession.[8] Whereas citizenship for Jewish-Israelis was defined as a birthright and automatic, for Palestinians it was understood to be a "benevolent act by the state" and, therefore, always contingent.[9]

So, too, was Palestinian access to education. Concerned about Palestinian resistance to the strict military regime that ruled them and about schools as sites potentially fomenting national liberation ideas, Israel established tight control over Palestinian teachers in its first decades.[10] The Israeli Ministry of Education worked with the Department for Arab Affairs and the Israeli Security Agency, the Shin Bet, to screen, appoint, and monitor Palestinian teachers. The Israeli government fielded applicants and influenced their acceptance to teachers' training courses and colleges based on political affiliations.[11] The government continually screened Palestinian teachers when they applied for tenure, promotion, and transfer, and fostered an atmosphere of fear and suspicion among them by routinely dismissing teachers for airing opinions deemed unacceptable by the state.[12]

The surveillance of Palestinian teachers and their young students was soon extended to higher education. As a few dozen Palestinian students began enrolling at Israeli universities in the 1950s, they, too, were closely monitored for potential political "radicalization."[13] Israeli government concerns about politicization through education were heightened when, in 1958, Palestinian students established their own organization at Hebrew University: the Arab Students Committee. Early Palestinian student organizing focused on the military rule and permit system governing Palestinian citizens, which severely infringed on their fundamental rights, including freedom of movement.[14]

In response, Israeli security agencies worked with the Hebrew University to establish a penalty and reward system for Palestinian students based on their political leanings and organizing. The university regularly reported on its Palestinian students to the prime minister's advisor on Arab affairs. The government in turn established the "Jewish-Arab students' forum" on campus, a body whose Palestinian participants were rewarded for "good behavior" with travel passes, income, and job recommendations. Palestinian members of the forum were expected to partake in *hasbara* (state propaganda) and to assist Israel, as educated representatives, in dissipating dissent among Palestinian citizens.[15]

Throughout the state's military rule over Palestinian citizens, and for years after, Israeli government officials continued to debate whether their access to higher education should be allowed at all. They debated whether education would strengthen Palestinian resistance or could ultimately facilitate cultural assimilation into Israel as a Jewish state. With the end of military governance, Tolidano himself altered his strategic approach. At a 1968 Arab Affairs Committee meeting, he advocated for educating Palestinians, particularly women, as a mechanism to lower the Palestinian birth rate. He laid out the Israeli conundrum as the government understood it: "What is preferable—a large population with low [national] consciousness or small population, more educated and more nationalistic?"[16] Ultimately, as Tolidano articulated at the meeting, Israeli state priority was given to "the demographic issue." It was decided that Palestinian access to higher education should be expanded, partly as a form of birth control.[17]

These state policies have had long afterlives. Direct supervision by the Shin Bet of Palestinian citizen education persisted for decades, with the agency granted the decisive vote concerning the appointment of teachers, principals, and supervisors.[18] Until 2005, a Shin Bet agent served as the deputy director of the Arab Education Department at the Ministry of Education, when a successful petition to the Supreme Court compelled the ministry to cancel the position on the grounds of discrimination and a violation of due process.[19] Yet even through 2017, the Ministry of Education was found to be cooperating with the Shin Bet concerning the appointment of Palestinian teachers.[20] As recently as 2020, the director general of the Ministry of Education met with the Shin Bet to discuss screening Palestinian citizen teachers for "radicalism."[21]

In Israeli universities, too, these practices lived on. Well after the end of military rule in 1966, administrations across campuses continued to collaborate with the Israeli security state in fielding and monitoring their Palestinian students. Into the 1970s, the government directly intervened in the admissions process to facilitate the acceptance of Palestinians deemed loyal to Israel for university programs of their choice.[22] Today, Israeli university administrations continue to work with the Israeli government to contain the scope of Palestinian pedagogy, knowledge production, and critical expression.

This chapter explores the restrictions imposed on the rights of Palestinian students to study, speak, and protest across Israeli universities. It reveals how the university administrations persistently curtail and police the presence of Palestinian students on their campuses, and how they move in lockstep with the Israeli government to deny the fundamental academic freedoms of Palestinian students, and particularly student organizers, mobilizing on their campuses against the systems of oppression of the Israeli state.

The Outpost University

On March 28, 2022, two Palestinian students of Hebrew University sat on the Mt. Scopus campus lawn and sang in Arabic. They were approached by Jewish-Israeli students who demanded to know what they were singing. The Israeli students—who were also off-duty police officers—accused the Palestinian students of singing "nationalist" songs, forcefully escorted them to the campus gates, and summoned active-duty officers to arrest them.[23]

The Palestinian students were interrogated by the Israeli police "on suspicion of behavior that could violate the public peace" and were questioned about their political views and religious practices.[24] They were ultimately released but were barred from campus for six days. The Hebrew University administration did not intervene in the arrest and banning of its Palestinian students, nor did it declare support for the students and affirm their right to free expression on its campus. The university also failed to reprimand the student officers and campus security for violating the rights of its Palestinian students. Instead, the administration simply stated that the Jewish-Israeli students acted of their own accord and vaguely promised to "clarify university regulations."[25] Palestinian student groups protested the administration's response, which they claimed exemplifies their criminalization and ongoing violent repression on campus.

Situated atop the occupied East Jerusalem Palestinian neighborhood of al-Issawiyeh, Hebrew University Mt. Scopus is policed particularly vigilantly by the administration and campus security. Palestinian students describe in interviews how they are alienated by the university prohibitions on clothing and other items expressing their identity. Aseel, a BA student, was told by her supervisor she could not continue to wear a kaffiyeh while working her campus job. Yousef, her classmate, wore a shirt with a kaffiyeh to a protest just outside the campus gates and was later denied entry back into the university by the guards, despite providing his student identification. Across Israeli campuses, university administrations marginalize and criminalize Palestinian students by scrutinizing them for signs of national, religious, or political expression.

Israeli universities were designed as apparatuses in service of the state's program to "Judaize" Palestinian territory in their regions.[26] Their strategically located campuses were themselves directly built on Palestinian lands, constructed as isolated enclaves, sitting atop mountains or hills overlooking the cities below. Reflecting their national militarized role, Israeli universities are bordered and gated. Despite their status as public institutions, entry is conditioned on a display of identification or permit, passage through metal detectors, and a security check by military veteran armed guards. Israeli scholars of architecture have shown that this is not coincidental: designed to serve the state's territorial policy, campuses remain spatially segregated from their environments.[27] The architecture of Israeli universities constitutes a practice of racialized national ownership, demarcating campuses as Jewish space.[28]

This militarized campus infrastructure is the ongoing subject of Palestinian criticism and organizing. Palestinian students argue that the university gates are reminiscent of military checkpoints in the Occupied Palestinian Territory, complete with armed guards, turnstiles, and ID requirements.[29] Palestinian student organizations across institutions have repeatedly petitioned their administrations to address racial profiling by the guards and contested routine discriminatory practices such as demands that Palestinian students provide proof of university affiliation or refusing Palestinian students entry. Students describe in interviews the humiliation of being turned away at the campus gates and missing classes because they were seen as not belonging at the university. These encounters with Israeli security apparatuses cause students to create narrowly designated walking routes, all to avoid the labyrinth of checkpoints, or minimizing the time spent on campus altogether.[30] Such measures render indigenous Palestinians as foreigners on their own campuses.

Israeli universities are internally designed for the benefit of their Jewish community members. Buildings and campus streets are named after Israeli military and state leaders, including the architects of the mass expulsion of Palestinians in the Nakba and the illegal military occupation of Gaza and the West Bank, including East Jerusalem, in 1967. Hallways display Zionist symbols and narratives, showcasing photographs and texts celebrating Israeli military power and territorial expansion.[31] A permanent exhibit at the University of Haifa, for instance, continues to honor one of its founders, Abba Hushi, who likened educating Palestinians to "raising snakes."[32]

Universities not only curate their campuses to reflect state narratives but also leave little room for alternative representation. Besides limited numbers of billboards specifically designated for student flyers, campuses are tightly regulated spatially. As sociologist of education Yael Maayan shows, Israeli campuses' visual space is well managed—indeed, almost hermetically sealed—explicitly prohibiting students from meaningfully shaping their physical space while they are enrolled.[33] This spatial governance leads Jewish and Palestinian students to occupy the campus differently. Rather than congregate in central meeting areas, Palestinian students are compelled to carve out peripheral spaces where they might feel more safe or "at home" in their institutions. They seek out less conspicuous corners on their campuses that they can temporarily and informally shape as their own, and where they can listen to music, share food and coffee, and speak more or less freely. Geographer Yara Saʿdi-Ibraheem calls these spatial practices of resistance and subversion by Palestinians in the face of alienation on Israeli campuses "indigenous students' geographies."[34]

The physical design of Israeli universities' campus space reflects their structural exclusion of Palestinians. Although the Council for Higher Education claims that Palestinian matriculation is on an upward trend,[35] research by both the Israeli government and scholars of education shows otherwise. According to 2019 data from the Israeli Ministry of Finance, for example, Palestinian student enrollment is growing primarily in underfunded colleges and not in universities.[36] The data shows that Palestinian enrollment across Israeli institutions of higher education remains one-third the rate of Jews, and that while Palestinians constitute approximately 30 percent of the university age population in Israel, they accounted for just 18.1 percent of first-year bachelor's degree students.[37] Thus, while there is a rise in the absolute number of Palestinian students enrolled in higher education, the Ministry of Finance research concluded that the integration of Palestinians is in fact currently in decline and that the gaps between Palestinian and Jewish students are in fact widening.[38]

While the percentage of Jewish students obtaining their BA from Israeli institutions of higher education has risen exponentially since 2000, the percentage of Palestinian students has risen by only a few points, remaining almost stagnant between 2009 and 2019.[39] Only 22 percent of Palestinian women and under 10 percent of Palestinian men obtained their BA from Israeli institutions in 2019.[40] Government data for the academic year 2021–22 shows that Palestinian students remain underrepresented in Israeli universities.[41] Palestinians made up just over 16 percent of bachelor's degree students, just over 11 percent of master's degree students, and 8 percent of PhD students, and the enrollment rate of new Jewish bachelor's degree students remained three times higher than that of Palestinians.[42] That same year, Palestinians made up only 3.5 percent of university faculty.[43]

These disparities exist by design. The CHE and Israeli universities continue to shape admissions policies in ways that limit Palestinian student access to the academic programs of their choice.[44] Current admission for bachelor's degrees is based on an aggregation of high school baccalaureate grades and the grade on the Israeli standardized test for higher education, called "the psychometric exam." By both criteria of evaluation, Palestinian high school graduates are at a disadvantage.[45] Palestinian students face the persistent underfunding of their schools, the financial and geographic inaccessibility of private preparatory courses for the psychometric exam, and the linguistic and cultural bias of the exam catering to Jewish-Israelis.[46] For competitive programs, such as medicine and diverse medical fields, there is also an admissions interview. The interview process has been shown to function as another site of racialized screening to curb Palestinian enrollment. The Hebrew University Medical School, which was the state's only medical school until 1964, used the interview as a mechanism to maintain caps on Palestinian students during Israeli military rule, admitting no more than two or three Palestinians per cohort.[47] Though such explicit caps have not been in place since the late 1960s, admission of Palestinian students to medicine and other competitive fields continues to be manipulated by state and university administrations.

Beginning in 2000, the Knesset education committee intervened in university admissions policies, eliminating the mandatory psychometric exam. The amended policy was implemented as part of a larger effort to increase enrollment of Jewish students from Israel's social and geographic "periphery."[48] But admissions data soon revealed that the main beneficiaries of the new policy were Palestinian students, for whom the exam constituted a significant admissions barrier. Under the new policy, admission of Palestinian students to programs such as dentistry, nursing, and occupational therapy was expected to significantly increase. Once this expectation materialized, the committee of university presidents reinstated the original admissions policy, openly admitting their intent to curb Palestinian enrollment in competitive degree programs and prevent "undesirable" demographic changes on their campuses.[49]

Universities also immediately increased the weight of personal interviews and instituted minimum age requirements of twenty for enrollment in competitive degree programs such as medicine and paramedical studies.[50] The minimum age requirement directly benefited Jewish applicants, who cannot apply until completion of their mandatory military service. The policy therefore effectively targeted Palestinian applicants, most of whom are not required to enlist in the Israeli military and can attend university upon graduating from high school.[51] The Palestinian Civil Rights organization Adalah began petitioning against this policy in 2008, citing racial discrimination.[52] While the legal challenges were dismissed, the CHE finally conceded and revoked the minimum age requirement in 2014.[53]

Unofficial caps on Palestinian student enrollment in medical fields still persist, however. Interviewed faculty in these fields across universities reported that in department meetings and in conversations with university administrators, there are ongoing and explicit discussions about the number of Palestinian students and informal ways to regulate their admission, including through the use of interviews. As Ronit, a professor in a medical field, described in an interview: "At our department there were discussions about what to do because there were 'too many' Palestinian students. In our field it is mostly women, and we have a lot of women Palestinian students. I often heard faculty and senior admin describe this as a problem." Unofficial caps on Palestinian students in medical fields, regarded as an open secret across Israeli universities,

have failed to attract consistent media attention and remain institutionally uncontested. Most recently, with the election of a far-right government in 2023, this open secret was explicitly articulated and proposed
once more as formal policy. Coalitional agreements advanced by far-
right minister Itamar Ben-Gvir stipulated that military veterans should
be given preferential admissions to medicine, law, and other competitive
degree programs. The proposed policy is a thinly veiled mechanism to
further bar Palestinians from earning Israeli universities' most desirable
degrees.[54]

With admission to competitive programs tightly regulated by universities, Palestinian students are compelled to seek higher education
abroad to study their preferred field or enroll in Israeli institutions but
settle for other fields of study. Palestinian students are more likely than
their Jewish peers to report that they compromised on their field of study
because they had not been admitted to their field of choice.[55] Increasingly,
Palestinian citizens have turned to pursuing education in Palestinian
universities or abroad, particularly in Jordan. While only 5 percent of
Jewish-Israelis apply to foreign universities for their academic training,
as many as 18 to 24 percent of Palestinian citizens leave Israel in pursuit
of higher education.[56] The majority of those over the last decade studied
in Jordan, and many increasingly enroll in Palestinian universities in the
occupied West Bank.[57] Most Palestinian citizens who study at Palestinian
universities or abroad are pursuing medicine and other medical fields.[58]
Government data shows that over 75 percent of practicing Palestinian
citizen physicians were trained abroad,[59] and that Palestinians constitute
the majority of practitioners across the medical fields who trained
abroad.[60]

There is a clear correlation between discriminatory admissions policies and the choice to study abroad. Palestinian citizens consistently cite
the minimum age requirements, admissions interviews, and often structurally unattainable psychometric exam scores as pushing them to leave
Israel in pursuit of higher education.[61] But many also explicitly strive to
escape the experience of alienation, discrimination, and exclusion at
Israeli universities. Palestinian students studying in Jordan, whether
Muslim or Christian, report a welcoming experience of cultural,

religious, and linguistic affinity and belonging. They often describe feeling at home in Jordanian institutions, as well as a greater degree of freedom not only to study in their field of choice but to express their multifaceted identities and their full selves.[62] This was also the case for many Palestinian students enrolling in Palestinian universities in the OPT, who consistently report positive social and academic experiences; however, they often struggle to get their degrees recognized in Israel upon graduation.[63] For their part, Palestinian university administrations welcome Palestinian citizens of Israel and offer specialized courses designed to assist them in integrating into the Israeli labor market.[64]

It is noteworthy that Palestinian citizens of Israel choose to move to Jordan or travel across Israeli checkpoints to Palestinian universities under Israeli military rule rather than enroll in Israeli institutions. It is also indicative of yet another significant barrier to Palestinian higher education in Israel: physical access to campus.

Admission to Israeli universities marks the beginning, not the end, of Palestinian students' exclusion. At the University of Haifa, which serves the majority of Palestinians living in the Galilee, Palestinian students have long faced inefficient commutes and difficulty finding local accommodations. When Palestinian student organizing for improved physical access to campus gained little traction with the administration, students held a sit-in and demanded that the university work with a local public transit company to offer transportation from regional Palestinian villages. The university responded by bringing protesting students before a disciplinary committee.[65] Long commutes due to the state-planned underdevelopment of public transportation from their villages and towns increase Palestinian student reliance on university dorms to complete their education. Yet access to dorms is far from guaranteed, as university dorm policies broadly discriminate against Palestinian students.[66]

The University of Haifa has a history of denying dorm applications by Palestinian students. Research by the students revealed why: military service constituted as much as 41 percent of eligibility criteria.[67] Student organizers petitioned the Haifa Magistrate Court to remove military service as a criterion. The court ruled in their favor and acknowledged that the criterion discriminated against Palestinians, the majority of whom are not drafted into the military.[68] But the University of Haifa refused to accept the ruling and appealed, and in 2008 the Israeli Supreme Court upheld the university's right to give preference to military veterans in dorms.[69] The preference given to Jewish-Israelis in university dorms exacerbates long-standing barriers for Palestinian students of access to campuses.

Palestinian students attending Israeli universities consistently report a shortage in off-campus housing as a key barrier to higher education. The refusal of Jewish-Israeli landlords to rent to Palestinians is systemic and well documented and was frequently brought up in interviews with Palestinian students across institutions.[70] They described calling landlords in response to active apartment rental ads, only to be told the apartment was no longer available once they shared their Palestinian names. Safaa, an incoming student at Hebrew University from the Galilee, is one of many in her cohort who struggled to find housing in West Jerusalem. "As soon as they detected my accent it was over," she described her experience over dozens of inquiries in an interview, "and the university doesn't help us with this at all." Palestinian student organizers have repeatedly tried to mobilize their universities to offer housing solutions, either by facilitating off-campus rentals or expanding access to dorms, but administrations have offered no institutional response.

After enrolling and finding accommodations, Palestinian students must contend with Israeli campuses' lack of religious, cultural, or linguistic diversity. Though civil society organizations pushed the CHE to recommend that university websites and signage be fully translated into Arabic in 2013, no university has completed this process to date. Corresponding to the Knesset's 2018 "Israel as the Nation-State of the Jewish People Law," which retracted the status of Arabic as an official state language, campuses' virtual and physical spaces do not award Arabic full status as they do Hebrew and English.[71] Most university websites still have limited Arabic-language content, and campus signage is frequently partially or incorrectly translated.[72] This sustained linguistic exclusion relegates Palestinians to the status of second-class students who cannot fully belong at Israeli universities, a status Thair Abu Rass and Yael Maayan have called "present absentees."[73]

While enrolling Muslim, Christian, and Druze Palestinian students, Israeli universities continue to maintain their campuses as Jewish spaces that strictly regulate other forms of religious expression. Muslim prayer spaces across campuses have been inconsistently or temporarily provided, remotely located, and largely maintained by students and not by university staff.[74] At the University of Haifa, which houses two full-service synagogues and additional prayer spaces for Jewish students,[75] Muslim Palestinian students had to wage an extended campaign for a single space to pray on campus. After strenuous negotiations with the administration, students were ultimately allotted a prayer space in the university parking lot, which for years remained the only room for Muslim prayer on campus. Christian Palestinian students likewise had to file a legal petition requesting to put up a Christmas tree in the university's main building. The university fought back and the petition was rejected, after which the students were only permitted to place the tree in a remote area of campus.[76] At Tel Aviv University, which houses three synagogues and multiple additional Jewish prayer spaces, Muslim students petitioned for a prayer space only to be allotted time slots in a dorm basement.[77] Even this temporary allocation was met with a campaign by Jewish employees and students to monitor the space for "radical political activity" and "incitement."[78] Nevertheless, after years of student campaigning against the temporary allocations for Muslim prayer, the administration finally allotted two designated permanent rooms.[79]

Yet once established, designated prayer spaces themselves come to serve as mechanisms of containment. The university administrations' move to ultimately grant prayer spaces for Muslim students, as Yara Sa'di-Ibraheem argues, paradoxically further restricted Palestinian student use of campus space. In relegating them to remote corners on their campus, university administrations facilitate the redirection of Palestinians away from more central locations and entrench the differential spatial practices between Palestinian and Jewish students.[80]

The universities' policies on prayer spaces exemplifies their broader project to regulate Palestinian student presence on their campuses. Over

the past decade, both the CHE and university administrations have
outlined policies and implemented new programs ostensibly designed to
address disparities between Jewish and Palestinian students. These
include designated preparatory courses, Hebrew-language tutoring, and
select scholarships for Palestinians.[81] But these do not address the root
causes of Palestinian exclusion. What remains unaddressed and unspeak-
able for university administrations is their alignment and collaboration
with the Israeli regime of discriminatory policies. Expressing any aspect
of the Palestinian national identity, or even merely speaking or singing
in Arabic, is construed by the Israeli state and university administrations
alike as threatening the "public peace." As Palestinian students argue,
Palestinian identity itself has always been conceived of as a "security
threat" on Israeli campuses.

But the policing of Palestinian students has become more pronounced
with their growing political mobilization on campus. As Palestinian
sociologist and political activist Arees Bishara explained, "When the
Planning and Budgeting Committee began to fund these programs to
'advance' Palestinians in academia, they didn't expect that Palestinian
students would be politically aware or vocal. They assumed that if they
gave Palestinians educational opportunities they would be more support-
ive of the Zionist institutions. But this is part of the unintentional consequences." Palestinian student organizers contend that the violence
against them will endure until Israeli universities are democratized,
freed of systemic racial discrimination, and transformed from Jewish-
Zionist institutions into egalitarian ones that belong to all their students
and faculty.

Occupied Students: The Repression of
Palestinian Political Expression

In the early morning hours of May 11, 2022, Israeli military forces
invaded the occupied West Bank city of Jenin. In the course of that invasion, Israeli snipers targeted and shot leading Palestinian journalist
Shireen Abu-Akleh in what has since been deemed an extrajudicial

killing.[82] The next day, Palestinian students at Ben-Gurion University organized a protest against the Israeli military's killing of Abu-Akleh. The university administration initially recommended to the students that they hold the protest inside a closed classroom. The students did not relent, and the university ultimately permitted them to hold the protest outside, only to allow Israeli police and Shin Bet forces to enter the campus and arrest student organizers.

Maryam Abu Qwaider, one of the Palestinian student protestors, was forcibly dragged from campus by undercover police officers in front of her peers. She was detained for ten days. Later accused of "incitement" based on her social media profile, Abu Qwaider was sentenced to house arrest and prohibited from connecting to the internet, causing her to miss her final semester exams.[83]

The Ben-Gurion University administration responded by stating that the police and Shin Bet made the arrests on its campus at their own discretion. The administration made no public commitment to support Abu Qwaider's return to her studies or to guarantee that police forces would no longer be permitted to abduct students from its campus.[84] The implications of the administration's response were abundantly clear to Palestinian students. As one student organizer told the press: "We see that the university is like a rubber stamp for the police and the Shabak [the Shin Bet]."[85]

In the 1950s, the entry of Palestinian citizen students into Israeli academia was conditioned upon their loyalty to the Israeli state. Still under military rule, Palestinian students who joined Israeli institutions of higher education were surveilled and policed as political dissidents. University administrations worked with Israeli state security apparatuses to surveil and contain Palestinian dissent on campus.[86]

Israeli university administrations today institutionally ignore their histories of collaboration with the military rule of Palestinian citizens, as well as their ongoing partnerships with the Israeli Shin Bet and police. They now increasingly speak the language of diversity. Photographs on university websites feature groups of Jewish and Palestinian students conversing in lecture halls or around lab tables and laughing together on sunny campus lawns. Tel Aviv University recently set up an Equality and

Diversity Commission, while Hebrew University at Mt. Scopus now operates a Diversity and Multiculturalism unit.[87] The unit declares that Hebrew University "strives to nurture a community that expresses a broad range of stances, world views, and cultures," one that is representative of the diverse populations that make up Israeli society and is "free from discrimination and harassment based on affiliations of community, nationality, congregation, religion or sexual orientation."[88] These formal declarations about equality are rarely backed by substantive institutional policy or reflected in the everyday experiences of Palestinian faculty and students. But they ring entirely hollow in the face of university administrations' daily monitoring, policing, and repression of Palestinian political expression.

Scholar of education Andre Mazawi argues that the alienation and repression experienced by Palestinian citizens in Israeli higher education are a structural problem, wherein the educational setting itself is designed to foreclose their fundamental political and national aspirations.[89] Yet from their entry into Israeli universities decades ago, Palestinian students have refused to remain silent about the injustices of Israeli settler colonialism. They have consistently committed themselves to what Ibrahim Makkawi has called "engagement from the margin": political organizing against the racial policies of the Israeli state and university administrations.[90]

Palestinian students engaged in political education and advocacy today argue that they are still treated by campus security and state apparatuses not as rights-bearing citizens but as a colonized population that must be controlled and subjugated. Campus security is made up of former Israeli combat soldiers, many of whom still serve in combat reserve units. Campus security officers are therefore not only armed, but also militarized and trained in the Occupied Palestinian Territory. Palestinian students experience the intimidating effects of this training. In spring 2022, a progressive student group at Hebrew University booked a common space for a meeting only to have a campus security guard enter the room. He then refused to leave and even filmed some of the students on his phone. Palestinian students reported in an interview that these interactions with campus security exemplify how they are treated with suspicion by their university. Israeli campus security is backed by Israeli state security forces, which maintain a regular presence on campuses, including the Israeli National Police, the border police, and the Shin Bet, all agencies operating in the OPT. These state forces, whose daily practices have been repeatedly found to violate international human rights law, are summoned to campus by university administrations to limit Palestinian student speech and organizing.

Palestinian student organizers are keenly aware that they face institutional restrictions backed by state violence. They can only enter campus as individuals seeking degrees—Israeli universities have consistently made clear—never as members of a collective with political or national consciousness. Unlike Jewish students, who are allowed a wide range of political activity and expression on campus, Palestinian students are expected to check their national identity at the university gates and take on identifications that are palatable to Jewish-Israelis. As Samir, a student organizer at the University of Haifa, explained in an interview: "As soon as I arrive to campus I am only allowed to be an 'Israeli-Arab,' never a Palestinian."

Located in the Galilee, the most populous Palestinian region in Israel, and enrolling the highest number of Palestinian students, the University of Haifa has a notorious reputation among Palestinian students for its severe repression of political expression on campus. With the outbreak of the Second Palestinian Intifada in 2000, and throughout subsequent Israeli military operations in the OPT, the University of Haifa administration repeatedly repressed Palestinian expression. At the height of the Israeli military offensives in the occupied West Bank in 2002, Palestinian students were brought before disciplinary hearings and suspended for peacefully protesting on campus.[91] In 2008, when the Israeli attorney general closed the investigations into the Israeli police killing of Palestinian citizen protestors in 2000, Palestinian students who held a peaceful protest vigil were summoned to disciplinary hearings.[92] Over 90 percent of students summoned to disciplinary committees at the university between 2002 and 2010 were Palestinian. Between 2010 and 2015, Palestinians remained three times as likely as their Jewish peers to be summoned before disciplinary committees.[93] This use of disciplinary hearings as a mechanism to target and deter Palestinian organizing is well documented by Palestinian civil society organizations and even by the Israeli state comptroller, yet it remains common practice.[94]

Disciplinary hearings for individual Palestinian students were gradually supplemented with wholesale constraints on student activity codified into university policy. In 2002, the University of Haifa administration added a clause to its charter permitting the president to suspend all public activity on campus for an indefinite period. Over the decade that followed, the clause became so routinely used to prohibit the political activity of Palestinian students that student organizers and a number of faculty took the university to court. Their legal battle made it all the way to the Israeli Supreme Court, which in 2015 ordered that the clause be rewritten to place some limits on the university president's suspension of public activity.[95]

The university also curbed Palestinian organizing by selectively denying permits. A play commemorating the Nakba, authorized by the university in 2012, was canceled just hours before it was scheduled to begin, with the administration accusing the students of presenting the event as "cultural" when it was really "political."[96] After three years of being refused permits to commemorate the Nakba, two primarily Palestinian leftist student groups defied the unofficial university ban and held a protest in 2014. They were suspended until the end of the academic year. The primary Palestinian student group on campus was similarly accused of holding an unauthorized event and suspended for a month.[97] The student groups petitioned the university administration to protest the unequal enforcement of university policy, since Jewish-Israeli student groups were never suspended for unauthorized events.[98] Together with Palestinian civil rights organization Adalah, they also petitioned the Haifa Magistrate Court to appeal the suspension as an infringement of freedom of speech and as a violation of university regulations.[99] The Magistrate Court upheld the suspension. Only an appeal to the Israeli Supreme Court succeeded in compelling the university to permit the student groups to resume their public activities.[100] In the wake of repeated legal challenges to its restrictions on Palestinian student activity, the university administration further amended its official regulations governing public activity on its campus.

Public activity on the Haifa campus is the most restricted of any Israeli institution and is subject to such strict regulations that it is practically prohibited. As of the latest regulations in 2022, students are permitted to hold protests at only a single outdoor designated space during two thirty-minute recesses on Mondays, and for a single thirty-minute recess on Wednesdays.[101] Many of these restrictions are implicitly or explicitly directed at Palestinian students. No public student activity is permitted on Jewish holidays, including Friday evenings, state-designated memorial days for the Holocaust and Israeli soldiers, and all the days between the two, as well as during meeting days of the Board of Trustees. Requests by student groups for space for protests, events, tabling, or passing out flyers must be made twenty-four to forty-eight hours in advance, and the content of every flyer must be translated into Hebrew and approved by the university administration.

The cumbersome paperwork, restrictive scheduling, and escalating administrative repression has succeeded in significantly discouraging Palestinian student expression and activism. As Farraj, a student activist, explained in an interview: "It doesn't feel possible to protest or do anything on campus anymore. We just moved all our activities outside of the university to [the city of] Haifa." Many interviewed Palestinian students at the University of Haifa reported experiencing such hostility from fellow students and institutional silencing by the administration that they no longer mobilize or join political activity on campus.

The trajectory of administrative repression of Palestinian political expression at the University of Haifa showcases the broader procedural landscape in Israeli higher education. Palestinian student initiatives challenging the Israeli military are routinely framed and managed by university administrations as "security threats," in ways that parallel the military governance of the OPT. At Hebrew University in 2014, a primarily Palestinian leftist student group organized a talk critical of the military draft of Druze Palestinian citizens. The university administration refused to grant a permit for the event, claiming it was unlawful to hold a lecture calling for civil disobedience. Two weeks later, students staged a peaceful protest against a new bill proposing to extend the draft to Christian Palestinians.[102] The university administration deemed it "unlawful" and called the border police to disperse the event, during which they injured several students and detained others for questioning.[103] The dean of students later labeled such demonstrations harmful to the "delicate fabric of life at the university" and warned of a wholesale suspension of political activity on campus.[104]

Permits for Palestinian events are commonly refused or rescinded across Israeli university campuses. The Hebrew University administration canceled an academic conference about Palestinian political prisoners in 2017.[105] At Ben-Gurion University that same year, a Palestinian student group organized an exhibit on Israeli demolitions of Bedouin Palestinian homes in the Naqab. Following complaints from the student union, the university reversed its earlier decision to authorize the exhibit, citing "security constraints."[106] The administration demanded that students present the content of the exhibit in advance and ultimately authorized the display for only one day.[107] In 2018, the Tel Aviv University administration canceled a previously authorized series of meetings, tabling, and events scheduled as part of a "Week to End the Occupation" organized by a joint Palestinian-Jewish student group shortly before the week commenced.[108] More recently, the first event of the 2022 semester for Palestinian students at Ben-Gurion University was effectively canceled by the administration with one day's notice. The event was scheduled to include a fair and a musical performance, but the administration prohibited students from setting up stalls to sell stickers in Arabic and traditional art pieces and canceled the evening performance by Palestinian artists. Alongside claims of bureaucratic difficulties, the university also cited concern about potential "incitement" and violation of the "public peace" as the reasons for its last-minute cancellations.[109]

Palestinian students consistently mobilize to make their campuses sites of expression and education about Palestinian history, culture, and rights. Time and again, the boundaries of acceptable content and format are narrowly drawn around them.

When university administrations do grant permits for Palestinian student events, they consistently fail to protect their physical safety in holding them. When Palestinian and joint Palestinian-Israeli student groups organized ceremonies across campuses to commemorate the Nakba in May 2022, they were subjected to state and state-backed violence. At Tel Aviv University, Palestinian students coordinated their commemoration ceremony with university security and obtained a permit for the campus's Entin Square. But shortly before the event began—as Im Tirtzu and other right-wing Jewish student groups gathered at the site—the university notified the Palestinian organizers that it had passed off the authority to oversee the event to the Israeli police. This was in spite of the fact that Entin Square is officially designated by the university as the central site on campus grounds for student gatherings and organizing of all kinds.[110] At the event, Palestinian students held signs and spoke about the mass expulsion of Palestinians in 1948, including from the village of Al-Shaykh Muwannis, on whose lands Tel Aviv University now stands. Opposite them stood Jewish-Israeli students vigorously waving Israeli flags, jeering, and yelling racial slurs. Im Tirtzu members made an explicit call to "celebrate" the Nakba by handing out candy to passersby. Dozens of armed police officers stood between the student groups, some of whom spoke with Im Tirtzu members and passed the candy around.

Soon a Palestinian student who walked past to join the Nakba commemoration was lunged at by a group of Jewish-Israeli students, and the police immediately seized on the opportunity to violently shut down the event. Officers descended upon the Palestinian students, attacking them with pepper spray and pinning several to the ground.[111] One officer pushed his knee onto a Palestinian student's neck as he lay face down on the ground. The police arrested three Palestinian students and detained them for up to four days. No Jewish students were arrested; they were merely ushered by officers to a position behind the police barrier. When pressured to respond to an inquiry by Palestinian Knesset members, the university president faulted student groups on "both sides" for the escalation, and flatly refused Palestinian student demands to institute new guidelines limiting police authority on campus.

Just a week after the event at Tel Aviv University, Palestinian student groups held a Nakba Day commemoration event at Ben-Gurion

University. Coordinated with the university administration, students gathered on campus holding Palestinian flags and making speeches, many speaking of their own grandparents' expulsion from their homes in 1948.

The repression was immediate and came first in the form of threats from other students. Im Tirtzu and Jewish-Israeli student groups gathered around the Palestinian students and repeatedly chanted "Give up your citizenship" and "Death to the Arabs!" The mayor of Beersheba swiftly joined the attack, sending a letter to the university president demanding that he bar the Palestinian flag and such protests from campus. Minister of Education Yifat Shasha-Biton also issued a condemnation, calling photos of the event "unacceptable."[112] Following the backlash, and a complaint submitted by Im Tirtzu in the wake of the event, the Ben-Gurion academic secretariat summoned a Palestinian student organizer for a disciplinary hearing at the Council for Higher Education.

The student, Watan Madi, was accused of "behavior that involves disobeying, or refusing to obey the instructions of the university's designated authorities, including the regulations regarding political activity," based solely on her reading aloud an essay by Mahmoud Darwish that included the word *shaheed* ("martyr" in Arabic).[113] After a months-long investigation, the Ben-Gurion University disciplinary committee convicted Madi for disobeying campus authorities, determining that she should have refrained from using a term that much of the Jewish-Israeli public associates with their conception of "terrorism."[114]

Supported by a letter from several hundred faculty and aided by the Association of Civil Rights in Israel, Madi appealed her conviction, which was thrown out on procedural grounds.[115] Media coverage of the case and public support by faculty, coupled with legal representation that found significant irregularities in the disciplinary proceedings, eventually bore fruit. Several months later, the university announced it would not be pursuing an additional disciplinary procedure against Madi, though the administration emphasized that it stands behind its initial decision to prosecute her.[116]

The Palestinian civil rights organization Adalah, among other civil rights groups, has been at the forefront of offering legal representation to

Palestinian students facing silencing or punitive measures at their universities. But many such cases do not rise to the level of obtaining legal representation or receiving media attention, and are allowed to stand. The taxing bureaucratic negotiations over every event and looming threat of disciplinary proceedings operate to intimidate Palestinian students, deterring them from organizing events, containing their expression, and minimizing their political imprint on the university campus.

From their entry into Israeli higher education, Palestinian students have been criminalized, policed, and targeted by their universities in collusion with the state. Academic freedom in Israeli higher education does not apply to Palestinian students.

University administrations have consistently shown themselves to be agents of the state, collaborating with the government to shield it from criticism and accountability for its military occupation and regime of apartheid. The government is increasingly censoring discussion of the Nakba and the foundational injustices of the Israeli state, both by the Palestinians it governs through military rule in the OPT and those it counts among its citizens. Mirroring this escalating censorship, universities increasingly and forcefully repress Palestinian study, commemoration, or protest of ongoing Israeli state violence. In repeatedly repressing academic learning and student advocacy in pursuit of decolonization, universities serve as guardians of the Israeli settler-colonial order.

6

Academia Against Liberation

On July 14, 2021, Palestinian students from Birzeit University in the occupied West Bank organized a solidarity visit to the nearby village of Turmus Ayya. They came to see a Palestinian family whose home had been demolished by the Israeli military just days before. Returning that evening, they found the Israeli military waiting for them. Israeli soldiers forced the bus to pull over and the students to disembark. After a bodily search, soldiers arrested forty-five students—tightly handcuffing their wrists together with cable ties and blindfolding them—then took them into Israeli custody for interrogation and detention.[1]

This arbitrary detention was immediately condemned by Birzeit University as well as Palestinian prisoner support and human rights association Addameer as a means of repressing student expression and activism.[2] Addameer declared that these arrests constituted a violation of Israel's obligations as the occupying power to protect Palestinian students' right to education, as outlined in Article 26 of the Universal Declaration of Human Rights and Article 13 of the International Covenant on Economic, Social, and Cultural Rights. Yet Israel detained at least thirty-three of the students for days, and thirteen of them for over a month, accusing them of "incitement" against the Israeli occupation.[3]

These arrests came on the heels of Israeli violence directed at Palestinian student activists at Israeli universities. In May 2021, tens of thousands of Palestinian citizens of Israel took to the streets in protest, among them many university students. The protests were sparked by Israeli security forces and far-right settlers' campaigns across occupied East Jerusalem during the month of Ramadan, which subjected Palestinian residents to increased surveillance, movement restrictions, and physical abuse.[4] This intensified Israeli violence came to a peak on May 6, when Palestinians facing expulsion from the occupied neighborhood of Sheikh Jarrah reported to the Israeli Supreme Court that they rejected a deal with the Jewish-Israeli settlers that claimed their homes and sought to replace them.[5] On May 7, hundreds of Palestinian worshippers stayed on at the Al-Aqsa Mosque after Friday prayers, protesting the impending expulsions. Israeli forces shot protestors at the mosque compound, injuring over 200 Palestinians.[6] Shortly thereafter, on May 10, Israeli border police invaded the Al-Aqsa Mosque compound during Ramadan prayers, shooting worshippers with tear gas, stun grenades, and rubber-coated metal bullets and injuring over 300 Palestinians.[7]

The day after the raid on Al-Aqsa, on May 11, Palestinian students at Ben-Gurion University organized a protest of their own, rallying against Israeli military incursions and ongoing Palestinian dispossession across occupied East Jerusalem. They coordinated the protest with university security and even the Israeli police, and gathered with signs at the edge of campus, joined by a contingent of progressive Jewish-Israeli students who stood with them. Palestinian students addressed the crowd to explain the current expulsions in occupied East Jerusalem as part of the ongoing Nakba, which targets Palestinians under occupation as well as Palestinian citizens of Israel. They held signs and chanted to draw the attention of their fellow students to the injustices of Israeli occupation.

This display of Palestinian politics on an Israeli campus was immediately and violently repressed. Shortly into the demonstration, Jewish-Israeli local residents gathered around the Palestinian students, threatening to assault them. Within minutes, Israeli police and undercover forces joined campus security to descend upon the Palestinian students. A stun grenade was fired into the crowd, and students were pinned to the ground, shoved, and beaten. Seven Palestinian students were arrested and detained for days.

One Palestinian student was so severely beaten by Israeli police that he passed out and was hospitalized overnight.[8] He awoke surrounded by officers. He was then illegally interrogated for hours while denied adequate food and sleep, questioned about his student organizing, and falsely accused of assaulting police officers. Hani, an undergraduate engineering student who was also arrested, described police intimidation tactics and threats during his detention. "The officer told me, 'Say bye-bye to your studies,'" he recalled. "'You wanted to go to demonstrations, huh? You will never be an engineer in your life.'"[9]

Yet despite its repression, the demonstration at Ben-Gurion University proved only the beginning. In the weeks that followed, Palestinian student groups across Israeli university campuses staged protests against Israeli military assaults on Palestinians in the besieged Gaza Strip and the occupied West Bank, including East Jerusalem, as well as against Israeli police operations targeting Palestinian citizens of Israel.[10]

This student mobilization was part of a historic popular uprising by Palestinians across both Israel and the Occupied Palestinian Territory, which would become known as the "Unity Intifada."[11] Dozens of protests erupted with tens of thousands of participants over the course of a week, culminating in a general strike on May 18 to interrupt the Israeli economy and everyday life that depend upon apartheid rule.[12] The day of the strike, Palestinians shuttered their storefronts and refused to arrive at the schools, hospitals, and businesses at which they work.[13] They instead took to the streets to take part in demonstrations and creative resistance. With the Unity Intifada, Palestinians with Israeli citizenship and Palestinians under Israeli military rule came together to resist their fragmentation by the Israeli state and articulate collective demands for liberation from its system of racialized domination.[14]

In their "Manifesto for Dignity and Hope," Palestinian citizens of Israel committed to a united struggle against Israeli settler colonialism and for the reunification of Palestinian society from across Israeli-created "isolated prisons," including the "citizenship prison."[15] Drawing on a long tradition of Palestinian citizen student activism articulating their politics as part of an anticolonial struggle, Palestinian student organizers on Israeli campuses in 2021 protested and challenged Israeli rule across all the territories it governs, also reminding the world of the plight of Palestinian refugees. As Lana Tatour shows, Palestinian citizens refused to limit their activism to the liberal politics of inclusion or equality within the Israeli state. Instead, they asserted their identity as Palestinians and their demands in terms of decolonization and an end to Israeli apartheid.[16]

This chapter traces the Israeli suppression of Palestinian student mobilization, from universities in Israel to those in the Occupied Palestinian Territory (OPT). Israel's continuous war against Palestinian presence, as Khaled Furani argues, is directed at *all* Palestinian students. He shows that Israeli repression of Palestinian students forms a single continuum, from the detention and killing of Palestinian organizers in universities across the OPT to Shin Bet interrogations and disciplinary hearings for Palestinian citizens at Israeli institutions.[17]

This targeting of Palestinian students serves Israel's settler-colonial project of eliminating the indigenous Palestinians. It is part of a decades-long campaign to repress Palestinian higher education, both within the Israeli state and under Israeli military rule, as a site of Palestinian resistance. Palestinian universities in the occupied West Bank, including East Jerusalem, face obstructive bureaucratic restrictions and recurrent military raids resulting in abduction, torture, and detention of students and faculty. In the besieged Gaza Strip, Palestinian universities are subjected to debilitating economic and structural isolation as well as repeated Israeli aerial bombardments that destroy their already depleted infrastructure. This systemic destruction of Palestinian centers of education is what Karma Nabulsi has called "scholasticide," which Nabulsi and others argue is a colonial tactic to keep Palestinians uneducated and therefore more susceptible to subjugation.[18]

The Israeli state targets Palestinian universities, scholars, and students to suppress the Palestinian movement for liberation, and the Israeli system of higher education is complicit. Institutionally, university campuses, knowledge production, and pedagogy directly serve the Israeli security state that maintains the military rule over Palestinians in the OPT. University administrations consistently—and sometimes violently—suppress Palestinian students mobilizing for the rights of scholars and students under Israeli occupation, as Jewish-Israeli faculty and students overwhelmingly stand by. Israeli universities are thus partners in the state's oppressive campaign directed at Palestinian academic freedoms, both those under military occupation and on their own campuses. This chapter, then, will show how Israeli academia is put to work against Palestinian freedom and the demands for justice and equality.

Higher Education under Occupation

Before the mass expulsion of Palestinians in the Nakba and the founding of Israel, Palestinians pursued higher education at leading universities in Beirut, Damascus, and Cairo. After 1948, Palestinians displaced from their homes and lands—whether to the Gaza Strip, under Egyptian governance, or to the West Bank, under Jordanian authority—continued to travel for study at universities across the Middle East as well as in the Soviet Union, Europe, and the United States.[19] Yet with the 1967 military occupation of the Gaza Strip and the West Bank, including East Jerusalem, Israel immediately escalated its war on Palestinian education. Palestinians were severed from neighboring Arab states and their travel severely restricted, closing off their opportunities to pursue higher education abroad. Forcibly isolated from the intellectual and political life offered at universities across the Middle East and beyond,[20] Palestinians in the OPT were compelled to establish their own system of higher education under the Israeli military government and despite its many obstacles.[21]

The first comprehensive Palestinian institution of higher education was Birzeit University, on the outskirts of Ramallah. First opening its doors in 1924, the school of Birzeit later became one of several Palestinian institutions to offer associate's degrees. But with Israel's occupation, the institution's administration began preparations to offer full four-year degree programs.[22] Several years later, after waging a struggle against

Israel's military government to overcome its restrictive orders and demands for permit applications, the institution began enrolling students for bachelor's degrees in 1972.[23] Birzeit University became the first Palestinian university and has been a major center of Palestinian intellectual and political life for generations of Palestinian students.[24]

From its early years, the Birzeit University campus was a site of Palestinian protest and a symbol of youthful civic resistance to Israeli military occupation. A hub of student activists advocating for Palestinian self-determination and articulating revolutionary anticolonial politics, the university was immediately regarded by Israel as a threat to its rule.[25] The Israeli state was also particularly concerned about the university enrolling and potentially radicalizing Palestinian citizens of Israel and thereby fueling a broader Palestinian mobilization and liberatory politics.[26] Almost immediately after Birzeit University opened its doors to enroll bachelor's degree students, Israel began deploying the military to destabilize its educational programming. In 1973, the Israeli military closed the Birzeit University campus for two weeks, the first of fifteen such closures.[27] Upon its reopening, the Israeli military governor of the occupied West Bank routinely invaded the campus to inspect classes, demanding copies of all assigned reading lists and textbooks for review and Israeli authorization.[28]

This campaign of harassment and suppression of academic freedom escalated with the Israeli military and Shin Bet arresting and interrogating senior Palestinian faculty and administrators and ousting and deporting the university's president, Hanna Nasir, to Lebanon in 1974.[29] Birzeit University and other institutions of higher education across the OPT have since become sites of continued struggle: the Israeli government has waged persistent campaigns to limit Palestinian education and repress resistance to its military rule, while Palestinian students and faculty have repeatedly defied Israeli military orders and continue to insist on their inalienable rights to education and to academic freedom.[30]

Israel escalated its repression of Palestinian universities, then, in tandem with Palestinian popular uprisings. When the First Intifada erupted in 1987, Israel immediately targeted universities, labeling them sites of rebellion. Between 1988 and 1992, the Israeli military ordered the closure of Birzeit University, along with all Palestinian institutions of higher education, forcing faculty and students into underground study groups operating entirely off campus.[31] The Israeli military surveilled and raided these study groups, terming them "cells of illegal education."[32] Students and faculty were arrested, interrogated, and sentenced to military prison for "public order" offenses for their participation in study groups, or even just for possession of a textbook.[33] Nevertheless, Palestinian students and faculty continued to hold classes in defiance of Israeli military orders and kept the university alive. Sustained resistance across the OPT and the Palestinian Academic Freedom Network campaign in the United States that generated Congressional pressure ultimately forced Israel to permit Palestinians to return to their campuses.[34]

With the outbreak of the Second Intifada in 2000, Israel tightened its control over Palestinian movement and further limited opportunities for students to travel within and outside the OPT to pursue higher education. The Israeli government severed ties between academic institutions in the occupied West Bank and the Gaza Strip, preventing joint research, teaching, and collaboration across Palestinian universities. In the occupied Gaza Strip, the Israeli military issued a blanket travel ban, preventing students from studying at West Bank universities or at institutions abroad.[35] In the occupied West Bank, the Israeli military constructed a checkpoint on the main road to Birzeit University to hinder student access to campus, limiting their window for learning and using their commute to class as an opportunity to surveil and interrogate them.[36] While Birzeit University was most frequently targeted throughout the Second Intifada, the Israeli military routinely invaded all Palestinian universities to intimidate and arrest both faculty and students.

Israeli military invasions of Palestinian campuses remain routine, including the use of tear gas, rubber bullets, and live ammunition. In 2014, the Israeli military raided the campuses of Birzeit University, the Arab American University in Jenin, and the Palestine Polytechnic University in Hebron, confiscating computers, banners, and student union materials.[37] In 2016 and 2017, the Israeli military raided student union offices and other buildings at Birzeit University and Al-Quds University, damaging property and confiscating computers, flags, banners, and political materials.[38] Following repeated raids on the Palestine Technical University in Tulkarm, in 2015 the Israeli military formed a temporary base and shooting range for military training on campus.[39] Throughout its use of the base, the Israeli military injured at least 138 faculty and students with live ammunition, and the campus became a site of regular student protest met with violent repression by the Israeli military.[40] In 2018, the Israeli military regularly stationed soldiers outside the Palestine Technical University campus in the Al-Arroub refugee camp, where they surveilled, interrogated, and injured students.[41] The Israeli military raided the Al-Quds University campus in the occupied East Jerusalem neighborhood of Abu Dis every year between 2015 and 2019, confiscating political materials and injuring students.[42] At Al-Quds University's Hind al-Husseini women's college in Sheikh Jarrah, Israel banned an academic conference in 2018, detaining conference participants and temporarily shutting down the campus as punishment.[43]

In offensives on the Gaza Strip, the Israeli military has repeatedly targeted Palestinian universities and colleges in aerial and land strikes, killing and injuring students, faculty, and staff. The strikes continually destroy campus infrastructure, which is rebuilt and then again devastated. In the 2008–9 offensive, fourteen of the fifteen institutions of higher education in Gaza were damaged by Israeli military fire, with six of them directly targeted.[44] Three colleges and six campus buildings were entirely destroyed.[45] In the 2012 bombardment, seven universities were damaged by Israeli airstrikes.[46] In the 2014 offensive, Israel targeted Gaza from the land, sea, and air over the course of fifty-one days, destroying or severely damaging over 18,000 homes and vital infrastructure, including 148 schools and eleven higher education facilities of three universities.[47] Israeli missiles struck the campus of Al-Quds University in the Gaza Strip, killing twenty-two Palestinian students.[48] A missile fired at the campus of the Islamic University in Gaza left its facilities in ruins.[49] The University College of Applied Sciences was also targeted by missiles, destroying its administration building, conference hall, computer laboratories, and many classrooms.[50] These aerial strikes inflicted millions of dollars of damage on these universities, plunging them into an even deeper financial crisis generated by the Israeli siege.[51]

On May 11, 2021, with the start of the Unity Intifada, Israel launched an eleven-day aerial offensive on the Gaza Strip. The bombardment killed 252 Palestinians, including 66 children and 5 university students.[52] Israeli fire wounded over 1,948 Palestinians and internally displaced over 107,000 during that campaign alone.[53] Aerial strikes made over 2,400 homes uninhabitable and damaged over 50,000 units, including the headquarters of major Palestinian, Arab, and International media outlets.[54] The targeting of civilian buildings, some of which Israel claimed—without evidence—were headquarters of military activity, was deemed a war crime by Human Rights Watch and B'Tselem, and was condemned by the UN and international civil society organizations.[55] Among the damaged buildings were also fifty-eight educational facilities, including those of Al-Aqsa University and the Islamic University in Gaza.[56]

Samir Mansour watched his printing house and bookshop reduced to rubble as the Israeli military destroyed the Kahil building adjacent to the Islamic University, which also housed several major cultural and educational centers and labs with expensive equipment.[57] The bookshop was beloved by the university community and frequented by its students. It housed diverse collections of academic and literary texts, some of which were originally translated by the bookshop. Mansour had carefully collected and printed over 100,000 books across genres, proudly serving his community for decades.[58] He described arriving at his bookshop after the bombing:

> The scene was frightening, as the building had come to ruins with only a few books covered by thick dust spared from the destruction. Some books could be seen to be strewn across the floor at great distances from the place, as they washed away 40 years' worth of memories since the founding of a library that served as a beacon and outlet for academics, intellectuals and science students in Gaza.[59]

During the eleven-day offensive, all seven universities in the Gaza Strip were forced shut. In the wake of the campaign, they faced a long struggle to fully reopen. Israeli forces had bombed the Gaza Strip data center and communications network, disrupting internet service and forcing universities to suspend all online educational activity, which was essential throughout the pandemic. The Palestinian Minister of Communication reported that bringing in the necessary equipment to restore internet service in the Gaza Strip was impeded by Israeli restrictions, which he called "inhumane."[60] University students in the Gaza Strip decried the devastating effects of Israeli strikes. Iman Safi, a student at Al-Aqsa University, described the bombings as "causing a complete paralysis of life," immediately derailing the academic trajectories of the hundreds of students who were maimed, whose homes were destroyed, and who lost family members in the aerial strikes.[61] These students, Safi reported, were "in a state of dispersion, instability and homelessness."[62] Palestinian faculty and students know that the repeated aerial strikes on their universities are not coincidental. As Adnan Abu Amer, a professor at Ummah Open University, explained: "Educational buildings have always been primary targets for the Israeli forces in any attack on the Gaza Strip."[63] With Palestinian education regarded as a threat to Israeli rule, Palestinian universities are defined as military targets.

Bureaucratic Violence and the Isolation of Palestinian Universities

In 2016, ten physics students from Al-Azhar University in the Gaza Strip were accepted to a training program at the Augusta Victoria Hospital in occupied East Jerusalem. Five of the students were denied permits by Israel, and the others were granted only short-term permits to leave the Gaza Strip. None of the students were able to complete the training, which was critical for their education and professional development, since the necessary devices and radiation material are unavailable in the Gaza Strip.[64] One of the students described the effect of missing the training after his permit was denied: "I feel I studied for five years for nothing, that my life has stopped."[65] Students and scholars from across the OPT face strict travel restrictions that prevent them from pursuing educational opportunities and training.

Isolating Palestinian universities has long been an Israeli tactic to paralyze them. But the Israeli campaign to stifle Palestinian universities' academic programs through curtailing their international exchanges is now intensifying.

In the Gaza Strip, longstanding restrictions on the movement of peoples and equipment have become sweeping since the 2007 Israeli military blockade began. Drawing condemnations from international human rights organizations, the blockade has sealed off the Gaza Strip from the world, ending local universities' academic exchanges with West Bank and international institutions.[66] Restrictions on the entry of lecturers and scholars from the West Bank and abroad limit opportunities for universities in the Gaza Strip to collaborate on conferences and research or hire external faculty, exacerbating a shortage of graduate degree programs across disciplines.[67] Scholars from the Gaza Strip are prohibited from participating in academic and research activities abroad and are therefore prohibited from staying informed on developments in their field, participating in new research, and expanding their degree programs.[68] This is a particularly acute problem in the medical fields and a range of paramedical studies programs that, consequently, are not offered in the Gaza Strip. The Israeli blockade has limited the scope of medical and paramedical academic programs and compromises the medical training offered to Palestinian students, who are also routinely denied permits to complete their training abroad.[69]

In the occupied West Bank, including East Jerusalem, Israel has found other ways to seal off Palestinian universities. In 2019, the Israeli military raided the home of Ubai Aboudi, director of the Bisan Center for Research and Development in Ramallah.[70] The center produces research and policy papers on Palestinian education and democracy and engages in advocacy for the rights to education, academic freedom, and freedom of expression in the OPT. After his arrest, Aboudi was sentenced by an Israeli military court to four months of administrative detention.[71]

Israel has since officially criminalized the Bisan Center in its entirety. In 2021, Israel designated Bisan, alongside five Palestinian civil society organizations, as "terrorist groups."[72] Despite Israel offering no evidence for this designation, it triggered immediate repercussions for Bisan, precluding Palestinian and international scholars from continued joint engagement and drying up the center's international funding.[73] International human rights groups condemned the designation, and independent investigations, including by the US security state, conclusively determined that Israel had failed to supply evidence to back its claims. Only after these outside interventions was the designation rejected and Bisan's funding and international exchanges resumed.[74]

As documented by Palestinian civil society organizations, the Israeli Civil Administration—the Israeli military government of the OPT—has escalated visa refusals and increasingly tightened restrictions on international faculty since at least 2016.[75] The Civil Administration refuses to issue visas for the length of the academic year and denies entry to international scholars and to Palestinians with international passports with contracts at Palestinian universities.[76] In the absence of transparent Israeli criteria, these international scholars are subjected to arbitrary and varying visa procedures and invasive Israeli "security" vetting.[77] They are often compelled to submit legal petitions to the Israeli Civil Administration, and to pay up to tens of thousands of dollars in security deposits to the Israeli state.[78]

These visa delays and denials continually disrupt Palestinian university programming, creating uncertainty for faculty and students and obstructing international cooperation and institutional development.[79] On these grounds, Palestinian human rights and legal advocacy organizations Al-Haq and Adalah petitioned the Israeli minister of the interior, attorney general, and the Israeli Civil Administration on behalf of Birzeit University in 2019. They demanded that Israel lift restrictions on international academics employed by Birzeit University, refrain from imposing future arbitrary restrictions on international academics, and publish clear and lawful procedures for issuing visas and work permits for international academics in the occupied West Bank.[80] They contended that the restrictions—meant to isolate the university and diminish the quality of education—constitute a violation of the right to "sovereignty of education" stipulated in Article 43 of The Hague Regulations of 1907.[81] In a letter to the Israeli government amplifying this petition, six major American academic associations called on Israel to respect Palestinian academic freedom.[82] They implored Israel to respect Palestinian rights guaranteed by international humanitarian and human rights law, as enshrined in Article 26 of the Universal Declaration of Human Rights (1948) and Article 13 of the International Covenant on Economic, Social, and Cultural Rights (1966).[83]

Instead, Israel has only since escalated and codified its restrictions. In February 2022, the Israeli Civil Administration announced the "Procedure for Entry and Residence of Foreigners in Judea and Samaria Area," which expanded Israeli military control over Palestinian universities in the occupied West Bank.[84] The directive allowed the Israeli military to select which international faculty, researchers, and students may attend Palestinian universities, including Palestinians with foreign passports, and authorized the Civil Administration to assess their academic qualifications and potential contributions. The directive further required applicants to submit to Israeli interrogation and pay expensive bonds. Crucially, it also limited the annual number of international students at Palestinian universities to 150 and international faculty to 100, while capping the duration of international faculty employment to five nonconsecutive years. Finally, the directive compelled foreign nationals to report to the Israeli Civil Administration if they become romantically involved with a local Palestinian.

Birzeit University immediately protested this directive, calling it a deliberate attempt to "isolate Palestinian universities from the outside world, and to determine the future course of Palestinian higher education," divesting them of basic control over their academic programming and international exchanges.[85] International criticism and diplomatic pressure soon followed. Academic associations and advocacy organizations, including the Middle East Studies Association of North America, the American Anthropological Association, the British Society of Middle Eastern Studies, and Scholars at Risk, among others, condemned this escalated violation of Palestinian academic freedom.[86] Human Rights

Watch decried this directive as another instance of Israeli failure to meet the requirements of international humanitarian law as the occupying power.[87] Even US ambassador to Israel Tom Nides stated that he "aggressively engaged with the Government of Israel on these draft rules," while the US State Department expressed concern over its "adverse impacts" on Palestinian academic institutions.[88] Following this international pressure, Israel amended the directive to remove the caps on international students and faculty permitted at Palestinian universities, as well as the requirement to report on relationships with Palestinians.[89]

Sustained international attention and pressure, particularly from the US government, have proven to serve as the only effective check on Israeli authority. Even then, the arduous and opaque Israeli military vetting process to access Palestinian universities as foreign passport holders remains codified under the new directive.

Israeli universities have remained silent over the decades as Israeli policies have continued to stifle Palestinian universities. With the sole exception of former Tel Aviv University president Chaim Ben-Shahar, who agreed to meet with Birzeit University President Gabi Baramki in 1979, no Israeli university president or senior administrator has offered to intervene on their behalf. Ben-Shahar initially seemed amenable to Baramki's request for assistance in importing books and journals but reportedly never followed through and was not heard from again. A later Tel Aviv University president even called, in 1986, for Birzeit to be closed by the Israeli military government.[90]

Solidarity from Jewish-Israeli faculty and students has also been sparse.[91] A marginal group of Jewish-Israeli faculty and students formed the Solidarity Committee with Birzeit University and was active in the 1970s and 1980s. Yet its campus rallies to protest the prolonged closure of Birzeit University were poorly attended, and the group failed to initiate any practical collective action beyond a few petitions and solidarity visits.[92] Shortly after it formed, the sole Israeli academic solidarity group disbanded. Describing his experience as a graduate student at Hebrew University during the First Palestinian Intifada, Neve Gordon recounts that the administration and students overwhelmingly considered themselves bystanders, removed from the violence unfolding daily right outside their campus in occupied East Jerusalem. "While the Palestinians fought for their liberation," Gordon writes, "we continued our classes on Immanuel Kant, John Stuart Mill, and G. E. Moore."[93]

It is only the growing traction of the academic boycott and increased international advocacy that has recently moved some Israeli university faculty and administrators to respond to campaigns by Palestinian universities. Following Birzeit University's legal petition in 2019 and the international amplification it received, thirty-three faculty members at the University of Haifa asked Ron Rubin, the head of the Israeli committee of university presidents, to address Israeli restrictions on international faculty and students at Palestinian universities. In an unequivocal response, the Israeli committee of university presidents announced that the governance of Palestinian universities by the Israeli military, including visa policies, is a "political matter" outside its mandate, and declared that it does not intend to intervene.[94]

But shortly thereafter, in February 2022—when the Israeli Civil Administration's new restrictions on Palestinian universities were met with broad coverage and international condemnation—the response from Israeli university presidents was starkly different.[95] Now, they moved themselves to act. The presidents of Hebrew University and Tel Aviv University wrote to Israeli Chief of Staff Benny Gantz, arguing that the "procedure violates academic freedom without adequate justification."[96]

Even then, however, the letter made clear that their objective was self-preservation. Israeli military restrictions on Palestinian universities were only a matter of concern because they rose to the threshold of international attention. The university presidents reasoned that this procedure "could come back to us like a boomerang" by strengthening the academic boycott and implored Gantz not to provide the BDS movement "with 'ammunition' against us."[97] International attention likewise induced many university faculty to speak out for the first time. The Hebrew University Faculty Senate and the Scientific Council of the Weizmann Institute of Science sent a letter to the Civil Administration asking it to amend the procedure. But this request fell far short of the demands of Birzeit University for full Israeli compliance with international law in regard to the Palestinian right to education.[98] The Israeli faculty letter merely asked the military government to refrain from intervening in the fields of study and research, and instead limit its intervention to "security considerations," including the military vetting of international faculty, researchers, and students.[99] The prevailing response from Israeli universities, then, has ultimately legitimated and naturalized Israel's right to restrict and control Palestinian higher education.

There is currently no movement in Israeli universities campaigning to sever ties with the Israeli military and security state for its repeated violations of the inalienable Palestinian right to education and other human rights. Even progressive organizations that work across Israeli campuses—such as the Joint Democratic Initiative or Academia for Equality, comprised of Jewish-Israeli and Palestinian (citizen) faculty and students—overwhelmingly fall short of addressing the demands of Palestinian universities. These activist groups have thus far refused to organizationally endorse Palestinian calls to hold Israeli universities accountable for their complicity in Israel's violations of international law.[100] Even the most progressive of Israeli-led initiatives, as Lana Tatour explains, operates within the framework of Israeli politics, and not within the Palestinian-led movement to end Israeli apartheid.[101]

Palestinian Resistance and Israeli Universities

Just before dawn on August 28, 2019, the Israeli military raided the family home of Mays Abu Ghosh in the Qalandia refugee camp. An undergraduate journalism student at Birzeit University, Abu Ghosh was handcuffed and blindfolded before being forcibly taken by soldiers to a military facility. There she was interrogated about her membership in the Democratic Progressive Student Pole (DPSP). While in detention, she was forced into painful pressure positions, deprived of sleep, and beaten, while made to hear the screaming of other detainees.[102] Abu Ghosh endured interrogations and torture for weeks and was denied access to a lawyer.[103] She was repeatedly threatened that she would be released paralyzed or mentally broken, if she would make it home alive at all.[104] After eight months of detention, Abu Ghosh was sentenced to sixteen months in Israeli military prison for her student activism.[105] Upon her release in November 2020, Abu Ghosh insisted on speaking openly about the brutal treatment she endured at the hands of Israeli Shin Bet and military personnel, and on continuing her studies and advocacy for the Palestinian right to education. "All over the world, participation in student activities is a right," Abu Ghosh stated in an interview, "but here we were arrested for it and subjected to criminal torture in Israeli jails."[106]

Abu Ghosh is one of many in her cohort to have been apprehended by the Israeli military. During the 2019–20 academic year, Israel detained and interrogated at least seventy-four students based on their membership in student groups.[107] In March 2019, Israeli soldiers invaded the Birzeit University campus disguised as Palestinians and abducted three students, who were later detained based on their student group association.[108] In December 2019, the Israeli military raided the home of Birzeit University student council president Shatha Hassan in the middle of the night.[109] Hassan was arrested and imprisoned for five months without charge or trial.[110]

Since 1967, Israel has declared over 411 Palestinian groups and associations—including all main political parties—unlawful.[111] The Israeli military routinely raids university campuses to abduct and arrest students for interrogation and detention, often through infiltration with undercover units disguised as students or journalists.[112] Through these arrests, Israel systematically targets Palestinian students based on their campus organizing or affiliation with student groups or political parties.[113] Palestinian prisoner support and human rights association Addameer argues that Israel practices political detention through criminalizing "any activities that Palestinian citizens partake in, including peaceful assembly, party affiliations, and any acts of resistance against the Israeli occupation."[114] Political detention is a violation of numerous international conventions, including Article 19 of the Universal Declaration of Human Rights, and Articles 19 and 26 of the International Covenant on Civil and Political Rights.[115]

In violation of the UN Convention Against Torture, Israel subjects the majority of Palestinian students to torture and ill-treatment during their detention, including beatings, stress positions for prolonged periods of time, and threats of long detainment that would derail their academic studies.[116] Students are often held in administrative detention, by which Palestinians can be indefinitely incarcerated in Israeli military prisons without charge or trial, based on undisclosed evidence.[117] Israel's systematic use of administrative detention, too, has been found by Palestinian human rights organizations and international legal experts to be in violation of international humanitarian law and the Fourth Geneva Convention.[118]

With total disregard to these international condemnations, the Israeli military has only increased its crackdown on student organizing in recent years, criminalizing additional student groups and arresting their members. In July 2020, the Israeli military arrested Birzeit University undergraduate Ruba Dar Assi in her home in the middle of the night. She was threatened by Israeli security state personnel that her academic career was over, and interrogated about participation in routine activities of the student council and the Democratic Progressive Student Pole (DPSP), including selling snacks and school supplies. She was sentenced to twenty-two months in military prison. In August 2020, Israel officially designated the DPSP as an "unlawful association" and escalated the targeting of its members.[119] Birzeit University undergraduate Layan Nasir was another such student. Arrested in her home in July 2021, Nasir was interrogated and detained for nearly two months in Israeli military prison before being released on bail. As of 2023, the trial for her student organizing with DPSP is ongoing, and she is forced to navigate the Israeli military legal system alongside her academic studies.[120] Nasir and her fellow student activists recognize Israel's thinly veiled attempts to criminalize their organizing, as she explains: "My arrest was part of a systematic campaign targeting Birzeit students. The list of charges against Birzeit students includes regular student activities on campus that students around the world organize and participate in, but for Birzeit students it is considered a crime and a "'security' offense."[121]

In 2021, the UN Working Group on Arbitrary Detention determined that the arrest of students on the basis of their involvement with DPSP did indeed constitute arbitrary detention.[122] Addameer has shown that these practices amount to illegal collective punishment, violating Palestinian students' rights to education and freedom of association, assembly, and expression.[123] Assi and Nasir, as well as dozens of other Palestinian students, have described how detention has derailed their academic studies, causing them to fall behind in their programs, delay their graduation, and interrupt their plans to apply to graduate school.

Yet this repression of Palestinian student organizing continues. In January 2022, Israeli military forces raided a student council meeting at Birzeit University, arresting five student group leaders and targeting and wounding one of them with live ammunition.[124] As of the 2022–23 academic year, Israel continues to hold over seventy Palestinian university students in military prisons.[125]

Israeli universities serve as part of the state apparatus to quell Palestinian student dissent. Defying the Israeli security state comes at a heavy cost in Palestinian universities, but so does challenging it on Israeli campuses. Universities in the OPT have been physically isolated, financially suffocated, raided by the military, and bombarded with heavy fire. In the face of this repression by the Israeli state, not only have Israeli universities continued to willingly collaborate with the Israeli military and security apparatuses, on their own campuses their administrations actively repress Palestinian student mobilization to protest these injustices.

The obstruction of Palestinian student mobilization by Israeli universities has been ongoing for decades, but it became apparent to many when the Unity Intifada broke out in 2021. The mass protest of Palestinian citizens fundamentally challenged Israeli rule, and the Israeli state and its universities worked in tandem to subdue it.

The institutional response of Israeli universities to the historic Palestinian mobilization was clear right from the first student protest at Ben-Gurion University on May 11. As soon as student demonstrators expressed an unapologetic politics of Palestinian struggle against Israeli apartheid and settler colonialism, they were violently suppressed. Shortly after they gathered, Palestinian students were surrounded by an angry crowd of Jewish-Israeli university students and local Beersheba residents, who formed a counterdemonstration. They vigorously waved Israeli flags and repeatedly shouted "Death to the Arabs!" and "Your village will burn!," as well as other racial slurs. Verbal threats turned physical, as counterdemonstrators drew knives and batons and menacingly displayed the guns they were carrying, with some even pelting Palestinian protestors with rocks. Fearing for their safety, Palestinian student organizers hurriedly directed protestors to seek refuge in a dorm building. But campus security guards at first refused them entry. Ultimately, the security personnel let dozens of Palestinian students in. But they then kept students contained and barricaded in the building for over five hours, claiming it was for their own safety.

Outside the dorm entrance, police forces seized Palestinian students, piling on them, holding them down, and beating them. Many officers hid their names tags and wore full face masks so they could not be identified. One officer threw a stun grenade into the crowd of students. The officers in uniform were joined by undercover security personnel and campus security, who seized Palestinian students and forcefully dragged them into police vehicles. One Palestinian student was arrested by campus security and police officers—all without name tags—who cursed him with racial slurs as they beat and arrested him. They did not explain the cause for his arrest, and they prevented students from documenting the events or speaking to him as they took him away. Even while being arrested, Palestinian students were beaten by Jewish-Israeli counterprotestors, one of them while he was pinned down by Israeli police. He sustained a head injury and was hospitalized overnight.

In the wake of the protest, Palestinian students left the dorms in droves. They returned home on rented buses coordinated by student organizers and their local councils. Weeks later, many reported being too afraid to return to Beersheba. At meetings organized by Palestinian students and a number of faculty members, which hundreds of students attended, Palestinian students said they did not feel safe to stay in their dorm rooms and could not trust their university.[126]

As students were beaten, detained, and fled its campus, the Ben-Gurion University administration issued a statement refusing to take any responsibility for the events.[127] The administration claimed that the violence was instigated by "unknown parties" and not members of the university community, and that the police did not act in coordination with campus security. Despite comprehensive footage and student testimony to the contrary, the university denied that its own Jewish-Israeli students and campus security took any part in the violence inflicted on Palestinian students. The university statement instead asked all students to "behave responsibly, with mutual respect and to maintain social cohesion."[128] Civility was all the administration called for, even amid a swell of racial violence directed at its own Palestinian students on its campus.

The events at Ben-Gurion University proved just the beginning. Within days, Palestinian citizens who mobilized in the Unity Intifada met the full force of the Israeli state and Jewish-Israeli mobs. Emboldened by state representatives from the far right, Jewish supremacists took up arms and took to the streets to enact vigilante repression. Across major cities in Israel, Palestinian communities came under attack.[129] In Ramle, Lydd, and Acre, Palestinians were assaulted and their stores vandalized and set on fire.[130] In Haifa, groups of men went door to door, beating Palestinians and attempting to break into their homes.[131] In Bat-Yam, an angry crowd descended on a Palestinian passerby and lynched him, critically injuring and nearly killing him.[132] Attacks turned fatal in Lydd, when a Jewish-Israeli shot and killed Musa Hasuna, a Palestinian citizen living in the city.[133] Augmenting this mob violence, Israel launched "Operation Law and Order" with the declared aim to "restore deterrence and strengthen governance."[134] Thousands of police and border patrol officers armed with military gear raided Palestinian communities. They beat protestors and arrested 531 Palestinians within days and nearly 2,000 over three weeks.[135] Palestinian civil rights organization Adalah declared the operation's mass and arbitrary arrests as illegal collective punishment of Palestinian citizens, and Amnesty International condemned Israel's discriminatory arrest, torture, and unlawful use of force.[136] Among those targeted by state and state-backed violence were Palestinian university student protestors.

Amid the surge of attacks by Jewish-Israeli mobs, campus security, and Israeli police, Palestinian students across campuses barricaded themselves in the dormitories. But the dorms offered no refuge. Palestinians who displayed signs in support of the uprising on their room doors got marked with red paint or had racial slurs and threats of violence tacked on instead. Online forums and group chats of dorm residents were soon filled with threats toward Palestinian students, often addressing them by name. Some Jewish-Israeli students threateningly exposed their weapons in dorm hallways as Palestinian peers passed by them. Palestinian students feared wearing their hijab or speaking in Arabic, since they had heard of peers verbally harassed and physically assaulted. They created chat groups to coordinate accompanying each other when walking across campus and back to their dorms.

Within a week, Israeli campuses were nearly emptied of their Palestinian students. Amid mob violence against Palestinians on public transportation and on the streets, students collectively organized to leave.[137] Student activists rented buses and shared transportation to bring Palestinians students home, mostly to their cities and towns in the Galilee. Students evacuated their campuses in a sense of fear and urgency, unsure of how they would complete their exams, scheduled to begin shortly thereafter, or if their university would offer them any protection or space to express their identities and politics. Fadi, an undergraduate student organizer at Tel Aviv University, explained it thus in an interview: "There is a terrible fear. We are still processing everything we are going through. Our dorm rooms were one of the few places we felt protected on campus and in this city, but now we understand we have to protect ourselves on our own. We entered the university with a feeling of alienation and this feeling still accompanies us every day . . . But now with these attacks we are supposed to be silent and normalize this reality. How can we do this?"

The campus violence followed Palestinian students home. During the summer weeks, Jewish-Israeli students used course websites and online student forums with wide campus readership to express racial hatred, often addressing or threatening Palestinian classmates directly. "You are all terrorists," "We will come for you," "You will die," "Death to all Arabs!" were common threats posted online, which received amplification by hundreds of students. Some teaching assistants joined in, with several explicitly calling for violence against Palestinians. "Go study at Birzeit," and "You should be grateful that you're even allowed to be at the university" were also comments that recurred online.[138]

Palestinian students witnessed this implosion of racial hatred in their universities' virtual spaces, directly communicating to them that they can never belong. These comments posted across campuses betray the sense of ownership that Jewish-Israeli students have over the universities, which they understand to be designed exclusively to serve them.

Incensed at the displays of Palestinian resistance and protest on campus, Jewish-Israeli students sought to remind Palestinians that their presence at Israeli institutions depended on their political allegiance to the state and, thus, is not guaranteed. The intended effect was sometimes achieved. Samir, a Palestinian undergraduate from the Galilee, was one of many who evacuated his campus in fear, following the violent arrests of his classmates and the threats his student group received online. In an interview, he described the summer weeks that followed as an experience of total alienation: "I don't feel like I belong in Ben-Gurion or in Beersheba anymore, and I don't want to go back." Samir had already lost critical weeks of the spring semester and was not certain he would ever return.

In the face of physical and verbal attacks by Jewish-Israeli students and mass exodus of Palestinians from their campuses, university administrations were slow—and reluctant—to respond. Footage of violent assaults and screenshots of verbal harassment were provided by Palestinian student activists, yet administrations did not act immediately to ensure the safety of their students.[139] Throughout the violent summer of 2021, rather than defending the safety and freedoms of their community members, Israeli universities worked alongside the Israeli state to repress Palestinian students.

To many Palestinian faculty and students, this escalated aggression on their campuses was unprecedented. And they believe it profoundly destabilized their already precarious position in Israeli higher education. Riham, a graduate student and seasoned organizer at Tel Aviv University, explained in an interview, "The mask has come off. We learned that we ultimately can't count on most of the Israeli academic institutions and students for support." Palestinian students across campuses described the summer of 2021 as a moment of further disillusionment with their institutions, but also as a transformative opportunity for the rearticulation of their politics. As Bushra, a Palestinian student at Ben-Gurion University put it in an interview, "there is a before and an after the summer of 2021. We are a new generation of Palestinian students with a different understanding of our place at the university. We know we have to advocate for ourselves because no one else will protect us. But the Palestinian people have been resisting for generations, and we will not back down."

The Unity Intifada that broke out in 2021 revealed in full force the interconnected repression of Palestinian students across both Palestinian and Israeli universities. In all the territories that it controls, Israel has targeted Palestinian higher education as a site of politicization and resistance to its settler-colonial rule. Palestinians armed with an education and unapologetically challenging the apartheid regime are regarded by Israel as a threat. Palestinian students are therefore subdued with disciplinary hearings, interrogations, and arrests on Israeli campuses, and with abductions, torture, military detention, and even killing on Palestinian campuses.

Israeli universities are critical pillars of this regime. They not only conduct research, train, and collaborate with the Israeli security forces that maintain the military occupation over Palestinian students and scholars. They also work in lockstep with the Israeli government to stifle Palestinian students mobilizing on their own campuses.

Ultimately, Israeli universities have played a direct role in the Israeli state repression of the Palestinian student movements for liberation—and in its denial of academic freedom to Palestinians—for over seventy-five years. A reckoning with this complicity is overdue.

Epilogue

"No one can speak up all the time on all the issues. But, I believe,
there is a special duty to address the constituted and authorized
powers of one's own society, which are accountable to its citizenry,
particularly when those powers are exercised in a manifestly disproportionate and immoral war, or in a deliberate program of discrimination, repression, and collective cruelty." —Edward Said[1]

The Palestinian call for the institutional academic boycott of Israel builds
on long-standing global movements by Indigenous peoples. These movements seek to decolonize the universities of the settler states that govern
them and to hold universities accountable for their role in perpetuating
violence against Indigenous peoples and in seizing their land.[2]

Institutions of higher education have indeed played a critical role in the
expropriation of Indigenous lands and the expansion of colonial settlements, particularly in Anglo-dominant settler societies established under
the aegis of the British Empire. From the United States and Canada to
Australia, New Zealand, and South Africa, Anglo settler states developed
their institutions of higher education through appropriating unceded
Indigenous territory. Facilitated by the British Empire, over 15 million acres
of Indigenous lands across three continents were transferred to settler

universities.[3] These settler states used the lands to either build or finance their institutions of higher education, which became known as land-grant universities, termed "land-grab universities" by Indigenous peoples.[4]

In the United States, the Morrill Land-Grant College Act of 1862 facilitated the violent expropriation of Indigenous lands to American universities and colleges. Eastern, Southern, and some Midwestern states received funding from the sale of appropriated Indigenous lands granted by the government; Western states, meanwhile, built their universities directly upon tribal lands.[5] The lands were seized through violence-backed cessions, sometimes in the wake of massacres of tribal members: 245 Indigenous tribes lost 10.7 million acres of their lands to facilitate the expansion of US higher education, worth nearly USD 500 million.[6] Africans captured and enslaved in the Americas were used to further accumulate wealth by colonial universities, which were often themselves built with enslaved peoples' labor or funded by the slave trade.[7]

Canadian universities, too, were built through the seizure of Indigenous territory. From Ontario through Manitoba to British Columbia, land-grants by the British Crown and later by provincial Canadian governments transferred over 450,000 acres of dispossessed Indigenous lands to establish Canada's major universities.[8] In New Zealand, Maori land confiscation and government land-granting served as the basis for the development of nearly all the state's colonial universities, while Aboriginal lands in Australia were directly expropriated to build a number of settler universities.[9]

In South Africa, the 1913 and 1936 Land Acts legislated land alienation and dispossessed Black South Africans. These acts laid the groundwork for the establishment of strategically placed, historically white universities in South Africa. These, in turn, sustained white settlement and facilitated the segregation of higher education and the formation of historically Black institutions.[10] As part of the South African government's suppression of mobilization for Black liberation, the state developed historically Black universities to establish new structures of administrative control and the Bantustan system. The segregated university system, from its campus infrastructure to its academic training programs, was designed to enforce apartheid.[11] As Pedro Mzileni and Nomalanga Mkhize argue, South African universities were deliberately "set into 'the land,' as immovable and concrete physical infrastructures," their locations and spatial positioning making their transformation in the post-apartheid era all the more challenging.[12]

Across these settler states, the project of Indigenous land expropriation and colonial settlement fueled the expansion of higher education. Founded on lands seized from Indigenous peoples, universities have, in turn, served as settlement strongholds amid Indigenous communities the state sought to contain and eliminate.[13] Holding universities accountable for their imbrication with colonialism, Indigenous scholars and student activists argue, must begin with addressing the very lands upon which they were founded and the ways in which they themselves serve as infrastructure of Indigenous dispossession and violent oppression.[14]

Built on indigenous Palestinian land and designed as vehicles of Jewish settlement expansion and Palestinian dispossession, Israeli institutions of higher education were founded in the tradition of land-grab universities. Like other settler institutions, Israeli universities were established to uphold the colonial infrastructure of the Israeli state. Where they stand apart, however, is in their explicit and ongoing role in sustaining a regime now overwhelmingly recognized by the international community as apartheid. Israeli universities continue not only to actively participate in the violence of the Israeli state against Palestinians but also to contribute their resources, research, and scholarship to maintain, defend, and justify this oppression.

It need not be this way. Indeed, it can and should be otherwise. The Palestinian Campaign for the Cultural and Academic Boycott of Israel (PACBI) has offered guidelines for the boycott. Read correctly, these offer Israeli universities a road map for a way forward and extend an invitation to Israeli academics to address their institutions' complicity.

Israeli universities could stop denying that their campuses stand on expropriated Palestinians lands and cease to serve as engines of "Judaization," colonization, and Palestinian dispossession in their regions.

Academic disciplines could end research programs that lend expertise to sustain Israel's systematic violations of international law, in the service of the Israeli military government of the Occupied Palestinian Territory. Departments could close their military, police, and Shin Bet degree programs that offer academic training to hone the work of illegal detention, investigation, and torture of Palestinians. Laboratories could sever their ties with Israeli military industries and no longer direct their resources and research toward designing technologies and weapons that are field-tested on occupied Palestinians and exported worldwide.

Israeli universities could cease to serve as the scaffolding to repress the Palestinian movement for liberation and transform themselves into the infrastructure that anchors free academic exploration and debate for all its students. Administrations could offer institutional support for and allocate resources toward critical research on the structural racialized violence of the Israeli state and the study of Palestinian experiences of dispossession and oppression. Presidents and deans could work with Palestinian faculty and students to rebuild their institutions as democratic centers founded on equality and operating in service of all people. Jewish-Israeli faculty could honor and support the courageous Palestinian students mobilizing for their inalienable human rights.

Israeli universities have yet to embark on this path on their own. The movement for the academic boycott calls on the international academic community to guide Israeli universities to take the first, most difficult, steps toward decolonization.

The Palestinian BDS movement carries forward the vision and tactics from the struggle against apartheid in South Africa and the Civil Rights movement in the United States. It is joining in common struggle and building alliances with activists working toward justice across the world. The Palestinian campaign for the academic boycott is part of a global movement, led by Indigenous scholars and students, that challenges the terms of the colonial university. They are calling to fundamentally reimagine the university: the relationship to the land on which it stands, the knowledge it produces, and the pedagogy it practices.

Israeli academics and students need not be confined to their status as settlers or occupy the position of those in the way of change. They can challenge the institutional complicity of their universities in Israeli settler colonialism and apartheid and join the movement to remake higher education for liberation. For, as PACBI teaches us, there is no academic freedom until it applies to all.

Afterword
Robin D. G. Kelley

"It can never be business as usual. Israeli Universities are an intimate part of the Israeli regime, by active choice." —Archbishop Desmond Tutu

I read *Towers of Ivory and Steel* just as the right-wing attack on education in the US had reached a fever pitch. The US Supreme Court ruled that colleges and universities can no longer consider race as a factor in the admissions process. At least forty-two states have passed laws prohibiting or limiting the teaching of race, racism, gender, or anything considered "divisive." Diversity, equity, and inclusion programs are being demolished and their administrators are not only subject to dismissal but death threats. Conservative activists in the guise of parent advocacy are banning books from schools and libraries. Florida governor and presidential candidate Ron DeSantis used the power of his office to take over the state's progressive public liberal arts institution, New College, in order to turn it into a conservative *Christian* college. In the name of purging the school of "ideology," DeSantis appointed handpicked allies to the board of trustees, who immediately installed Republican politician Richard Corcoran as president, eliminated all vestiges of diversity, equity, and inclusion, and pressed faculty to align with the school's new orientation. Within six months of the takeover, one-third of the faculty had been either dismissed, denied tenure, or pushed to leave on their own.[1]

Meanwhile, as outraged liberals remonstrate over the demise of academic freedom, Fatima Mousa Mohammed faced death threats for criticizing Israel in her commencement address to fellow graduates of the City University of New York (CUNY) School of Law. The Yemeni-born Mohammed condemned the illegal occupation, settlement building, and violent raids and described Israel as an apartheid state. Despite unwavering support from CUNY's faculty and student groups, including the Jewish Law Students Association, she has been roundly attacked as an antisemitic zealot who should be banned from practicing law. Democrats and Republicans have proposed cutting funding to CUNY, and one Republican congressman introduced the "Stop Anti-Semitism on College Campuses Act," which would defund institutions permitting organizations or events to criticize Israel or Zionism.[2] Even the left-leaning *Nation* magazine, a leading voice against the right-wing war on academic freedom, ran an especially vitriolic article accusing Mohammed of anti-Semitism.[3] Like clockwork, the loudest liberal defenders of academic freedom usually fall silent when it comes to critiques of Israel. This is not surprising. The "Palestine exception" still holds, even when Israel proves its critics right. In the weeks following Mohammed's commencement address, the editorial board of *Ha'aretz* labeled Benjamin Netanyahu and his cabinet "fascist." Its forewarning of Israel's march toward fascism was confirmed when the Knesset voted to weaken the power of the Supreme Court. Settlement building and settler violence escalated. Israeli military incursions in the West Bank, most spectacularly in Jenin, took the lives of more than 130 Palestinians, displaced thousands, and forced some 250 Palestinian students from West Bank universities. In the wake of such slaughter, President Joe Biden hosted Israel's president Isaac Herzog at the White House to "reaffirm the iron-clad commitment of the United States to Israel's security."[4]

As Maya Wind's remarkable and timely book demonstrates, this iron-clad commitment extends to higher education, effectively bludgeoning academic freedom in both countries in the name of security. She

painstakingly details the innumerable ways in which Israeli universities
participated in the dispossession of Palestinians, the illegal occupation,
and the creation of an apartheid state and its maintenance through military, carceral, juridical, architectural, demographic, medical, and educational means. She lays out the horrendous consequences for Palestinian
students and faculty, both in the occupied territories and inside the '48
borders, as well as the costs of challenging the status quo—whether it be
university policies, official narratives, state laws, Israel's violation of
international law, or Zionism itself. For Palestinians the price is exorbi-
tant, ranging from censure and expulsion to beatings, detention, torture,
even death. Israeli intellectuals willing to stand up for academic freedom, expose the country's history of settler colonial violence, and resist
apartheid are often disciplined by their university administration,
harassed by right-wing groups such as Im Tirtzu, or forced into exile.[5]
Or they are ignored, which is what happened in 2008 when several Israeli
scholars at Tel Aviv University issued a petition calling on the government to rescind laws restricting "freedom of movement, study and
instruction" for students and lecturers so they can access campuses in
the West Bank and Israel without risking the withdrawal of residence
visas. The petition only garnered a little over 400 signatures out of more
than 8,500 faculty and lecturers (less than 5 percent).[6]

The vast majority of Israeli faculty members, Wind argues, either
defend the status quo, are indifferent, or choose to stay silent, while
many of their colleagues willingly and actively participate in projects
designed to maintain the oppressive status quo. Armed with overwhelming evidence of academia's complicity with the apartheid state, she
presents a compelling case for the academic boycott of Israel. To critics
who argue that an academic boycott hurts progressive Israeli scholars
and deters others from opposing the regime, Wind not only reminds
readers that the boycott applies to institutions and not individual faculty
members participating in events or projects outside of official Israeli
channels; she also records the long, unbroken history of university
administrations actively sustaining and backing state repression and
arresting the very intellectual freedoms to which all scholars believe they
are entitled.

Where was the resistance? Why are Israeli faculty reluctant to fight for change within their own institutions, to challenge the decades-long complicity of their universities in Israeli settler colonialism and apartheid? How do we explain the absence of Jewish-Israeli student protest? By 1968, universities around the world had become epicenters of rebellion. Just look at Prague, Paris, Mexico City, London, Rome, Madrid, West Berlin, Tokyo, Jamaica, Johannesburg and Cape Town, Montreal, and yes, all across the United States. Palestinian students were certainly in revolt, challenged of course by Israel's 1967 military occupation. In the US, a mass student movement arose to resist the military draft, oppose US imperial wars in Southeast Asia and Southern Africa, demand an end to the cozy relationship between universities and the corporate-military complex, imagine new forms of democracy both within the academy and beyond, and open the vaunted doors of academia to the people who had been excluded. Some student activists denounced Israel's occupation of the Palestinian West Bank (including East Jerusalem), Gaza, and the Syrian Golan Heights, comparing the 1967 invasion with other colonial wars. Israeli students, for the most part, celebrated the nation's latest conquest and swelled with nationalist pride. The state spent the next decade further entrenching its apartheid system of education.

Palestinian campuses have been anything but silent. They are the real epicenter of the long and protracted struggle for *freedom*, not just the academic variety. Wind's vivid descriptions of the state of college campuses under occupation and the persistence of student militancy in the face of Israeli military violence remind us that the point of the boycott is not simply to protect scholars' rights to free speech, free association, critical inquiry, and mobility; rather, the point is to end the occupation, dismantle the apartheid system, respect the UN-stipulated rights of Palestinian refugees, extend civil rights to all, and end military detentions, the frequent invasions and surveillance of Palestinian institutions, and the deliberate disruption of learning. Her observation that the repression of Palestinian students has become normalized confirmed my own experience during my second trip to the West Bank in March of 2018. I was part of a delegation organized by Professor Rabab Abdulhadi that held symposia on the theme of "teaching Palestine and the indivisi-bility of justice" at Birzeit University in Ramallah and An-Najah National University in Nablus. We arrived in Ramallah just days after Israeli armed forces had detained Omar Kiswani, president of the student council at Birzeit University. The question of Kiswani's freedom weighed heavily on the proceedings. At An-Najah National University we learned that a twenty-one-year-old student activist and journalist named Ola Marshoud had just been placed in the Hawara detention center without charge. On March 21, one day before our symposium, Israeli forces raided her house in the Balata refugee camp in Nablus, searched for her phone, and questioned members of her family. Four months later, a mili-tary court convicted and sentenced her to seven months in prison on undisclosed charges.[7]

Israeli apartheid could not exist without the massive financial support, political legitimacy, and legal protection the US provides. The annual $3.8 billion in military funding (Israel is the largest overall recipient of US military aid in history) helps finance ongoing state violence, oppres-sion, and inequity without an iota of accountability. And every US administration, Republican and Democratic alike, has worked overtime to shield Israel from international law and UN condemnation. Israeli colleges and universities, in particular, have enjoyed unwavering support from US college presidents and high-profile administrators.[8] These same leaders oversee institutions that have suppressed Palestine advocacy on their campuses, decertified chapters of Students for Justice in Palestine (SJP), condemned legitimate criticisms of Israeli policies as anti-Semitic, fired or refused to hire faculty for criticizing Israel, and overturned BDS resolutions that had overwhelming student support. Although support for BDS has grown among college students and academic organizations, especially since 2014, the rather feeble defense of Fatima Mohammed points to another problem: liberal silence.

Israeli apartheid could not exist without liberal silence. This, I believe, is Wind's most astute observation, one that sits at the very core of *Ivory and Steel*. The silence, indifference, or cowardice of liberals facilitates occupation and enables the subjugation of Palestinian and anti-Zionist Jewish intellectuals. Liberal silence, not just the Zionist lobby, explains why thirty-five states in the US have passed laws, condemned by the ACLU as undemocratic if not McCarthyite, demonizing BDS or criticism of Israel and advocacy for Palestine as anti-Semitic and conditioning any contract with the state on commitment to rejecting BDS.[9] And the silence of liberals has hastened the deteriorating intellectual and political climate. The assault on democracy in Israel and the US was neither sudden nor surprising. Both are settler colonial states founded on ethnonationalism, racial hierarchy, and the subjugation and dispossession of Indigenous people. But if democracy in the US has always been fragile and incomplete, Israel's democracy has always coexisted with what leading Israeli human rights organization B'Tselem has called apartheid, a "regime of Jewish supremacy from the Jordan River to the Mediterranean Sea"—a democracy for some, and military rule and systematic subjugation for others. A democracy that subjects a segment of the population to dictatorial rule is always flawed, partial, and susceptible to authoritarianism. The concentration of executive power; the weakening (or weaponizing) of a judiciary; the stripping of the right to bodily autonomy, reproductive rights, and gender identity; voter suppression; and the like should not surprise anyone. It is a classic case of the chickens coming home to roost.

Once again, Florida provides a textbook case for how the unraveling of democracy in both Israel and the US are mutually reinforcing. Predictably, the leading adversary of so-called "woke" education, Governor Ron DeSantis, is a staunch opponent of BDS. In an address sponsored by Christians United for Israel (CUFI), DeSantis boasted of his efforts to defund the UN Relief and Works Agency (UNRWA), which he called anti-Semitic and accused of "fomenting terrorism." He also echoes the Zionist view that the West Bank is not "occupied territory" but "disputed territory," adding, "I don't care what the State Department says," let alone what international law says.[10] As governor he built close ties with Israeli universities, notably Ariel University, which is illegally located in the West Bank near Nablus. In 2019, Ariel and Florida Atlantic University signed a memorandum of understanding committing to joint research projects and campus exchanges.[11]

DeSantis, like so many right-wing extremists, regards Israel as a model for the kind of authoritarian power they hope to wield. Indeed, DeSantis's so-called "war on woke" and draconian curricula reforms arguably found inspiration in the Knesset's 2011 law prohibiting the teaching the Nakba or mentioning it in school textbooks. The minister of finance can reduce government funding to any institution (including schools and universities, civic organizations, and local governments) that violates the law. Similarly, Florida's Stop W.O.K.E. Act banned the teaching of Nikole Hannah-Jones's *The 1619 Project* published by the *New York Times*. Conservatives nationwide considered it an affront because it challenged the founding myth that America was born out of a war for liberty rather than a colonial economy based on racial slavery, plantation production, and the buying, selling, mortgaging, and insuring of human beings. Several Republican-dominated state legislatures voted to cut funding to schools that use materials or concepts from *The 1619 Project*, and Florida went further by imposing a blanket ban on material from the project in *any* educational curriculum.[12] The Florida Department of Education imposed an alternative interpretation of chattel slavery. Under the state's latest social studies guidelines, slavery taught Black people valuable skills which "could be applied for their personal benefit."[13] Finally, it is ironic, though consistent with Republican extremists, that DeSantis's "war on woke" led some schools to ban books on the Holocaust, a graphic novel version of Anne Frank's diary, a Purim book about a Jewish family, and anything on Jewish culture that smacks of diversity or critical race theory.[14]

In our struggle to rebuild democracy and contest the rise of authoritarianism, *Towers of Ivory and Steel* is an invaluable weapon in our arsenal. Wind cautions us that universities are not necessarily bastions of democracy, equity, or inclusion. They are, however, sites of power. Thus, what appears to be a fight to secure intellectual freedom within the academy is fundamentally a struggle for power. The truth is, there will never be genuine academic freedom in the region without a free Palestine, and there cannot be a free Palestine so long as universities are under occupation or remain bastions of Zionism and settler colonialism. And as long as the majority of Israeli intellectuals remain silent or fail to grasp that their own freedom is bound up with the freedom of Palestine, we will continue to boycott Israeli institutions. Silence = Complicity.

Acknowledgments

This book was written in response to a call from Palestinian civil society and is a collective project made possible by the labor of many researchers, activists, and scholars. Since the 2004 Palestinian Campaign for the Academic and Cultural Boycott of Israel (PACBI) call to boycott complicit Israeli academic institutions, the Palestinian-led BDS movement has researched, exposed, and raised awareness about the role of Israeli universities as a pillar of Israel's system of settler colonialism and apartheid. Palestinian activists and academics have since led a global campaign to end international academic and cultural support for Israel's oppressive regime. This book builds on this crucial work of over two decades and seeks to offer a new window into the complicity of Israeli universities in the ongoing denial of Palestinian freedom.

The courageous and principled Palestinian leadership of the BDS movement is a deep source of inspiration and a guide to me, as it is to thousands across the world. It has been an honor to learn from Omar Barghouti, one of the most profound thinkers of our time, as well as other brilliant thinkers and scholars from PACBI whom I cannot name to protect their safety. They have transformed my thinking about the questions that prompted this book.

I am immensely grateful and humbled that Nadia Abu El-Haj and Robin D. G. Kelley are part of this book. Nadia has deeply shaped our understanding of Israeli colonialism and epistemology and has demonstrated how to theorize politically and with integrity. In addition to generously offering the foreword, Nadia's incisive comments shaped and sharpened the manuscript. Robin has taught us to write for liberation and has led us to take seriously the material conditions that make our universities. I join generations of students and scholars in learning from Robin how to center justice in our work in the university and reimagine it anew.

I am deeply indebted to the brilliance and generosity of scholars from whom I have learned so much over many years, and who served as expert advisors and reviewers for the project. I thank Nadera Shalhoub-Kevorkian, Lana Tatour, Noura Erakat, Sherene Seikaly, and Haidar Eid for offering invaluable insights and comments that immeasurably improved the manuscript.

I am profoundly grateful for the generosity of Hugh Gusterson, whose mentorship and support made it possible for me to complete this project. Hugh offered his advice and expertise and provided invaluable critique. Discussions with Hugh sharpened the arguments and writing and made this a much more rigorous book. I am grateful to the Department of Anthropology at the University of British Columbia, which offered me a scholarly home in the book's final year. My UBC colleagues offered intellectual community to think through questions of decolonization and the university. M. V. Ramana and Elif Sari gave much appreciated encouragement and advice.

I thank Niko Besnier, who offered instructive comments and editorial advice that clarified and organized the manuscript. I am very grateful to Arees Bishara and Tom Pessah, who read sections of the manuscript and offered sharp analysis and illuminating comments, edits, and additional sources. Kobi Snitz was an appreciated interlocutor, as always. Many thanks are owed to Elyse Crystall for her edits to an earlier iteration of the project, and to Sarah Schulman for her comments and edits to early drafts and for consistent advice and support for this project. Discussions with and organizing alongside members of the AnthroBoycott collective were inspiring and energizing in the project's last months.

It is an honor that this book found its home at Verso. I am so grateful for Rosie Warren, who believed in this project from the beginning and shepherded the book over several years. Rosie offered crucial insights and expertly shaped the arc of the manuscript, keeping it focused and bringing out its best version. I also thank Jeanne Tao, Steven Hiatt, and the entire Verso team for guiding the manuscript through production. In the final stretch, Ben Platt offered guidance, encouragement, and astute advice that brought clarity and shaped the introduction. Ben's expert and careful editing gave the manuscript its final polish.

The research and writing of this book began as I was at the Department of Social and Cultural Analysis at New York University, which offered me a cherished scholarly and political home. For their immeasurable generosity and for so profoundly shaping my thinking and writing over many years, I thank Caitlin Zaloom, Neferti Xina M. Tadiar, Nikhil Pal Singh, and Thuy Linh Tu. I have been fortunate to think and write alongside treasured colleagues from whom I have learned so much, particularly Emma Shaw Crane, Brittany Meché, María José Méndez Gutiérrez, Dean Mohammed Chahim, Kaitlin Noss, and Dylan Brown.

Eran Efrati, my partner in all things, has made this book possible. This book is the result of a project we began together years ago, and he has remained indispensable to the research and analysis throughout. Eran brought his brilliance as an investigative researcher and movement organizer to the innumerable hours he spent thinking and talking through ideas with me. I am grateful to have him as a partner and a comrade every day.

Finally, I thank the Palestinian and Jewish-Israeli faculty, researchers, and students whom I cannot name, who freely gave their time for interviews, who offered reading recommendations, and who invited me to attend events on their campuses. I especially thank Palestinian student organizers across Israeli institutions who shared their stories and analyses about the universities they currently inhabit and the ones they seek to build. Palestinian students in universities across Israel and the Occupied Palestinian Territory are on the front lines of the struggle for freedom, justice, and equality. May we heed their call to decolonize higher education and remake universities with academic freedom for all.

The work on this book began in the Occupied Palestinian Territory and was completed in the traditional, ancestral, and unceded territories of the Musqueam, Squamish, and Tsleil-Waututh nations. This book was materially made possible by my status as a settler in both places. It is written in service of the movements that seek to dismantle these systems of violence and build a future in which, in the words of Ruth Wilson Gilmore, life is precious.

Notes

Foreword

1 See Patrick Kingsley, "Israel's Identity Hangs in the Balance Ahead of Key Vote on New Law," *New York Times*, July 23, 2023; Isabel Kershner and Patrick Kingsley, "What's Next for Israel's Judicial Overhaul," *New York Times*, July 26, 2023.

2 A state without a formal constitution, Israel's Basic Laws serve as a de facto one.

3 The Knesset, "Basic-Law: Israel—The Nation State of the Jewish People," knes set.gov.il.

4 Adam Shinar, "In Israel, the Worst May Be Yet to Come," *New York Times*, July 26, 2023.

5 Human Rights Watch, "A Threshold Crossed: Israeli Authorities and the Crimes of Apartheid and Persecution," April 27, 2021, hrw.org; Amnesty International, "Israel's Apartheid Against Palestinians: Cruel System of Domination and Crime Against Humanity," February 1, 2022, amnesty.org; Michael Sfard, *The Israeli Occupation of the West Bank and the Crime of Apartheid: Legal Opinion* (Yesh Din, June 2022), yesh-din.org; B'Tselem, "A Regime of Jewish Supremacy from the Jordan River to the Mediterranean Sea: This Is Apartheid," position paper, January 12, 2021, btselem.org.

6 Oren Ziv, "The Problem with 'Reclaiming' the Israeli Flag," *+972 Magazine*, April 27, 2023, 972mag.com.

7 Ben Reiff, "Israel's Justice Minister Gives Away the Realm Aim of the Judicial Coup's First Law," *+972 Magazine*, July 25, 2023, 972mag.com. Although the settler movement sees it as an impediment to its ultimate goal of annexation, the High Court has been an essential pillar in upholding the occupation. See, for example, "The Supreme Court of the Occupation," B'Tselem, February 25, 2020, btselem.org.

Introduction

1 Al-Haq, "Al-Haq Condemns Attack by the Israeli Occupying Forces on Birzeit University Students," January 10, 2022, alhaq.org; Addameer, "Undercover Israeli Occupation Forces Storm Birzeit University, Arresting Five Palestinian Students and Shot Live Ammunition," January 12, 2022, addameer.org; Qassam Muadi, "Israeli Forces Raid Student Strike at Birzeit University Campus in the West Bank," The New Arab, January 11, 2022, newarab.com.
2 Al-Haq, "Al-Haq Condemns Attack."
3 The Public Inquiries Unit, "Response by Israeli Ministry of Justice to February 8 Letter," Middle East Studies Association Committee on Academic Freedom, February 28, 2022, mesana.org.
4 Ibid. These arrests were widely condemned by Palestinian and international human rights organizations, as well as by Scholars at Risk and the Middle East Association of North America.
5 Addameer, "Palestinian Students under Suspended Detention," January 24, 2023, addameer.org.
6 Ibid.
7 Oren Ziv, "The only detainee in the demonstration for the Palestinian prisoners: A young Arab" [in Hebrew], Local Call, April 18, 2022; Neta Golan, "I was supposed to get arrested, but I am Jewish" [in Hebrew], Ha'aretz, April 20, 2022; Amir Ali Buyrat, "The release of the student Rami Salman after his arrest from the student dorms in Tel Aviv" [in Arabic], Arab48, April 18, 2022, arab48.com.
8 Salman was taken in for questioning on the suspicion of "obstructing and assaulting police officers" and detained overnight. When footage shown the next morning disproved the charges, he was released on bail but forbidden from attending any protest for the following fourteen days. Oren Ziv, "The only detainee."
9 Ministry of Defense, "Public tender for the procurement of undergraduate studies the 'Erez' program for the Israeli ground forces," privately provided; Lior Detel, "Commanders in the infantry will study for a degree at Tel Aviv University already during their mandatory service" [in Hebrew], TheMarker, July 5, 2023, themarker.com.
10 Ministry of Defense, "Public tender," 16.
11 Ibid., 26.
12 Ibid., 14.
13 "Living in Tel Aviv," Tel Aviv University–Columbia University dual degree program website, tau.gs.columbia.edu.
14 Lee Bollinger, "President of Columbia University Lee Bollinger Addresses the Israel Summit 2021," February 7, 2021, video, Israel Summit, March 4, 2021, youtube.com.
15 While Northwestern and Georgetown operate their own stand-alone campuses in Qatar, they offer student exchanges and study abroad programs at Israeli universities. New York University likewise operates a satellite campus in Abu Dhabi but has a robust exchange program with Tel Aviv University.
16 Freedom House, "Freedom in the World 2022: Israel," freedomhouse.org.
17 Katrin Kinzelbach et al., Academic Freedom Index 2022 Update (FAU Erlangen-Nürnberg and V-Dem Institute, March 2022), fau.eu.

18 This is from Hebrew University (American Friends of Hebrew University, "About HU," afhu.org), but others have similar statements. For more examples of this narrative, see also Cary Nelson and Gabriel Brahm, eds., *The Case Against Academic Boycotts of Israel* (MLA Members for Scholars' Rights, 2014).

19 PACBI, "PACBI Guidelines for the International Academic Boycott of Israel," July 9, 2014, bdsmovement.net; BDS Movement, "Academic Boycott," bdsmovement.net.

20 Omar Barghouti, *BDS: Boycott, Divestment, Sanctions: The Global Struggle for Palestinian Rights* (Chicago: Haymarket, 2011).

21 BDS Movement, "What Is BDS?," bdsmovement.net.

22 US Campaign for the Academic and Cultural Boycott of Israel, "Academic Associations Endorsing Boycott and Resolutions," usacbi.org; Sunaina Maira, *Boycott! The Academy and Justice for Palestine* (Oakland: University of California Press, 2018); Canadians for Justice and Peace in the Middle East, "Who Supports BDS in Canada?" June 2023, cjmpe.org; American Anthropological Association, "AAA Membership Endorses Academic Boycott Resolution," July 24, 2023, americananthro.org.

23 BDS Movement, "British Society for Middle Eastern Studies Endorses Palestinian Call to Boycott Complicit Israeli Academic Institutions," June 24, 2019, bdsmovement.net; Dania Akkad, "UK Student Union Pro-BDS Vote Causes Major Stir in Israel," June 4, 2015, middleeasteye.net; John Hedges, "Palestinian Teachers Welcome Teachers' Union of Ireland 'Boycott Israel' Call," April 9, 2013, anphoblacht.com.

24 Maira, *Boycott!*; *The Palestine Exception to Free Speech: A Movement Under Attack in the US* (Palestine Legal and Center for Constitutional Rights, September 2015), palestinelegal.org; Steven Salaita, *Uncivil Rites: Palestine and the Limits of Academic Freedom* (Chicago: Haymarket, 2015); Piya Chatterjee and Sunaina Maira, eds., *The Imperial University: Academic Repression and Scholarly Dissent* (Minneapolis: University of Minnesota Press, 2014).

25 See, for example, Academic Engagement Network, "Pamphlet Series," academicengagement.org.

26 Dan Rabinowitz, "Why the BDS Campaign Can't Tolerate Israeli Moderates," *Ha'aretz*, November 3, 2015.

27 Association for Israel Studies, "AIS Statement on MESA Proposed Resolution Regarding BDS."

28 Philosopher Anat Biletzky encapsulated this recurring argument, contending that "there is an obvious injustice in collective punishment, and more specifically, in harming [Israeli] academics who are committed to the Palestinian cause." Andris Barblan et al., "Mixed Perspectives," *Academe* 92, no. 5 (September–October 2006): 73–4.

29 Barghouti, *BDS: Boycott, Divestment, Sanctions*; Omar Barghouti and Lisa Taraki, "Academic Boycott and the Israeli Left," Electronic Intifada, April 15, 2005.

30 Baruch Kimmerling, "The Meaning of Academic Boycott," Miftah, April 27, 2005, miftah.org.

31 Ibid.

32 Israeli Anthropological Association, "A Response to the Proposed Resolution to the American Anthropological Association (AAA) to Boycott Israeli Academic Institutions," April 3, 2023, americananthro.org.

33 Sarab Abu-Rabia-Queder, "Epistemology of Surveillance: Revealing Unmarked Forms of Discipline and Punishment in Israeli Academia," *British Journal of Sociology* 73, no. 2 (March 2022): 387–40; Adalah, "Israel Forcing International Lecturers Out of West Bank Palestinian Universities," April 20, 2021, adalah .org; Adalah, "Inequality Report: The Palestinian Arab Minority in Israel," February 2011, adalah.org; Addameer, "Commemorating the International Day of Education by Highlighting the Reality of the Right to Education for Palestinian Political Prisoners," January 24, 2023; Addameer, "Suspended Graduation: The Targeting and Political Detention of Palestinian University Students," February 3, 2020, addameer.org; Ismael Abu-Saad, "Palestinian Education in Israel: The Legacy of the Military Government," *Holy Land Studies* 5, no. 1 (May 2006): 21–56; Khalid Arar and Kussai Haj-Yehia, *Higher Education and the Palestinian Arab Minority* (Basingstoke, UK: Palgrave Macmillan, 2016); Ahmad Sa'di, *Through Surveillance: The Genesis of Israeli Policies of Population Management, Surveillance and Political Control Towards the Palestinian Minority* (Manchester: Manchester University Press, 2013); Omar Barghouti, *BDS: Boycott, Divestment, Sanctions*; Mossawa Center, "Analysis of the Ministry of Education's Budget for 2016," mossawa.org.

34 See, for example, Andre Mazawi, "Education as Spaces of Community Engagement and a 'Capacity to Aspire,'" in Educator of the Mediterranean: Up Close and Personal, ed. R. G. Sultana (Malta: Sense Publishers, 2011); Khaled Jamal Furani and Yara Sa'di-Ibraheem, eds., *Inside the leviathan: Palestinian experiences in Israeli universities* [in Arabic] (Jerusalem and Haifa: Van Leer Institute Press, Dar Laila Publishing, 2022); Ayman Agbaria, "To be a Palestinian researcher at the Israeli university" [in Arabic], *Fusha*, December 15, 2017; Abu-Rabia-Queder, "Epistemology of Surveillance"; Areej Sabbagh-Khoury, "Tracing Settler Colonialism: A Genealogy of a Paradigm in the Sociology of Knowledge Production in Israel," *Politics and Society* 50, no. 1 (March 2022): 44–83; Nadera Shalhoub-Kevorkian, "Palestinian Women and the Politics of Invisibility: Towards a Feminist Methodology," *Peace Prints: South Asian Journal of Peacebuilding* 3, no. 1 (Spring 2010); Rema Hammami, "On the Importance of Thugs: The Moral Economy of a Checkpoint," *Middle East Report* 231 (2004): 16–28; Eileen Kuttab, "Reflections on Education as Political Practice," in *Universities and Conflict: The Role of Higher Education in Peacebuilding and Resistance*, ed. Juliet Millican (New York: Routledge, 2019).

35 See, for example, Uri Cohen, *The mountain and the hill: The Hebrew university in Jerusalem during the pre-independence period and early years of the state of Israel* [in Hebrew] (Tel Aviv: Am Oved, 2006); Haim Yacobi, "Academic Fortress: The Planning of the Hebrew University Campus on Mount Scopus," in *Global Universities and Urban Development: Case Studies and Analysis*, ed. Wim Wiewel and David C. Perry (London: Routledge, 2015); Yael Maayan, "From a racialized space to social sustainability: faculty members' perceptions of their influence on campus climate" [in Hebrew] (master's thesis, University of Haifa, 2013); Yali Hashash, *Who's daughter are you? Ways of speaking Mizrahi feminism* [in Hebrew] (Tel Aviv: HaKibbutz Hameuhad, 2022); Ella Habiba Shohat, "A Voyage to Toledo: Twenty-Five Years after the 'Jews of the Orient and Palestinians' Meeting," *Jadaliyya*, September 30, 2019; Yehouda Shenhav, "Sociologists and the Occupation," *Israeli Sociology*, 9, no. 2 (2008): 263–70.

36 For a detailed history and legal analysis of the development of this recognition, see Rania Muhareb et al., *Israeli Apartheid: Tool of Zionist Settler Colonialism* (Al-Haq, November 29, 2022), alhaq.org.

37 Human Rights Watch, "A Threshold Crossed: Israeli Authorities and the Crimes of Apartheid and Persecution," April 27, 2021, hrw.org.

38 Amnesty International, "Israel's Apartheid Against Palestinians: Cruel System of Domination and Crime Against Humanity," February 1, 2022, amnesty.org.

39 For an analysis of these limitations, see Lana Tatour, "Why Calling Israel an Apartheid State Is Not Enough," Middle East Eye, January 18, 2021. Michael Sfard, *The Israeli Occupation of the West Bank and the Crime of Apartheid: Legal Opinion* (Yesh Din, June 2022), yesh-din.org; B'Tselem, "A Regime of Jewish Supremacy from the Jordan River to the Mediterranean Sea: This Is Apartheid," position paper, January 12, 2021, btselem.org.

40 Muhareb et al., *Israeli Apartheid*.

41 Ibid.

42 Michael Lynk, "UN Doc A/HRC/49/87," March 21, 2022, un.org.

43 Francesca Albanese, "UN Doc A/77/356," September 21, 2022, un.org.

44 Ibid., paragraph 9.

45 Muhareb et al., *Israeli Apartheid*; BDS Movement, "Historic Palestinian Anti-Apartheid Call," January 25, 2023, bdsmovement.net.

46 BDS Movement, "Historic Palestinian Anti-Apartheid Call."

47 Ibid.

48 Netanel Koprak, "The system of higher education in Israel—data and budgeting" [in Hebrew], March 10, 2022, fs.knesset.gov.il.

49 Patrick Wolfe, "Settler Colonialism and the Elimination of the Native," *Journal of Genocide Research* 8, no. 4 (2006): 387–409.

50 Ibid.; Patrick Wolfe, *Traces of History: Elementary Structures of Race* (New York: Verso, 2016); Eve Tuck and K. Wang Yang, "Decolonization Is Not a Metaphor," *Decolonization: Indigeneity, Education and Society* 1, no. 1 (2012): 1–40.

51 Audra Simpson, "Sovereignty, Sympathy, and Indigeneity," in *Ethnographies of US Empire*, ed. Carole McGranahan and John E. Collins (Durham, NC: Duke University Press, 2018), 72.

52 Nur Masalha, *Expulsion of the Palestinians: The Concept of "Transfer" in Zionist Political Thought, 1882–1948* (Washington, DC: Institute for Palestine Studies, 1992); Wolfe, *Traces of History*; see also official Zionist documents and statements concerning the elimination and replacement of Palestinians in Benny Morris, "Yosef Weitz and the Transfer Committees, 1948–49," *Middle Eastern Studies* 22, no. 4 (October 1986): 522–61.

53 These include Zionist leaders such as Ze'ev Jabotinsky, who explicitly conceptualized Zionist conquest of Palestine as a colonialist project comparable to other forms of European colonialism: Ze'ev Jabotinsky, "The Iron Wall," jabotinsky.org. Multiple Zionist organizations conceived of their work in colonialist terms, such as the Jewish Colonization Association, a philanthropic association that funded Jewish colonies and educational programs in Mandatory Palestine: Nirit Raichel and Tali Tadmor-Shimony, "Jewish Philanthropy, Zionist Culture, and the Civilizing Mission of Hebrew Education," *Modern Judaism* 34, no. 1 (February 2014): 60–85. See also Masalha, *Expulsion of the Palestinians*; Ilan Pappé, *Ten Myths about Israel* (New York: Verso, 2017); Ilan Pappé, "Zionism as Colonialism: A Comparative View of Diluted

Colonialism in Asia and Africa," *South Atlantic Quarterly* 107, no. 4 (October 2008): 611–33.

54 Walid Khalidi, ed., *All That Remains: The Palestinian Villages Occupied and Depopulated by Israel in 1948* (Washington, DC: Institute for Palestine Studies, 1992); Rashid Khalidi, *The Hundred Years' War on Palestine: A History of Settler Colonialism and Resistance, 1917–2017*, 1st ed. (New York: Metropolitan Books, 2020); Wolfe, *Traces of History*.

55 Oren Yiftachel, "'Ethnocracy': The Politics of Judaizing Israel/Palestine," *Constellations* 6, no. 3 (September 1999): 355; Yinon Cohen and Neve Gordon, "Israel's Biospatial Politics: Territory, Demography, and Effective Control," *Public Culture* 30, no. 2 (May 2018): 199–220; Elisha Efrat, *National planning and development in Israel in the twenty-first century* [in Hebrew] (Tel-Aviv: Ramot, Tel-Aviv University, 2003); Ahmad Amara, "The Negev Land Question: Between Denial and Recognition," *Journal of Palestine Studies* 42, no. 4 (Summer 2013): 27–47; Ghazi Falah, "Israeli 'Judaization' Policy in Galilee," *Journal of Palestine Studies* 20, no. 4 (Summer 1991): 69–85.

56 Ibid.

57 Diana Dolev, *The Planning and Building of the Hebrew University, 1919–1948: Facing the Temple Mount* (London: Lexington Books, 2016).

58 Uri Cohen, *Laboratory, research institute, city of science: From the Daniel Sieff Research Institute to the Weizmann Institute of Science, 1934–1949* [in Hebrew] (Jerusalem: Bialik Institute, 2016).

59 Ibid.; Uri Cohen, The *mountain and the hill*.

60 Uri Cohen, *Laboratory, research institute, city of science;* Uriel Bachrach, *The Power of Knowledge: HEMED the Israeli Science Corps* (Monterey, CA: Samual Wachtman's and Sons, 2016).

61 Moshe Lissak and Uri Cohen, "Scientific Strategists in the Period of Mamlakhtiyut: Interaction between the Academic Community and Political Power Centers," *Journal of Israeli History* 30, no. 2 (September 2011): 189–210.

62 Sa'di, *Through Surveillance;* Abu-Saad, "Palestinian Education in Israel."

63 Palestinian Federation of Unions of University Professors and Employees, "PFUUPE Letter to AAA," May 4, 2023, americananthro.org.

64 For an analysis of this refusal, see Barghouti, *BDS: Boycott, Divestment, Sanctions;* Barghouti and Taraki, "Academic Boycott and the Israeli Left."

65 Tuck and Yang, "Decolonization Is Not a Metaphor."

66 Ibid., 9.

67 Suriamurthee Moonsamy Maistry, "The Higher Education Decolonisation Project: Negotiating Cognitive Dissonance," *Transformation: Critical Perspectives on Southern Africa* 100, no. 1 (2019): 181.

68 Nick Mitchell, "(Critical Ethnic Studies) Intellectual," *Critical Ethnic Studies* 1, no. 1 (Spring 2015): 86–94.

69 Sharon Stein, *Unsettling the University: Confronting the Colonial Foundations of US Higher Education* (Baltimore, MD: Johns Hopkins University Press, 2022); Maistry, "The Higher Education Decolonisation Project."

70 Barghouti, *BDS: Boycott, Divestment, Sanctions*.

71 Ian Bunting, "The Higher Education Landscape under Apartheid," in *Transformation in Higher Education: Global Pressures and Local Realities in South Africa*, ed. N. Cloete et al. (Dordrecht: Kluwer Academic Publishers, 2004), 35–52.

1. Expertise of Subjugation

1 Amos Harel, "Prof. Asa Kosher: If it's the neighbor or the soldier, the priority is the soldier" [in Hebrew], *Ha'aretz*, February 6, 2009.

2 Uri Blau and Yotam Feldman, "Operation 'cast lead': This is how the military attorney's office gave the IDF victory" [in Hebrew], *Ha'aretz*, January 23, 2009.

3 Human Rights Watch, "Israel/Gaza: Civilians Must Not Be Targets," December 30, 2008, hwr.org.

4 Blau and Feldman, "Operation 'cast lead.'"

5 Craig Jones, *The War Lawyers* (New York: Oxford University Press, 2020); Noura Erakat, *Justice for Some: Law and the Question of Palestine* (Stanford, CA: Stanford University Press, 2020); Eyal Weizman, *The Least of All Possible Evils: A Short History of Humanitarian Violence* (New York: Verso, 2017).

6 Blau and Feldman, "Operation 'cast lead.'"

7 See also Erakat, *Justice for Some*. Bar-Ilan University law professor Abraham Bell retrospectively offered a similar justification for this strike. According to Israel, Bell argues, Gazan police cadets are armed forces "tasked with engaging in military and quasi-military operations," making them legitimate targets. Abraham Bell, "A Critique of the Goldstone Report and Its Treatment of International Humanitarian Law," *American Society of International Law Proceedings* 104 (2010): 1–9.

8 Human Rights Watch, "Israel/Gaza: Civilians Must Not Be Targets"; Erakat, *Justice for Some*.

9 Blau and Feldman, "Operation 'cast lead'"; United Nations, "UN Fact Finding Mission Finds Strong Evidence of War Crimes and Crimes Against Humanity Committed during the Gaza Conflict; Calls for an End to Impunity," September 15, 2009, ohchr.org.

10 Li-or Averbach, "Attorney Sharvit Baruch: I did not expect an attack against me" [in Hebrew], *NRG*, February 1, 2009.

11 Ofri Ilany, "Lecturers: Prevent the employment of Col. Pnina Sharvit Baruch who sanctioned combat" [in Hebrew], *Ha'aretz*, January 26, 2009.

12 Averbach, "Attorney Sharvit Baruch."

13 Ibid.

14 Blau and Feldman, "Operation 'cast lead.'"

15 Human Rights Council, "The United Nations Independent Commission of Inquiry on the 2014 Gaza Conflict," June 24, 2015, ohchr.org; David Halbfinger, "Israeli 'Warning' Shot Killed Two Boys in Gaza, Rights Groups Say," *New York Times*, December 17, 2018.

16 Avner Shemla Kadosh, "The Practice of 'Roof Knocking' from the Perspective of International Law," *Strategic Assessment* 24, no. 4 (November 2021): 61–77.

17 Ibid. Following Israeli attempts to legalize the practice, it was reported that roof knocks were adopted by the US military in 2016 operations in Iraq. Adam Taylor, "Israel's Controversial 'Roof Knocking' Tactic Appears in Iraq. And This Time, It's the US Doing It," *Washington Post*, April 27, 2016.

18 B'Tselem, "ISA Detains and Interrogates B'Tselem Field Researcher; B'Tselem: 'Disgraceful Arrest Aimed at Hampering the Work of a Human Rights Organization,'" August 12, 2022, btselem.org; Gideon Levy and Alex Levac, "Why This Palestinian Activist Was Subjected to an Israeli Army Raid and 14 Hours in Detention," *Ha'aretz*, August 12, 2022.

19 Levy and Levac, "Why This Palestinian Activist."

20 B'Tselem, "Chronicles of Dispossession: The Facts about Susia," July 29, 2015, btselem.org.

21 Emek Shaveh, "Susya: The Displacement of Residents Following the Discovery of an Ancient Synagogue," September 12, 2016, emekshaveh.org.

22 Institute of Archaeology, "About the institute" [in Hebrew], archaeology.huji. ac.il; Yonathan Mizrachi, "The Temple Mount/Haram al-Sharif: Archaeology in a Political Context" (Emek Shaveh, 2017), emekshaveh.org.

23 Susya, "Welcome to Susya" [in Hebrew], atarsusya.co.il; Ziv Stahl, "Appropriating the Past: Israel's Archaeological Practices in the West Bank," report (Emek Shaveh and Yesh Din, December 2017), emekshaveh.org.

24 Chen Gilad, "Akiva London" [in Hebrew], Yesha Council, May 4, 2016, myesha .org.il.

25 Emek Shaveh, "Susya"; Susya, "About" [in Hebrew], atarsusya.co.il.

26 Gilad, "Akiva London."

27 B'Tselem, "Chronicles of Dispossession."

28 Stahl, "Appropriating the Past"; Raphael Greenberg and Adi Keinan, *Israeli Archaeological Activity in the West Bank 1967–2007: A Sourcebook* (Ostracon, 2009).

29 Ibid.; Emek Shaveh, "Susya."

30 Emek Shaveh, "Susya."

31 B'Tselem, "Khirbet Susiya: A Village Under Threat of Demolition," August 19, 2012, btselem.org; OCHA, "Susiya: A Community in Immediate Danger of Forced Transfer," June 2015, ochaopt.org.

32 Akiva London, "About truth and lies in Susiya" [in Hebrew], Ynet, July 24, 2012, ynet.co.il.

33 Ibid.

34 Ibid.

35 B'Tselem, "Settler Violence = State Violence," btselem.org.

36 B'Tselem, "Khirbet Susiya"; Yotam Berger, "Senior security official: The Palestinian village of Susya will be evacuated within a few months" [in Hebrew], *Haaretz*, September 25, 2017.

37 Yolande Knell, "Susiya: Palestinian West Bank Village Faces Bleak End," *BBC News*, July 25, 2015.

38 Jen Marlowe, "'We Lived in Constant Suffering': The Secret Life of a Palestinian Refugee," *Salon*, June 13, 2015.

39 Susya, "What we do on the site" [in Hebrew], atarsusya.co.il.

40 Nadia Abu El-Haj, *Facts on the Ground: Archaeological Practice and Territorial Self-Fashioning in Israeli Society* (Chicago: University of Chicago Press, 2001), 18.

41 Ibid.

42 See also Aseil Abu-Baker and Marya Farah, "Established Practice: Palestinian Exclusion at the Dead Sea," *Journal of Palestine Studies* 49, no. 2 (February 1, 2020): 48–64.

43 Hamdan Taha, "Jerusalem's Palestinian Archeological Museum," *Jerusalem Quarterly* 91 (2022): 59–78.

44 Ibid.

45 Ibid. The Palestinian Ministry of Tourism and Antiquities and Israeli sources estimates that between 1967 and 1992 approximately 200,000 artifacts were

removed annually from the OPT: Gabriel Fahel, "Repatriating Palestinian Patrimony: An Overview of Palestinian Preparations for Negotiations on Archaeology," *Present Pasts* 2, no. 1 (August 15, 2010).

46 Taha, "Jerusalem's Palestinian Archeological Museum"; Valentina Azarova and Nidal Sliman, "Activating Palestine's UNESCO Membership," Al-Shabaka, October 23, 2013, al-shabaka.org; Beatrice St. Laurent, "Reconciling National and International Interests: The Rockefeller Museum and Its Collections," *Journal of Eastern Mediterranean Archaeology and Heritage Studies* 5, no. 1 (2017): 35–57.

47 Israel Museum, "The Qumran Scroll at the Shrine of the Book," imj.org.il.

48 David Keane and Valentina Azarov, "UNESCO, Palestine and Archaeology in Conflict," *Denver Journal of International Law and Policy* 41, no. 3 (Spring 2013): 309–44; Joanna Overdiran, *Plunder, Destruction and Despoliation: An Analysis of Israel's Violations of the International Law of Cultural Property in the Occupied West Bank and Gaza Strip* (Ramallah: Al-Haq, 1997); Fahel, "Repatriating Palestinian Patrimony"; Hamdan Taha, "The Current State of Archaeology in Palestine," *Present Pasts* 2, no. 1 (2010), presentpasts.info.

49 Joel Greenberg, "In the West Bank, a Contested Heritage," *Washington Post*, November 21, 2011. See also Keane and Azarov, "UNESCO, Palestine and Archaeology in Conflict"; Valentina Azarov and Nidal Sliman, "Can Palestinians Advance Their Rights Through UNESCO?," *Foreign Policy*, November 11, 2013, foreignpolicy.com.

50 Israel Museum, "The Qumran Scroll"; Israel Museum, "Israel Museum Studies in Archaeology," imj.org.il; Joel Greenberg, "Museum Exhibit Becomes Front in Israeli-Palestinian Struggle," *Washington Post*, February 13, 2013.

51 Nir Hasson, "The good news: A hidden scroll was discovered in Qumran. The bad news: It is empty" [in Hebrew], *Ha'aretz*, February 8, 2017; Oren Gutfeld, "Bandits or monks? The mystery of the missing scrolls from cave 53/XII in the Qumran," in *Desert Archaeology: Proceedings of the 16th South Conference* [in Hebrew], ed. Yael Abadi-Reis, Daniel Varga, and Gunnar Lehmann (Beer-Sheva: Israel Antiquities Authority, 2020), 71–80.

52 Ruth Schuster and Ariel David, "Israel finds new Dead Sea scrolls, first such discovery in 60 years" [in Hebrew], *Ha'aretz*, March 16, 2021.

53 Greenberg and Keinan, *Israeli Archaeological Activity in the West Bank*.

54 Ibid.; Stahl, "Appropriating the Past," 23.

55 Ibid.

56 Ibid; Keane and Azarov, "UNESCO, Palestine and Archaeology in Conflict."

57 Hague Convention respecting the Laws and Customs of War on Land (1907), Article 43 of its Annexed Regulations. International law limits the occupying military to rescue or salvage excavations for preservation of antiquities in occupied territory, and explicitly prohibits the occupying power from destroying, transferring ownership, or expending these assets. Israeli archaeological activity significantly deviates from these restrictions. The transfer of ancient sites to Israeli control violates Palestinian rights to property and cultural rights under international law. Moreover, Israel has included some archaeological sites in the jurisdiction areas of settlements, thereby expropriating sites bearing historical, cultural, religious, and economic significance from Palestinians. Karma Nabulsi, *Traditions of War: Occupation, Resistance, and the Law* (Oxford:

Oxford University Press, 2005); Stahl, "Appropriating the Past"; Keane and Azarov, "UNESCO, Palestine and Archaeology in Conflict."

58 Coordination of Government Actions in the Territories, "Archaeology" [in Hebrew], gov.il; Stahl, "Appropriating the Past."

59 The Staff Officer of Archaeology is authorized to decide where archaeological excavations will take place, how archaeological sites will be run and which audiences they will serve, and the content and display of findings. Stahl, "Appropriating the Past."

60 An excavation was conducted at Tel Shiloh-Khirbet Seilun by Bar-Ilan University in 1981, and in 2010 excavations were resumed by the Staff Officer of Archaeology and Ariel University. The site is located on the lands of the Palestinian village of Qaryut in the OPT, some of which are privately owned. At Khirbet al-Mazra'a, an archaeological excavation was supported by Bar-Ilan University in 1998, which served as a cover for the establishment of the illegal settlement outpost of Amona. Stahl, "Appropriating the Past."

61 Sonia and Marco Nadler Institute of Archaeology, "Tel Aviv University Institute of Archaeology" [in Hebrew], tau.ac.il.

62 Greenberg and Keinan, *Israeli Archaeological Activity in the West Bank*; Stahl, "Appropriating the Past."

63 Nir Hasson, "The state finances an initiative of Hebron settlers to establish an archaeological park in Tel Rumeida" [in Hebrew], *Ha'aretz*, January 9, 2014.

64 Ahikam Moshe David and Efrat Zemer Bronfman, "Starting next year: Students will tour Hebron" [in Hebrew], *NRG*, February 15, 2011; Channel 2 News, "Education Minister Gideon Sa'ar: 'We will continue the heritage tours in Hebron'" [in Hebrew], *Mako*, August 27, 2012, mako.co.il.

65 Zinman Institute of Archaeology, "Previous projects" [in Hebrew], arch.haifa.ac.il.

66 Department of Land of Israel Studies and Archaeology, "The Department of Land of Israel Studies and Archaeology at Bar-Ilan University" [in Hebrew], lisa.biu.ac.il; Department of Land of Israel Studies and Archaeology, "New archaeological finds from the Bar Kochba Period" [in Hebrew], December 14, 2022, biu.ac.il.

67 Hagar Shezaf and Nir Hasson, "Bar-Ilan University conducts an archaeological dig in the West Bank. Palestinians claim that the territory belongs to them" [in Hebrew], *Ha'aretz*, August 10, 2022.

68 UNESCO criticized the demolition of the Maghariba Quarter, which had featured some of Jerusalem's most ancient and important Islamic structures. Mizrachi, *The Temple Mount*; Abu El-Haj, *Facts on the Ground*.

69 Ibid.

70 Ibid.

71 Abu El-Haj, *Facts on the Ground*.

72 Mizrachi, *The Temple Mount*; Stahl, "Appropriating the Past."

73 City of David, "Archaeology" [in Hebrew], cityofdavid.org.il

74 City of David, "About City of David" [in Hebrew], cityofdavid.org.il; Registrar of Associations, "Verbal account for the year 2017" [in Hebrew], Israeli Corporations Authority, November 5, 2018, guidestar.org.il.

75 State Comptroller, "Annual report 67A" [in Hebrew], November 1, 2016, mevaker.gov.il; see also Mahmoud Hawari, "Silwan: Biblical Archaeology, Cultural Appropriation, and Settler Colonialism," *Jerusalem Quarterly* 90 (2022): 75–97.

76 These were ruled illegal by Israeli courts, who found that deceit, fraud, and manipulation of Israeli absentee property laws enabled the settlers to transfer the properties to Jewish ownership. Despite court rulings, the properties remain in Jewish hands. Tal Sagi, "City of David: When archaeology and politics mix" [in Hebrew], *Ynet*, February 29, 2008, ynet.co.il.

77 The archaeological site and visitor center crafted an ahistorical narrative that describes only Jewish presence at the site, drawing a direct line from the era of King David to the first Zionist settlement in Palestine. Ibid.

78 Emek Shaveh, "Six Feet Under: The Cultural Heritage of Minorities in Jerusalem," May 21, 2019, emekshaveh.org.il.

79 Emek Shaveh, "Wall from Early Islamic Period Prevents Continued Excavation of Tunnel Between Silwan and the Old City," March 20, 2019, emekshaveh.org.

80 Nir Hasson, "Jerusalem's 'landlords' are digging away again" [in Hebrew], *Ha'aretz*, February 21, 2017.

81 Nir Hasson, "Silwan residents blame right-wing group for collapse of tunnel near mosque" [in Hebrew], *Ha'aretz*, December 28, 2011.

82 Emek Shaveh, "Fissures and Cracks: Damage to Homes in the Wadi Hilweh Neighborhood in Silwan," March 18, 2020, emekshaveh.org; Nir Hasson, "25 Residents of Silwan were removed from an apartment building after archaeological excavations began under it" [in Hebrew], *Ha'aretz*, April 6, 2017.

83 Nir Hasson, "US envoys break open tunnel running under Palestinian village in East Jerusalem" [in Hebrew], *Ha'aretz*, June 30, 2019.

84 Sagi, "City of David"; Emek Shaveh, "Six Feet Under"; City of David, cityofdavid .org.il [in Hebrew].

85 Megalim, "Academia" [in Hebrew], megalim.org.il; Talila Nesher and Nir Hasson, "Tel Aviv University will excavate in East Jerusalem, funded by a right-wing organization" [in Hebrew], *Ha'aretz*, October 25, 2012; Ir Amim, "Shady Business in Silwan," May 2009, ir-amim.org; City of David, "From the sources" [in Hebrew], cityofdavid.org.il.

86 Nir Hasson, "Fearing an academic boycott, the Supreme Court forbade publishing information about archeological excavations in the West Bank" [in Hebrew], *Ha'aretz*, May 19, 2019; Haggai Matar, "Because of the boycott: A judge authorized the state to hide the identity of archaeologists digging in the territories" [in Hebrew], *Local Call*, November 21, 2016.

87 Hasson, "Fearing an academic boycott."

88 Shezaf and Hasson, "Bar-Ilan University conducts an archaeological dig in the West Bank."

89 Erakat, *Justice for Some*; Lisa Hajjar, "International Humanitarian Law and 'Wars on Terror': A Comparative Analysis of Israeli and American Doctrines and Policies," *Journal of Palestine Studies* 36 (Autumn 2006): 21–42; Lisa Hajjar, "Israel as Innovator in the Attempted Mainstreaming of Extreme Violence," *Middle East Report* 279 (Summer 2016): 38–45; Weizman, *The Least of All Possible Evils*.

90 Erakat, *Justice for Some*.

91 Ibid., 179.

92 Ibid.; Hajjar, "International Humanitarian Law"; Hajjar, "Israel as Innovator."

93 Hajjar, "Israel as Innovator"; Weizman, *The Least of All Possible Evils*; Jones, *The War Lawyers*.

94 Avi Sagi, "The spirit of the IDF and the value of statism" [in Hebrew], Israel Democracy Institute, February 10, 2019, idi.org.il.

95 Ibid.

96 Jones, *The War Lawyers*.

97 Blau and Feldman, "Operation 'cast lead.'"

98 Asa Kasher and Amos Yadlin, "The Military Ethics of Fighting Terror: An Israeli Perspective," *Journal of Military Ethics* 4, no. 1 (2005).

99 Asa Kasher and Amos Yadlin, "Determining Norms for Warfare in New Situations," *Military and Strategic Affairs* 5, no. 1 (2013): 79–97.

100 Erakat, *Justice for Some*; Hajjar, "International Humanitarian Law."

101 See for example, Amnesty International, "Israel and the Occupied Territories: Shielded from Scrutiny: IDF Violations in Jenin and Nablus: Executive Summary," November 4, 2002, amnesty.org; Amnesty International, "Eight-Day Gaza 2012 Conflict/Accountability for Alleged War Crimes and Human Rights Violations," February 21, 2013, un.org; UN Office for the Coordination of Humanitarian Affairs, *Fragmented Lives: Humanitarian Overview 2014* (East Jerusalem: OCHA, March 2015), ocha.org.

102 Kasher and Yadlin, "Determining Norms for Warfare."

103 Asa Kasher, "Proper approach to the third population—not combatants and not civilians" [in Hebrew], *Military and Strategic Affairs* 5, Special Issue (April 2014): 47–50.

104 Asa Kasher and Amos Yadlin, "Assassination and Preventive Killing," *SAIS Review of International Affairs* 25, no. 1 (2005): 41–57. This argument was echoed by Israeli legal scholars; see also Iddo Porat and Ziv Bohrer, "Preferring One's Own Civilians: May Soldiers Endanger Enemy Civilians More Than They Would Endanger Their State's Civilians?," *George Washington International Law Review* (2015): 99–158

105 Erakat, *Justice for Some*.

106 Human Rights Watch, "White Flag Deaths: Killing of Palestinian Civilians During Operation Cast Lead," August 13, 2009, hrw.org; Amnesty International, "Eight-Day Gaza 2012 Conflict/Accountability for Alleged War Crimes and Human Rights Violations," February 21, 2013, un.org; OCHA, "Gaza: Initial Rapid Assessment," August 27, 2014, ochaopt.org; UN Office for the Coordination of Humanitarian Affairs, *Fragmented Lives: Humanitarian Overview 2014* (East Jerusalem: OCHA, March 2015), ocha.org.

107 Breaking the Silence, *This Is How We Fought in Gaza 2014: Soldiers' Testimonies from Operation "Protective Edge"* (2015), breakingthesilence.org; Yoav Zeitoun et al., "The IDF entered Gaza with large ground forces" [in Hebrew], Ynet, July 18, 2014, ynet.co.il.

108 Breaking the Silence, *This Is How We Fought*.

109 Asa Kasher, "Operation Cast Lead and the Ethics of Just War," *Azure* 37 (2009): 43–75; Kasher, "Proper Approach to the Third Population."

110 Pnina Sharvit Baruch, "The Legitimacy Component in the 'IDF Strategy,'" in *The IDF Strategy in the National Security Review*, ed. Meir Elran, Gabi Siboni, and Kobi Michael (Tel Aviv: Institute for National Security Studies, 2016).

111 Ibid.

112 Pnina Sharvit Baruch, "The report of the Human Rights Council Commission of Inquiry of the 2014 operation in the Gaza Strip: A critical analysis" [in Hebrew], *INSS Memorandum* 160, September 2016, inss.org.il.

113 Ibid.
114 Pnina Sharvit Baruch, "Operation Guardian of Walls: A Legal Angle," *INSS Insight* 1478 (May 2021).
115 Pnina Sharvit Baruch and Ori Beeri, "The Amnesty Report: Charges of Apartheid and the Denial of Israel's Right to Exist," *INSS Insight* 1555 (February 2022); Pnina Sharvit Baruch and Ori Beeri, "The International Criminal Court: A general guide and the Israeli angle" [in Hebrew], *INSS Memorandum* 222, July 2022, inss.org.il.
116 Sharvit Baruch and Beeri, "The International Criminal Court."
117 Eilat Maoz, *Living law: Police and sovereignty in an occupation regime* [in Hebrew] (Jerusalem and Tel Aviv: Van Leer Press and Hakibbutz Hameuhad, 2020).
118 Roni Alsheich, *Police commissioner at the forefront: In defense of values* [in Hebrew] (Israel: Tchelet Books, 2020); Israeli Police, "The annual statistics" [in Hebrew], 2019, Planning and Organization Department, gov.il.
119 Eilat Maoz, *Living law*; Lisa Hajjar, *Courting Conflict: The Israeli Military Court System in the West Bank and Gaza* (Berkeley: University of California Press, 2005); Nery Ramati and Karin Torn Hibler, "The cooperation between the police and the Israeli Security Agency in investigating security offenses" [in Hebrew], *Law, Society and Culture* 4 (2021): 459–86.
120 Hajjar, *Courting Conflict*; Addameer, "Presumed Guilty: Failures of the Israeli Military Courts System," November 2009, addameer.org; Lior Yavne, "Backyard Proceedings: The Implementation of Due Process Rights in the Military Courts in the Occupied Territories," Yesh Din, December 2007, yesh-din.org.
121 Ramati and Torn Hibler, "Cooperation between the police and the Israeli Security Agency."
122 Ibid.; Addameer, "I've Been There: A Study of Torture and Inhumane Treatment in Al-Mosqobiyeh Interrogation Center," 2018. addameer.org.
123 Ibid.
124 Tal Jonathan-Zamir, David Weisburd, and Badi Hasisi, "Editors' Introduction," in *Policing in Israel: Studying Crime Control, Community and Counterterrorism*, ed. T. Jonathan-Zamir, D. Weisburd, and B. Hasisi (Boca Raton, FL: CRC Press, 2015).
125 See, for example, Simon Perry et al., "The Situational Prevention of Terrorism: An Evaluation of the Israeli West Bank Barrier," *Journal of Quantitative Criminology* 33 (2017): 727–51; Simon Perry et al., "Who Is the Lone Terrorist? A Study of Vehicle-Borne Attackers in Israel and the West Bank," *Studies in Conflict and Terrorism* 41, no. 11 (2017): 899–913; Badi Hasisi and David Weisburd, "Policing Terrorism and Police-Community Relations: Views of the Arab Minority in Israel," *Police Practice and Research* 15, no. 2 (2014): 158–72; David Weisburd et al., "Terrorist Threats and Police Performance: A Study of Israeli Communities," *British Journal of Criminology* 50 (2010): 725–47.
126 Alsheich, *Police commissioner at the forefront*.
127 Ibid.
128 Israeli Police, "For the first time in the Israel Police—an academic forum advising the commissioner" [in Hebrew], December 8, 2016, facebook.com.
129 Moshe Nussbaum, "The academics letter: Keep Alsheich" [in Hebrew], *Mako*, May 31, 2018.

130 Institute of Criminology, "Prof. Weisburd's speech at the farewell ceremony for the Police Commissioner" [in Hebrew], December 2, 2018, criminology.huji.ac.il.

131 Israeli Police, "Awarding of degrees to seventy graduates of the police academization track" [in Hebrew], July 4, 2023, gov.il.

132 Ibid.

133 Ibid.

134 Simon Perry at al., "The Ten Commandments for Effective Counterterrorism," in *Handbook of the Criminology of Terrorism*, ed. Gary LaFree and Joshua D. Freilich (Chichester, UK: Wiley Press, 2016), 482–3.

135 Ibid., 484–8.

136 It is well documented that Palestinians are forced through extortion and torture to become informants for the Israeli police and Shin Bet. This includes children in occupied East Jerusalem arrested by the INP. Noga Kadman, "Backed by the System: Abuse and Torture at the Shikma Interrogation Facility," B'Tselem and HaMoked, December 2015, btselem.org; Yael Stein, "Unprotected: Detention of Palestinian Minors in East Jerusalem," B'Tselem, October 2017, btselem.org.

137 Weisburd et al., "Terrorist Threats and Police Performance"; Researching the Israeli-American Alliance and Jewish Voice for Peace, "Deadly Exchange: The Dangerous Consequences of American Law Enforcement Training in Israel," September 2018, deadlyexchange.org.

138 Researching the Israeli-American Alliance and Jewish Voice for Peace, "Deadly Exchange."

139 Jonathan-Zamir, Weisburd, and Hasisi, "Editors' Introduction."

140 Simon Perry and Tal Jonathan-Zamir, "Lessons from Empirical Research on Policing in Israel," in Jonathan-Zamir, Weisburd, and Hasisi, *Policing in Israel.*

141 Eyal Clyne, *Orientalism, Zionism, and Academic Practice: Middle East and Islam Studies in Israeli Universities* (New York: Routledge, 2019), 527.

142 Edward W. Said, *Orientalism* (New York: Vintage Books, 1979); Nadia Abu El-Haj, "Edward Said and the Political Present," *American Ethnologist* 32, no. 4 (2005): 538–55.

143 Said, *Orientalism*; Gil Eyal, *Disenchantment of the Orient: Expertise in Arab Affairs and the Israeli State* (Stanford, CA: Stanford University Press, 2006), 22–3.

144 Eyal, *Disenchantment of the Orient.* All major Israeli news media employ one or more full-time experts under the job title of "commentator/correspondent on Arab affairs." Diverse government agencies such as intelligence and security bodies, the Ministries of Justice, Education, and Religions, and diplomatic offices employ officially titled *Mizrahanim* in advisory positions, as do independent think tanks, research institutions, and NGOs. Clyne, *Orientalism, Zionism, and Academic Practice*, 550.

145 Clyne, *Orientalism, Zionism, and Academic Practice*; Eyal, *Disenchantment of the Orient.*

146 Clyne, *Orientalism, Zionism, and Academic Practice.*

147 Ibid.

148 Ibid.; Moshe Dayan Center for Middle Eastern and African Studies, "About Moshe Dayan Center" [in Hebrew], dayan.org.

149 Ibid.; Eyal, *Disenchantment of the Orient.*

150 Eyal, *Disenchantment of the Orient.*

151 Ibid.

152 Ibid.

153 Clyne, *Orientalism, Zionism, and Academic Practice.*

154 Ibid.

155 Assaf David and Eyal Clyne, "On criticism and self-awareness of Israeli *Mizrahanut*" [in Hebrew], *Israeli Readings* 3 (January 2023): 1–10.

156 Moshe Dayan Center, "About Moshe Dayan Center."

157 Moshe Dayan Center for Middle Eastern and African Studies, "Experts" [in Hebrew], dayan.org.

158 Ibid.; Idan Ring, "Our commander is with us . . . Ah, our commentator" [in Hebrew], *Ha'aretz*, March 4, 2008.

159 Moshe Dayan Center, "About Moshe Dayan Center."

160 See, for example, Michael Milshtein, *Neither here nor there: The portrait of the young Palestinian generation* [in Hebrew] (Tel-Aviv: IDF Maarachot and Moshe Dayan Center, 2022).

161 Clyne, *Orientalism, Zionism, and Academic Practice.*

162 Moshe Dayan Center for Middle Eastern and African Studies, "New books" [in Hebrew], "New articles" [in Hebrew], "External articles" [in Hebrew], dayan.org.

163 See, for example, Eyal Zisser, "Hizbollah: Never-ending jihad," in *The jihad: Ideological roots* [in Hebrew], ed. Yossef Kostiner (Tel Aviv: Dayan Center, 2012); Meir Litvak, "Jihad and sacrifice in Hamas's teaching" [in Hebrew], in Kostiner, *The jihad.*

164 Asher Susser, "Israel and Hamas: On the limits of force" [in Hebrew], *Middle East Intersection* 4, no. 10, October 5, 2014, dayan.org.

165 Or Kashti, "Mizrahan from Bar Ilan: The only thing that will deter terrorists is the knowledge that their sister or mother will be raped" [in Hebrew], *Ha'aretz*, July 21, 2014.

166 Uzi Rabi, Radio Galey Israel [in Hebrew], November 19, 2018, gly.co.il.

167 In a notable partial exception, Keidar's comments in 2014 received some criticism from several feminist scholars and organizations, though not from Middle East studies departments. Tellingly, both Keidar and Bar-Ilan University issued a statement of affirmation in response. They claimed that Keidar did not *directly* advocate that Israel use rape as a weapon of war but was simply describing what they construed as the "death culture of the terrorist organizations" in the Middle East. Elinor Davidov, "A lecturer at Bar-Ilan University calls for the rape of terrorist wives" [in Hebrew], *Local Call*, July 21, 2014; Kashti, "Mizrahan from Bar Ilan."

168 MEISAI was founded as the Israeli Oriental Society in 1949; it was established as a bridge between Jewish-Israeli scholars of the Middle East and government officials. The society received government subsidies, and dozens of its inaugural members were notable state officials and senior military officers. Clyne, *Orientalism, Zionism, and Academic Practice.*

169 Yonatan Mendel, "Arabic language in Israel" [in Hebrew], *Mafte'akh: Lexical Review of Political Thought* 9 (2015): 31–52.

170 Clyne, *Orientalism, Zionism, and Academic Practice.*

171 Mendel, "Arabic language in Israel."

172 Israeli academics have also found that serving in the Intelligence Corps constitutes both a central selling point and motivation for Israeli high school students to study Arabic. Ibid.; Muhammad Amara et al., *Arabic in the Israeli academy: Historical absence, current challenged and future possibilities* [in Hebrew] (Jerusalem: Van Leer Institute, 2016).

173 Yonatan Mendel, *The Creation of Israeli Arabic* (London: Routledge, 2014), 8.
174 Amara et al., *Arabic in the Israeli Academy*; Mandel, "Arabic language in Israel."
175 Tamara Traubmann, "The BA program for Shin Bet personnel at the Hebrew University has been canceled" [in Hebrew], *TheMarker*, June 1, 2006.
176 Ibid.
177 Ibid.; Tamara Traubmann, "The degree program for Shin Bet personnel is contrary to the decision of the Council for Higher Education" [in Hebrew], *Ha'aretz*, April 23, 2006; Tamara Traubmann, "The University in Jerusalem will approve the program for Shin Bet personnel' [in Hebrew], *Ha'aretz*, May 26, 2006.
178 Yaniv Kubovich, "The IDF is working to establish a fenced base inside a university" [in Hebrew], *Ha'aretz*, March 25, 2019; Havatzalot, "Havatzalot: The flagship program of the IDF intelligence division" [in Hebrew], havatzalot.org.
179 The program was conceptualized and initiated by Tel Aviv University professor Eviatar Matania. Eviatar Matania and Lt. Col. 'Y', "The other within us: Adapting the training of the intelligence officer to the current era" [in Hebrew], *Ma'arachot* 402, August 2005.
180 Havatzalot, "The stages of training" [in Hebrew], havatzalot.org.
181 Ami Rojkes, "The Hebrew University will lead the intelligence corps' Havatzalot program" [in Hebrew], *Israel Defense*, April 14, 2019.
182 Kubovich, "The IDF is working to establish"; Anat Matar, "The campus is a civilian space, there is no place for those wearing uniforms" [in Hebrew], *Local Call*, March 31, 2019.
183 Ibid.
184 Rojkes, "Hebrew University."
185 Barak Medina, "Continuous Updates – April 2019," April 7, 2019, rector .huji.ac.il.
186 See chapter 3 for more on Talpiot.
187 Matar, "The campus is a civilian space."
188 Ibid.
189 Havatzalot, "Questions and answers" [in Hebrew], havatzalot.org.
190 Kubovich, "The IDF is working to establish."
191 Havatzalot, "Havatzalot compound" [in Hebrew], havatzalot.org.
192 Tomi Shtukman, "To be a 'Havatzalon': The desired path of the intelligence division" [in Hebrew], *Arutz Sheva*, November 24, 2019.
193 Havatzalot, "Havatzalot: The flagship program of the IDF intelligence division."
194 Ibid.
195 Oren Ziv, "The Hadash chapter at Hebrew U came out against the militarization on campus and caused outrage" [in Hebrew], *Local Call*, May 25, 2020.
196 Ibid.

2. Outpost Campus

1 Uri Cohen, *The mountain and the hill: The Hebrew university in Jerusalem during the pre-independence period and early years of the state of Israel* [in Hebrew] (Tel Aviv: Am Oved, 2006), 33.
2 Ibid.

3 Ayala Levin, "The mountain and the fortress: The Mt. Scopus Campus in the Imagination of Israeli National Space" [in Hebrew], *Theory and Criticism* (Winter 2011): 11–34.

4 Hebrew University of Jerusalem, "History" [in Hebrew], huji.ac.il.

5 Israeli Defense Forces Archive, "Yitzhak Rabin: Mt. Scopus speech" [in Hebrew], mod.gov.il.

6 Ibid.

7 Levin, "The mountain and the fortress."

8 Ze'ev Jabotinsky, "The Iron Wall," jabotinsky.org; Oren Yiftachel, "'Ethnocracy': The Politics of Judaizing Israel/Palestine," *Constellations* 6, no. 3 (September 1999): 355; Yinon Cohen and Neve Gordon, "Israel's Biospatial Politics: Territory, Demography, and Effective Control," *Public Culture* 30, no. 2 (May 2018): 199–220; Elisha Efrat, *National planning and development in Israel in the twenty-first century* [in Hebrew] (Tel-Aviv: Tel-Aviv University, 2003).

9 Yinon Cohen and Gordon, "Israel's Biospatial Politics"; Nur Masalha, *Expulsion of the Palestinians: The Concept of 'Transfer' in Zionist Political Thought, 1882–1948* (Washington, DC: Institute for Palestine Studies, 1992).

10 Yinon Cohen and Gordon, "Israel's Biospatial Politics"; Walid Khalidi, ed., *All That Remains: The Palestinian Villages Occupied and Depopulated by Israel in 1948* (Washington, DC: Institute for Palestine Studies, 1992); UN Human Rights Council, *Report of the Special Rapporteur on Adequate Housing as a Component of the Right to an Adequate Standard of Living, and on the Right to Non-discrimination in This Context: Addendum, Mission to Israel and the Occupied Palestinian Territory*, December 24, 2012, A/HRC/22/46/Add.1; Ilan Pappé, *The Ethnic Cleansing of Palestine* (London: Oneworld, 2007).

11 UN Human Rights Council, *Report of the Special Rapporteur on Adequate Housing*; Yinon Cohen and Gordon, "Israel's Biospatial Politics"; Ahmad Amara, "The Negev Land Question: Between Denial and Recognition," *Journal of Palestine Studies* 42, no. 4 (August 1, 2013): 27–47; Ghazi Falah, "Israeli 'Judaization' Policy in Galilee," *Journal of Palestine Studies* 20, no. 4 (July 1, 1991): 69–85; Alexandre Kedar, Ahmad Amara, and Oren Yiftachel, *Emptied Lands: A Legal Geography of Bedouin Rights in the Negev* (Stanford, CA: Stanford University Press, 2018); Efrat, *National planning and development in Israel*.

12 Masalha, *Expulsion of the Palestinians*; Yinon Cohen and Gordon, "Israel's Biospatial Politics." This policy is based on an Israeli legal covenant, which declares that the state was established as the creation of "the entire Jewish people" and with the aim of developing the land for their benefit. World Zionist Organization, "Jewish Agency (Status) Law, 5713-1952," adalah.org.

13 Erez Tzfadia and Haim Yacobi, *Rethinking Israeli Space: Periphery and Identity* (New York: Routledge, 2011).

14 Ibid.; Efrat, *National planning and development in Israel*, 12.

15 Esther Zandberg, "The exhibition is about Aryeh Sharon, the only architect in the world who designed an entire country" [in Hebrew], *Ha'aretz*, October 10, 2018.

16 Tzfadia and Yacobi, *Rethinking Israeli Space*; Alexandre Kedar and Oren Yiftachel, "Land Regime and Social Relations in Israel," in *Realizing Property Rights*, vol. 1 of *Swiss Human Rights Book*, ed. Hernando de Soto and Francis Cheneval (Zurich: Rüffer and Rub, 2006); Efrat, *National planning and development in Israel*.

17 Kedar and Yiftachel, "Land Regime and Social Relations in Israel."

18 Yiftachel, "Ethnocracy"; Patrick Wolfe, *Traces of History: Elementary Structures of Race* (New York: Verso, 2016). This was made possible by granting organizations purportedly representing the Jewish people, such as the Jewish National Fund, the Jewish Agency, and the Zionist Federation, some sovereign powers to govern land, development, and settlement. Adalah, "Land Controlled by Jewish National Fund for Jews Only," July 29, 2007, adalah.org.

19 Yiftachel, "Ethnocracy"; Yinon Cohen and Gordon, "Israel's Biospatial Politics."

20 Ahmad El-Atrash, "Politics of Informal Urbanization and the Battle for Urban Rights in Jerusalem," *Jerusalem Quarterly* 65 (2016): 104–10; John Dugard and John Reynolds, "Apartheid, International Law, and the Occupied Palestinian Territory," *European Journal of International Law* 24, no. 3 (2013): 867–913.

21 Hebrew University of Jerusalem, "Constitution" [in Hebrew], huji.ac.il/constitution; Ben-Gurion University of the Negev, "Constitution and general regulations" [in Hebrew], bgu.ac.il.

22 Uri Cohen, *The mountain and the hill*, 19.

23 Ibid, 39.

24 Haim Yacobi, "Academic Fortress: The Planning of the Hebrew University Campus on Mount Scopus," in *Global Universities and Urban Development: Case Studies and Analysis*, ed. Wim Wiewel and David C. Perry (London: Routledge, 2015).

25 Uri Cohen, *The mountain and the hill*, 10.

26 Ibid.; Diana Dolev, *The Planning and Building of the Hebrew University, 1919–1948: Facing the Temple Mount* (London: Lexington Books, 2016).

27 Ibid.

28 Uri Cohen, *The mountain and the hill*.

29 Dolev, *The Planning and Building of the Hebrew University*.

30 Uri Cohen, *The mountain and the hill*; Gish Amit, *Ex libris: Chronicles of theft, preservation, and appropriating at the Jewish National Library* [in Hebrew] (Jerusalem: Van Leer Jerusalem Institute, 2014).

31 Uri Cohen, *The mountain and the hill*, 23.

32 Ibid.; Uriel Bachrach, *The Power of Knowledge: HEMED the Israeli Science Corps* (Monterey, CA: Samual Wachtman's and Sons, 2016).

33 Uri Cohen, *Laboratory, research institute, city of science*.

34 Uri Cohen, *The mountain and the hill*. Contemporary members of the governing board with state ties include Israeli Supreme Court Justice Dalia Dorner (who served years as a judge in the military court system) and Ephraim Halevi, former head of the Mossad. Hebrew University in Jerusalem, "Members of the executive committee" [in Hebrew], huji.ac.il.

35 Uri Cohen, *The mountain and the hill*.

36 Ami Volansky, *Academy in a changing environment: Higher education policy in Israel 1952–2004* [in Hebrew] (Tel Aviv: Hakibbutz Hameuḥad, 2005); Uri Cohen, *Laboratory, research institute, city of science*.

37 The nomination ultimately failed because of the American Board of Trustees' insistence on institutional autonomy. Uri Cohen, *Laboratory, research institute, city of science*.

38 Ibid.

39 Uri Cohen, *The mountain and the hill*.

40 National Library of Israel, "History of the National Library" [in Hebrew], nli.org.

41 Diana Dolev, "Architecture, education and belligerence: A feminist view of the Hebrew University campus on Mount Scopus," in *Militarism in education* [in Hebrew], ed. Hagit Gur (Tel Aviv: Babel, 2005); Uri Cohen, *The mountain and the hill.*

42 Uri Cohen, *The mountain and the hill.*

43 Hebrew University of Jerusalem, "History" [in Hebrew], huji.ac.il.

44 Dolev, *The Planning and Building of the Hebrew University.*

45 Hebrew University of Jerusalem, "History."

46 Nathan Krystall, "The Fall of the New City 1947–1950," in *Jerusalem 1948: The Arab Neighborhoods and Their Fate in the War,* ed. Salim Tamari (Jerusalem: Badil Resource Center, 1999); Esther Zandberg, "The campus of the green line," [in Hebrew] *Ha'aretz,* November 5, 2002.

47 Tamari, *Jerusalem 1948*; Amit, *Ex Libris.*

48 Amit, *Ex libris*; Tom Segev, "Did the National Library steal books or save them" [in Hebrew], *Ha'aretz,* January 29, 2015.

49 Amit, *Ex libris.*

50 Ibid, 112.

51 Ibid.

52 Ibid.

53 Karma Nabulsi, *Traditions of War: Occupation, Resistance, and the Law* (Oxford: Oxford University Press, 2005); Jeanette Greenfield, *The Return of Cultural Treasures* (Cambridge: Cambridge University Press, 2007).

54 Amit, *Ex libris.*

55 Ibid., 99.

56 Ibid.

57 Yifat Weiss, "This is how the village of Issawiya became a stage for the show of Israeli sovereignty even before 1967" [in Hebrew], *Ha'aretz,* November 30, 2016; Yuval Arnon-Ohana, *On guard Mt. Scopus* [in Hebrew] (Jerusalem: Ariel Books, 2008).

58 Uri Cohen, *The mountain and the hill*; Unit Matzof 247, "Unit 'Matzof 247'— Mt. Scopus enclave" [in Hebrew], matzof247.com; Yuval Arnon-Ohana, "The other side of the moon" [in Hebrew], *Mabat MALAM* 71 (2015): 26–7; Arnon-Ohana, *On guard Mt. Scopus.*

59 Arnon-Ohana, "The other side of the moon"; Arie Shnipper, "The story of Unit 'Matzof 247'—Mt. Scopus enclave" [in Hebrew], matzof247.com.

60 Yacobi, "Academic Fortress," 261–2; Dolev, *The Planning and Building of the Hebrew University.*

61 Yacobi, "Academic Fortress," 262.

62 Ibid, 262.

63 Ibid., 265.

64 Ibid.

65 Levin, "The mountain and the fortress"; Yacobi, "Academic Fortress."

66 Dolev, "Architecture, education and belligerence."

67 Ibid.

68 Ibid.

69 Ibid.; Yacobi, "Academic Fortress."

70 Tehila Bigman, "The height of the water tower" [in Hebrew], Jerusalem Institute blog, January 25, 2019, jerusaleminstitute.org.

71 Weiss, "This is how the village of Issawiya became a stage"; Bimkom, "Al-Issawiyeh—Neighborhood Card," June 2014, bimkom.org

72 Weiss, "This is how the village of Issawiya became a stage."

73 Ibid.

74 Bimkom, "Al-Issawiyeh—Neighborhood Card"; Eyal Hareuveni, "This Is Jerusalem: Violence and Dispossession in al-'Esawiyah," B'Tselem, May 2020, btselem.org.

75 Hareuveni, "This Is Jerusalem"; Bimkom, "The Kamniker Project to Plan Issawiyeh," June 2022, bimkom.org; Bimkom, "The Kamniker Project in the East Jerusalem Neighborhood of Issawiya," April 2006, bimkom.org.

76 Hareuveni, "This Is Jerusalem," 14.

77 Ibid.

78 Gideon Levy and Alex Libek, "The twilight zone: The police harassment of Issawiya residents did not end when the television cameras were turned off" [in Hebrew], Ha'aretz, August 9, 2019; Jodi Rudorin, "Unrest by Palestinians surges in Jerusalem Neighborhood," New York Times, September 17, 2014; Moriel Rothman-Zecher, "Hundreds of Palestinians, Israelis Protest Collective Punishment in East Jerusalem," +972 Magazine, November 13, 2014; Hareuveni, "This Is Jerusalem."

79 Nir Hasson, "The other side of the view from the top of Mount Scopus" [in Hebrew], Ha'aretz, April 3, 2016.

80 Hareuveni, "This Is Jerusalem." A toddler and a sixty-five-year-old woman both died in Issawiyeh as a result of tear gas inhalation in 2021 and 2015. Nir Yahav, "Report: A Palestinian toddler died from inhaling tear gas" [in Hebrew], Walla, September 24, 2010; Michael Salisbury-Corech, "A closed village at the foot of the Hebrew University" [in Hebrew], Local Call, October 22, 2015.

81 Nir Hasson, "12 residents of Issawiya were arrested in a night raid by the police on suspicion of throwing stones and shooting fireworks" [in Hebrew], Ha'aretz, November 25, 2019; Oren Ziv, "Daily Police Violence Is the New Norm in Issawiya—with No End in Sight," +972 Magazine, November 12, 2019; Levy and Libek, "The twilight zone."

82 Hasson, "12 residents of Issawiya were arrested"; Yudith Oppenheimer, "Under the guise of law enforcement, the police take Issawiya outside the fence" [in Hebrew], Local Call, July 30, 2019; Nir Hasson, "'They abused me in the police car': A complaint by a resident of Issawiya to the police department reveals a story of violence" [in Hebrew], Ha'aretz, November 18, 2019.

83 After this was exposed by Ha'aretz, the show was taken off the air, and both the INP and network producers apologized, but neither took full responsibility for using Palestinians as props for Israeli reality television. Nir Hasson, "Israeli Police Plant Gun in Palestinian's Home for TV Docudrama," Ha'aretz, August 6, 2019; Nir Haasson, "Police officers were recorded training in throwing stun grenades in the Issawiya neighborhood" [in Hebrew], Ha'aretz, October 16, 2016; Levy and Libek, "The twilight zone."

84 Nir Hasson, Jacky Khouri, and Aaron Rabinowitz, "A Palestinian youth was killed by live fire from police officers in East Jerusalem" [in Hebrew], Ha'aretz, June 27, 2019.

85 Hareuveni, "This Is Jerusalem."

86 See, for example, Tarabut-Hithabruth, "Everyday racism (3): Between Issawiya and the Hebrew University" [in Hebrew], November 12, 2009, tarabut.info.

87 Academia for Equality, "In solidarity with the residents of Issawiya" [in Hebrew], January 13, 2020, academia4equality.com.

88 Barak Medina, untitled letter [in Hebrew], January 28, 2020, academia4equal ity.com.

89 Academia for Equality, "In solidarity with the residents of Issawiya."

90 See also Nadav Aharoni, "Enough of oppression, enough of closing the Issawiya neighborhood" [in Hebrew], April 22, 2016, socialism.org.

91 Nir Hasson, "The road from Issawiya to the university has been blocked for 20 years. Now the residents are petitioning to open it" [in Hebrew], *Ha'aretz*, April 13, 2022.

92 Ibid.; HaMoked, "HaMoked to the high court: The police must remove the blockade of the access road to the Al-Issawiya neighborhood, which connects the neighborhood to the rest of the city" [in Hebrew], March 24, 2021, hamoked .org.il.

93 HaMoked, "Petition for granting a conditional order" [in Hebrew], 2021, hamoked.org.il.

94 HaMoked, "HaMoked to the high court."

95 Yael Freidson and Noa Shpigel, "The police broke up a meeting of parents in East Jerusalem on the grounds that it was funded by the Palestinian authority" [in Hebrew], *Ha'aretz*, January 7, 2023.

96 University of Haifa, "About—multiversity vision" [in Hebrew], haifa.ac.il.

97 University of Haifa, "About the university" [in Hebrew], haifa.ac.il.

98 Efrat, *National planning and development in Israel*, 85.

99 Baruch Kipnis, "Northern immigration field: The turning point in the late 1970s," in *The lands of Galilee* [in Hebrew], ed. Avshalom Shemu'eli, Arnon Sofer, and Nurit Kliot (Haifa: Society for Applied Scientific Research, 1983), 518.

100 Avraham Dor, "The mitspim enterprise in the Galilee twenty years later" [in Hebrew], *Studies in National Security: The Geostrategic Chair University of Haifa* 6 (2004); Oren Yiftachel, "State Policies, Land Control, and an Ethnic Minority: The Arabs in the Galilee Region, Israel," *Environment and Planning D: Society and Space* 9, no. 3 (1991): 335.

101 Ilan Gur-Zeev, "The 31st floor: University tower and Zionist phallocentrism" [in Hebrew], *Theory and Criticism* 16 (Spring 2000).

102 Khalidi, *All That Remains*; Benny Morris, *The Birth of the Palestinian Refugee Problem, 1947–1949* (Cambridge: Cambridge University Press, 1998).

103 Khalidi, *All That Remains*; see also Zochrot, "al-Khureiba," zochrot.org; Gur-Zeev, "The 31st floor."

104 Ibid.

105 Yossi Ben-Artzi, "On the tower at University of Haifa" [in Hebrew], *Theory and Criticism* 19 (Fall 2001): 277–80.

106 Gur-Zeev, "The 31st floor."

107 See, for example, Knesset, "Negative migration balance in the Galilee" [in Hebrew], July 12, 1988, knesset.gov.il.

108 Kipnis, "Northern immigration field," 509; Naomi Carmon et al., *The new settlement in the Galilee: An evaluation study* [in Hebrew] (Haifa: Technion Center for the Study of the City and the Area, 1990), 110.

109 University of Haifa geographers Arnon Sofer and Nurit Kliot argue that there has long been a "diverse mosaic" of populations in the Galilee, but that "more than any of the others, the Jews maintained a continuous connection to the Galilee . . . kept for 3,000 years." Palestinian Bedouins, by contrast, are presented

as having "infiltrated" and "settled" the Galilee only during the Ottoman period, and as predominantly residing in tents. Sofer argues further that Palestinians are "not yet aware" of the importance of nature preservation, and that they fail to plan their towns without compromising the Galilee's "authentic character." Jewish society, by contrast, "strictly preserves" landscape and nature reserves and identifies with the values of preservation." Introduction to Shemu'eli, Sofer, and Kliot, *The lands of Galilee*, 494; Arnon Sofer, "The development of the Galilee and its preservation—contradiction or coexistence?" [in Hebrew], in Shemu'eli, Sofer, and Kliot, *The lands of Galilee*, 655.

110 Arnon Sofer and Racheli Finkel, *The mitspim in the Galilee: Objectives, achievements, lessons* [in Hebrew] (Rehovot: Center for Rural and Urban Settlement Research, 1988), 33.

111 Dor, "The mitspim enterprise"; "Land Da7, 1976," *The Interactive Encyclopedia of the Palestinian Question*, palquest.org.

112 Sofer and Finkel, *The mitspim in the Galilee*.

113 Ibid., 35, 8; Oren Yiftachel, "Power Disparities in the Planning of a Mixed Region: Arabs and Jews in the Galilee, Israel," *Urban Studies* 30, no. 1 (1993): 157–82; Baruch Kipnis, "The development of Jewish urban settlement in the Galilee 1948–1980" [in Hebrew], in Shemu'eli, Sofer, and Kliot, *The lands of Galilee*.

114 Yiftachel, "Power Disparities in the Planning of a Mixed Region."

115 Sofer and Finkel, *The mitspim in the Galilee*.

116 Yiftachel, "Power Disparities in the Planning of a Mixed Region."

117 The admission committees were first legally challenged by the Association for Civil Rights in Israel in a petition to the Israeli Supreme Court in 1995 on the grounds that they are discriminatory against Palestinian citizens. They were challenged again on the grounds of discrimination in a 2011 petition, but rejected by the Israeli Supreme Court in 2014. ACRI, "Abolish the admissions committee law" [in Hebrew], September 17, 2014, acri.org.il; Galia Daor, "Admission committees for localities discriminate against the Arab public" [in Hebrew], Israeli Democracy Institute, October 27, 2010, idi.org.il; Revital Hovel and Jackie Houri, "By a narrow majority: The Supreme Court approved holding admissions committees in community settlements" [in Hebrew], *Ha'aretz*, September 17, 2014.

118 Chen Maanit, "The new generation of admissions committees: Come live with us! Unless you are religious, Arab, single or just look a little different" [in Hebrew], *Globes*, February 1, 2019; Daor, "Admission committees."

119 Noa Shpigel, "The Knesset finally approved the expansion of the Law on Admissions Committees to communal settlements" [in Hebrew], *Ha'aretz*, July 25, 2023.

120 Arnon Sofer, "Opposition to the admissions committees in small communities in the periphery: Is there justification for complaint?" [in Hebrew] (Haifa: Chaikin Chair in Geostrategy, University of Haifa, 2011), 6–7.

121 Ibid.

122 University of Haifa, "Chair founder, Professor Arnon Sofer" [in Hebrew], hevra .haifa.ac.il.

123 Lily Galili, "Jewish and demographic state" [in Hebrew], *Ha'aretz*, June 28, 2002.

124 Ibid.; Miron Rapaport, "A demonstration in Tel Aviv against the 'transfer' of the triangle: 'A crazy and harrowing idea'" [in Hebrew], *Local Call*, February 1,

2020; Joseph Jabarin, "When Trump suggests to transfer me" [in Hebrew], *Ha'aretz*, February 1, 2020.

125 Galili, "Jewish and demographic state."

126 Hovel and Houri, "By a narrow majority."

127 Baruch Kipnis, *Proposal for a municipal organization of the new settlements in the Galilee* [in Hebrew] (Haifa: Prepared for the Jewish Agency Settlement Division, April 1982).

128 Sofer and Finkel, *The mitspim in the Galilee.*

129 Carmon et al., *The new settlement in the Galilee.*

130 Dor, "The mitspim enterprise."

131 Diana Bachor, "The government approved the establishment of 14 new community settlements" [in Hebrew], Ynet, July 21, 2002, ynet.co.il.

132 Emily Amrousi, "My personal Zionism" [in Hebrew], *Israel Hayom*, August 8, 2019.

133 Nufar Avni and Nurit Alfasi, "UniverCity: The Vicious Cycle of Studentification in a Peripheral City," *City and Community* 17, no. 4 (December 2018): 1249.

134 Ibid.; Ben-Gurion University of the Negev, "Kiryat Bergman in the past, the Institute for Applied Research/Institute for Negev Research—History" [in Hebrew], bgu.ac.il. Palestinian civil society organizations have repeatedly decried the colonial ideology underwriting this slogan. Al-Haq, "Palestinian Civil Society Denounce EU Commission Statement," May 1, 2023, alhaq.org.

135 Yinon Cohen and Gordon, "Israel's Biospatial Politics."

136 Efrat, *National planning and development in Israel.*

137 Ibid., 136.

138 Ben-Gurion University, "Kiryat Bergman in the past."

139 Kedar, Amara, and Yiftachel, *Emptied Lands.*

140 Oren Yiftachel et al., "Urban Justice and Recognition: Affirmation and Hostility in Beer Sheva," in *Searching for the Just City*, ed. Peter Marcuse et al. (London: Routledge, 2009), 128.

141 The same can be said of the 1966 Negev Physical Plan, the 1975 National Plan 6, and the 1991 National Plan 31, which worked to concentrate Bedouins and reduce their numbers in the Negev and failed to address the legal status issues facing the residents of Bedouin villages. But it is also true of the 2000 District Plan 4/14, the 2005 National Plan 35, the 2006 District Plan 4/14/23, which all made incremental steps toward resolving the recognition problem for a minority of Bedouin towns while refusing to address the structural discrimination of Bedouins in the Naqab with regard to land ownership, rights to settlement, and participation in planning their own futures. Kedar, Amara, and Yiftachel, *Emptied Lands.*

142 While in recent years the government extended recognition to eleven Bedouin towns, it has not supplied them with adequate infrastructure, including running water, roads, or permanent schools. Over 65,000 Bedouin citizens reside in the remaining thirty-five villages classified by Israel as "unrecognized" and therefore "unlawful." Ibid.; Yinon Cohen and Gordon, "Israel's Biospatial Politics," 214; Efrat, *National planning and development in Israel.*

143 Israeli punitive measures against unrecognized villages have included spraying agricultural plots with poison or plowing them over and regularly demolishing communal structures and residential homes. Yiftachel et al., "Urban Justice and Recognition"; Kedar, Amara, and Yiftachel, *Emptied Lands*; Yinon Cohen and Gordon, "Israel's Biospatial Politics."

144 Human Rights Watch, "Israel: End Systemic Bias Against Bedouin," March 30, 2008, hrw.org.

145 Yiftachel et al., "Urban Justice and Recognition."

146 Efrat, *National planning and development in Israel*; Carmey Avdat Farm, "The Wine Route in the Negev" [in Hebrew], carmey-avdat.co.il.

147 Nufar Avni, Nurit Alfasi, and Lisa Bornstein, "City Profile: Beersheba," *Cities* 53 (April 2016): 18–29; Efrat, *National planning and development in Israel.*

148 Avni, Alfasi, and Bornstein, "City Profile: Beersheba."

149 Avni and Alfasi, "UniverCity."

150 Ismael Abu-Saad and Gali Shani, "Higher education among Bedouin-Arabs in the Negev," in *Science and humanities in the Negev: Ben-Gurion University in the Negev and its history in research* [in Hebrew], ed. Yehudah Gradus (Beersheba: Ben-Gurion University Publishing, 2014); Human Rights Watch, "Off the Map," March 30, 2008, hrw.org; Sikkuy, "The barriers to access to public transportation in disconnected settlements in the Negev" [in Hebrew], February 2018, sikkuy-afouq.org.il.

151 Ben-Gurion University of the Negev, "About Ben-Gurion University of the Negev" [in Hebrew], bgu.ac.il.

152 Erez Tzfadia, Yagil Levy, and Amiram Oren, "Moving the IDF south: Between Zionism and the market" [in Hebrew], *Mifne* (May 2008): 14–19.

153 Ben Shif, "Toward the move of IDF bases to the Negev: NIS 55 million will be invested in Ben Gurion University" [in Hebrew], Beer Sheva Net, October 11, 2018, b7net.co.il.

154 Adalah, "Opposition to the transfer of military bases to the Negev" [in Hebrew], adalah.org.

155 Ayalim, "Our story" [in Hebrew], ayalim.org.il; Ben-Gurion University Dean of Students, "Ayalim Association" [in Hebrew], bgu.ac.il;

156 Ayalim, "Student Villages," ayalim.org.il.

157 Ibid.

158 Arutz Sheva, "Rivlin: You are the embodiment of Zionism" [in Hebrew], June 4, 2017, inn.co.il.

159 The Student Association of Ben-Gurion University, "Ayalim Association" [in Hebrew], bgu4u.co.il; Ben-Gurion University Dean of Students, "Ayalim Association."

160 Kedma, "About Kedma" [in Hebrew], kedma-hityashvut.org; Kedma, "Student villages" [in Hebrew], kedma-hityashvut.org; Ayalim, "Student Villages."

161 Kedma, "Student villages."

162 Or Kashti, "After a decade-long struggle, the committee of university presidents adds Ariel" [in Hebrew], *Ha'aretz*, April 9, 2021.

163 Ariel University, "About Ariel University: A new spirit in academia" [in Hebrew], ariel.ac.il.

164 Hagai Amit and Shani Littman, "Ariel University: Research or just politics?" [in Hebrew], *TheMarker*, July 27, 2012, themarker.com.

165 Ariel Municipality, "Ariel archive—local story" [in Hebrew], ariel.localtimeline.com.

166 Yehezkel Lein, "Land Grab: Israel's Settlement Policy in the West Bank," B'Tselem, May 2002, btselem.org.

167 Tal Ariel Amir, "I have no intention of giving up: Ron Nachman's brave fight against cancer" [in Hebrew], *NRG*, May 19, 2012.

168 Ariel Municipality, "Ariel archive—local story."
169 Ibid.; Amir, "I have no intention of giving up."
170 Ariel Municipality, "Ariel archive—local story."
171 Nir Shalev, "Under the Guise of Legality: Israel's Declarations of State Land in the West Bank," B'Tselem, February 2012, btselem.org.
172 Amir, "I have no intention of giving up"; Ariel Municipality, "Ariel archive—local story."
173 Amir, "I have no intention of giving up."
174 Amit and Littman, "Ariel University: Research or just politics?"
175 Ibid. For his work to develop Ariel into a city and his service as mayor for almost three decades, as well as his initiation and development of Ariel University, Nachman was awarded the Israel Prize for his "special contribution to society and the state" in 2013. Shlomo Pyutrekovsky, "Israeli lifetime achievement award for the late Ron Nachman" [in Hebrew], *Arutz Sheva*, February 17, 2013.
176 Ibid.; Ariel Municipality, "Ariel archive—local story."
177 Ariel Noy, "Ariel: Investors follow the academy" [in Hebrew], *Calcalist*, September 13, 2012.
178 Amit and Littman, "Ariel University: Research or just politics?"; Ronen Niv, "A point of merit for Ariel: How did the university jump-start real estate in its vicinity?" [in Hebrew], *Calcalist*, March 5, 2020; Gili Melnitcki, "Who doesn't want a big house with a garden for a million shekels? The new hit with young adults" [in Hebrew], *TheMarker*, November 19, 2019, themarker.com; Erga Shilony, "These are the places that students in Ariel must know" [in Hebrew], *Mako*, January 16, 2019; Hila Sion, "How much does it cost to rent near the university?" [in Hebrew], Ynet, October 10, 2016, ynet.co.il; Ofer Petersburg, "For students' information: It is cheaper to live with your parents" [in Hebrew], *Israel Hayom*, October 18, 2020.
179 Rogel Alper, "The actors are right: Ariel is not in Israel" [in Hebrew], *Ha'aretz*, September 2, 2010.
180 Kedma, "Student villages"; Kedma, "About Kedma."
181 Israeli Ministry of Justice, "Together at Ariel: Registered association" [in Hebrew], Guidestar, guidestar.org.il.
182 Or Kashti and Hagar Shezaf, "Settlement university crediting students for volunteering at illegal Israeli outposts" [in Hebrew], *Ha'artez*, April 22, 2021.
183 Nir Shalev, "Under the Guise of Legality"; Lein, "Land Grab."
184 Ibid.; B'Tselem, "List of Military Checkpoints in the West Bank and Gaza Strip," November 2021, btselem.org.
185 B'Tselem, "Map of Palestinian Land in Ariel," btselem.org; Lein, "Land Grab."
186 Yotam Berger, "Construction waste from Ariel University is dumped in a nearby area in violation of the law" [in Hebrew], *Ha'aretz*, August 19, 2018.
187 United Nations, "UN Condemns Israel's Housing Plans in Occupied Palestinian Territory," UN News, August 16, 2011, un.org; Shabtay Bendet, "US on approval of housing units in settlements: A serious threat to peace" [in Hebrew], Walla, August 31, 2016; Tal Shalev, "The European Union joins the condemnations: 'Concerned about the expansion of construction in the settlements'" [in Hebrew], Walla, September 2, 2016.
188 Pinhas Wolf, "Netanyahu: 'Ariel, the capital of Samaria, will remain in Israel'" [in Hebrew], Walla, January 29, 2010.

189 David Makovsky, "Camp David II Aftermath: Options for the Next Ninety Days," Washington Institute for Near East Policy, August 4, 2000, washington institute.org; "Summary of Olmert's 'Package' Offer to Abu Mazen," Al Jazeera, August 31, 2008, ajtransparency.com.

190 Council for Higher Education, "About" [in Hebrew], che.org.il.

191 Council for Higher Education, "The working methods of the Council for Higher Education" [in Hebrew], March 2007, che.org.il. A 2005 CHE decision stipulated that CHE Judea and Samaria can only consist of active members in the governing committee of CHE. Council for Higher Education, "The Tenth Council for Higher Education: Compilation of fundamental decisions 2002–2007" [in Hebrew], March 2007, che.org.il. The CHE Israel and CHE Judea and Samaria also extended recognition to colleges in the West Bank settlements of Elkana and Alon Shvut. Or Kashti, "The academic annexation passes without any academic protest" [in Hebrew], Ha'aretz, February 27, 2018.

192 Yarden Skop, "Ariel University awards doctorate and professor degrees that are not recognized by the Council for Higher Education" [in Hebrew], Ha'aretz, February 3, 2015.

193 Itamar Fleishman and Shahar Chai, "The major general signed, the sign was updated: Ariel University" [in Hebrew], Ynet, 25, December 2012, ynet.co.il.

194 Council for Higher Education, "The plenary of the Council for Higher Education supports the establishment of the university in Ariel" [in Hebrew], January 8, 2013, che.org.il.

195 Skop, "Ariel University awards doctorate and professor degrees."

196 Knesset, "Book of laws: 2691" [in Hebrew], February 15, 2018, knesset.gov.il.

197 Kashti, "The academic annexation passes"; Knesset, "Final approval: The CHE will be able to exercise its powers in the Judea and Samaria region as well" [in Hebrew], February 12, 2018, Knesset News, knesset.gov.il.

198 Knesset, "Final approval."

199 Or Kashti, "Hours before its dissolution, CHE in the occupied territories approved the establishment of the Faculty of Medicine in Ariel," Ha'aretz, February 13, 2019; Shira Kadari-Ovadia, "The Higher Education Council approved the establishment of the Faculty of Medicine in Ariel" [in Hebrew], Ha'aretz, April 11, 2019.

200 Yotam Berger, "Bennett and Adelson inaugurated the department of medicine at Ariel; Bennett: 'There is a university cartel'" [in Hebrew], Ha'aretz, August 19, 2018.

201 Chen Pundak, "The committee of the heads of universities to Netanyahu: Do not build another university" [in Hebrew], Calcalist, June 27, 2012.

202 Israeli Supreme Court, "Ruling on Supreme Court case 6168/12" [in Hebrew], supremedecision.court.gov.il. The request of the Israeli nonprofit Peace Now to join the petition in order to raise independent objections to the accreditation of Ariel University grounded in international law concerning the governance of occupied territory was summarily rejected by the Supreme Court.

203 Ibid.

204 Kashti, "The academic annexation passes."

205 Ibid.

206 Kashti, "After a decade-long struggle."

207 Hebrew University of Jerusalem, "Constitution"; Ariel University, "About Ariel University."

3. The Scholarly Security State

1 Cyber Week, "Cyber Week 23–27 June, 2019 Tel Aviv University," cyberweek
.tau.ac.il.
2 Erez Raviv, "Vice president of research and development at Hebrew University:
Without is there is no mobileye," *Davar*, March 17, 2017, davar1.co.il.
3 Uri Cohen, *Laboratory, research institute, city of science: From the Daniel Sieff
Research Institute to the Weizmann Institute of Science, 1934–1949* [in Hebrew]
(Jerusalem: Bialik Institute, 2016).
4 Ibid.; Uriel Bachrach, *The Power of Knowledge: HEMED the Israeli Science Corps*
(Monterey, CA: Samuel Wachtman's and Sons, 2016).
5 Benny Morris and Benjamin Z. Kedar, "'Cast Thy Bread': Israeli Biological
Warfare during the 1948 War," *Middle Eastern Studies* (2022): 1–25.
6 Ibid.; Uri Cohen, *Laboratory, research institute, city of science*; Bachrach, *The
Power of Knowledge*.
7 Morris and Kedar, "'Cast Thy Bread.'"
8 Ibid.
9 Hospital reports from April and May 1948 reported a typhoid epidemic. Other
reports suggest that the infections in Acre were short lived, but they nonetheless
reportedly sowed panic and demoralized the Palestinian residents and were
believed by the Haganah to have helped in the occupation of the town. Morris
and Kedar, "'Cast Thy Bread.'"
10 Ibid.
11 Morris and Kedar, "'Cast Thy Bread,'" 12.
12 Ibid.
13 Ibid.; Uri Cohen, *Laboratory, research institute, city of science*.
14 Ibid.; Uri Kirsch, *Unique Aspects of the Technion's Development: Academic
Excellence, National Contribution and Managerial Culture* (Haifa: Samuel
Neaman Institute, 2013).
15 Moshe Lissak and Uri Cohen, "Scientific Strategists in the Period of
Mamlakhtiyut: Interaction between the Academic Community and Political
Power Centers," *Journal of Israeli History* 30, no. 2 (September 2011): 189–210.
16 Ibid.; Uri Cohen, *Laboratory, research institute, city of science*; Bachrach, *The
Power of Knowledge*.
17 Rafael, "Move Faster than Threats: Rafael for Dynamic Defense," rafael.co.il.
18 Rafael, "About," rafael.co.il.
19 Kirsch, *Unique Aspects of the Technion's Development*; Amnon Barzilai, "Israel
has a second authority to develop weapons. It's called the Technion" [in
Hebrew], *Ha'aretz*, April 11, 2004.
20 Israeli Aerospace Industries, "IAI Worldwide," iai.co.il.
21 Kirsch, *Unique Aspects of the Technion's Development*; Barzilai, "Israel has a
second authority to develop weapons."
22 UNWRA, "Gaza's 'Great March of Return' One Year On," 2019, unrwa.org.
23 Palestinian Centre for Human Rights, "Question and Answer: 1st Year Anniversary
of the March of Return Demonstrations," March 28, 2019, pchrgaza.org.
24 Amnesty International, "Six Months On: Gaza's Great March of Return," June 8,
2018, amnesty.org.
25 Ibid.

26 Palestinian Centre for Human Rights, "Question and Answer."
27 UNWRA, "Gaza's 'Great March of Return'"; Amnesty International, "Six Months On."
28 Médecins Sans Frontières, "Great March of Return: Shattered Limbs, Shattered Lives," msf.org.; UNWRA, "Gaza's 'Great March of Return.'"
29 Médecins Sans Frontières, "Shattered Limbs, Shattered Lives"; Amnesty International, "Six Months On."
30 Human Rights Council, "Report of the Independent International Commission of Inquiry on the Protests in the Occupied Palestinian Territory," February 25, 2019, ohchr.org.
31 INSS, "The battle for public opinion: Gaza as a case study" [in Hebrew], June 25, 2018, inss.org.il.
32 Ibid.
33 Ibid.
34 Ibid.
35 INSS, "Mission" [in Hebrew], inss.org.il.
36 INSS, "Team" [in Hebrew], inss.org.il.
37 INSS, "The annual international conference" [in Hebrew], inss.org.il.
38 INSS, "Publications in strategic survey for Israel" [in Hebrew], inss.org.il.
39 INSS, "The American Jewish Community and Israel's National Security," inss.org.il; INSS, "Delegitimization and BDS," inss.org.il.
40 Einav Yogev and Gallia Lindenstrauss, eds., "The Delegitimization Phenomenon: Challenges and Responses," *Memorandum* 169 (September 2017), inss.org.
41 Ibid.
42 Ibid.
43 Comper Center, "Ambassadors Online," compercenter.haifa.ac.il; Comper Center, "Ambassadors Online," shagririm.haifa.ac.il.
44 Ambassadors Online, "Shagririm Bareshet 2012: Syllabus," compercenter.haifa.ac.il.
45 Ambassadors Online, "Hurry up and sign up! Registration closes this week", October 7, 2018, Facebook.com/shagririmhaifa.
46 Comper Center, "Israel advocacy materials" [in Hebrew], compercenter.haifa.ac.il; Comper Center, "Theses, publications, and research" [in Hebrew], compercenter.haifa.ac.il.
47 Reut Cohen et al., "Strategies to Combat the Academic Boycott," Comper Center, July 2016, compercenter.haifa.ac.il.
48 Ibid., 10, 17.
49 "Ambassadors Online badge: Five Druze were awarded a medal" [in Hebrew], January 10, 2017, karmel.co.il.
50 Ibid.
51 "Members of Congress from Ohio visiting the University of Haifa: 'When you look at Israeli academia, you realize how much the BDS movement lies'" [in Hebrew], December 12, 2017, krcity.co.il.
52 Ibid.
53 Yair Altman, "A new track at the University of Haifa: Fight against anti-Semitism" [in Hebrew], May 16, 2019, israelhayom.co.il.
54 Ben-Gurion University of the Negev, "The Air Force academic program: Head of the program statement" [in Hebrew], in.bgu.ac.il.
55 Omri Zerachovitz, "10 million NIS per year: Haifa University won the tender

for military colleges" [in Hebrew], *Globes*, June 13, 2018, globes.co.il.

56 See also chapter 1.

57 Gil Baram and Isaac Ben-Israel, "The Academic Reserve," *Israel Studies Review* 34, no. 2 (September 1, 2019): 75-91.

58 Israel Defense Forces, "Majors and Fields of Study" [in Hebrew] atuda.org.il; Israel Defense Forces, "The academic reserve" [in Hebrew], December 20, 2020, mitgaisim.idf.il.

59 Academia for Commissioned Rank, "The elite unit of the reserve" [in Hebrew], atuda.org; Yaakov Katz and Amir Bohbot, *The Weapon Wizards: How Israel Became a High-Tech Military Superpower* (New York: St. Martin's Press, 2017).

60 Baram and Ben-Israel, "The Academic Reserve," 78.

61 Ibid.

62 Shahar Alon, "The University of Haifa will award academic degrees to the three military colleges" [in Hebrew], *Calcalist*, June 13, 2018.

63 School of Political Science, "National Security Programs," poli.haifa.hevra.ac.il; Pinhas Yehezkeli, "The National Security College" [in Hebrew], amutatmabal .org.

64 Alon, "The University of Haifa will award academic degrees."

65 Ben-Gurion University of the Negev, "The academic program for the air force course" [in Hebrew], bgu.ac.il.

66 Israeli Ministry of Defense, "The Talpiot program: About the program" [in Hebrew], "The Talpiot program: The training" [in Hebrew], talpiot.mod.gov.il.

67 Ibid.; Israeli Air Force, "49 'Talpiot' graduates completed the excellence program" [in Hebrew], November 10, 2022, idf.il.

68 Baram and Ben-Israel, "The Academic Reserve."

69 Ibid.

70 Technion Israel Institute of Technology, "The 2019 academic year—let's get started!" [in Hebrew], October 18, 2018, technion.ac.il; Faculty of Data and Decision Sciences, "Alonim program" [in Hebrew], technion.ac.il.

71 Israel Defense Forces, "The Brakim program: Academic atuda" [in Hebrew], January 24, 2023, mitgaisim.idf.il.

72 Technion Israel Institute of Technology, "The 2019 academic year."

73 Israel Defense Forces, "Academic officers" [in Hebrew], atuda.org.il.

74 Iby and Aladar Fleishman Faculty of Engineering, "Top secret! Galim program—the title that you can almost talk about" [in Hebrew], August 7, 2018, engineering.tau.ac.il.

75 N', shore officer and program student, "Havatzalot program: Pass it on" [in Hebrew], *Mabat MALAM* no. 72 (2015), 12.

76 Ibid., 13.

77 See chapter 1. Havatzalot, "Havatzalot," havatzalot.org; Military Intelligence Directorate, "The new program that nurtures intelligence personnel. The entry is for the excellent ones only" [in Hebrew], Israel Defense Forces, October 15, 2018, idf.il; Hanan Greenwood, "Military intelligence department presents: The outstanding program to prevent brain drain" [in Hebrew], *Israel Hayom*, October 13, 2018.

78 Ran Yaron, "Holding Health to Ransom: GSS Interrogation and Extortion of Palestinian Patients at Erez Crossing," Physicians for Human Rights–Israel, August 2008, phr.org.il.

79 Elior Levy, "'We were there, we did it, and we're unable to continue.' Refusers from unit 8200 speak" [in Hebrew], Ynet, September 12, 2014, ynet.co.il.

80 Ibid.; "Any Palestinian Is Exposed to Monitoring by the Israeli Big Brother," *Guardian*, September 12, 2014.

81 Letter of 8200 Refusers, "The letter" [in Hebrew], September 11, 2014, modiin-letter.wordpress.com.

82 Elior Levy, "The refusers from unit 8200: We won't aid the occupation" [in Hebrew], Ynet, September 12, 2014, ynet.co.il.

83 Elior Levy, "'We were there, we did it, and we're unable to continue.'"

84 Yaron, "Holding Health to Ransom," 51.

85 Ibid.

86 Al Mezan, "Israeli Authorities at Erez Arbitrarily Arrested a Cancer Patient on His Way Back to Gaza from Jerusalem Hospital," March 22, 2023, mezan.org; Al Mezan, "Israeli Authorities Continue to Extort and Arrest Palestinian Patients," April 19, 2016, mezan.org.

87 Yaron, "Holding Health to Ransom"; Al Mezan, "Israeli Authorities Continue to Extort."

88 Hayadan, "Elbit Systems and the Technion established a research center in the field of vision systems" [in Hebrew], June 16, 2008, hayadan.org.il.

89 Ibid.

90 Ibid.

91 Human Rights Watch, "Precisely Wrong: Gaza Civilians Killed by Israeli Drone-Launched Missiles," 2009, hrw.org.

92 "Elbit Systems Ltd," Investigate, a project of the American Friends Service Committee, investigate.afsc.org.

93 Ibid.

94 Udi Etsion, "Elbit sold the Philippines Merkava tanks that the IDF hasn't bought yet" [in Hebrew], Ynet, July 19, 2022, ynet.co.il; Katz and Bohbot, *The Weapon Wizards*.

95 UN Human Rights Council, "Report of the United Nations Fact Finding Mission on the Gaza Conflict," September 25, 2009, ohchr.org; Human Rights Watch, "Israel: Gaza Airstrikes Violated Laws of War," February 12, 2013, hrw.org; Human Rights Council, "Gaza Inquiry Finds Credible Allegations of War Crimes Committed in 2014 by Both Israel and Palestinian Armed Groups," June 22, 2015, ohchr.org; Human Rights Watch, "Israel's May Airstrikes on High-Rises," August 23, 2021, hrw.org.

96 Technion Israel Institute of Technology, "Technion president and board members visit Rafael" [in Hebrew], February 13, 2018, technion.ac.il.

97 Yuval Azulay, "Rafael will offer 150 students from the Technion a job until retirement" [in Hebrew], *Globes*, January 1, 2013.

98 Yossi Nissan, "Elbit Systems will provide research grants to the Technion in the amount of half a million dollars" [in Hebrew], *Globes*, June 15, 2008. Elbit has also collaborated with Tel Aviv University's Faculty of Engineering to establish InnoBit, a program aiming to develop the "future generation" of technology leaders and entrepreneurs in Israel. Through the program, students are mentored by Elbit experts and develop a technological project "with potential application" as the final assignment for their degree. Elbit Systems, "Innobit program" [in Hebrew], innobit-elbitsystems.com.

99 Technion Israel Institute of Technology, "Prizes were awarded in the competition for security innovations" [in Hebrew], March 12, 2017, technion.ac.il; Technion Israel Institute of Technology, "Technology-based security: The annual conference of the Defense Science and Technology Center" [in Hebrew], March 12, 2019, technion.ac.il; Nissan, "Elbit Systems will provide research grants."

100 Department of Aerospace Engineering, "History" [in Hebrew], aerospace.technion.ac.il.

101 Department of Aerospace Engineering, "Aeolus: Autonomous jet UAV" [in Hebrew], "Project Cornetto, second year" [in Hebrew], aerospace.technion.ac.il.

102 Department of Aerospace Engineering, "The 62nd Annual Conference on Aerospace Sciences" [in Hebrew], aerospace.technion.ac.il; Department of Aerospace Engineering, "History."

103 Uri Berkovitz, "The Technion's vision: To turn the north into a high-tech industrial powerhouse" [in Hebrew], *Globes*, May 3, 2021.

104 Israeli Ministry of Defense, "MAFAT" [in Hebrew], "The unit for research and technological infrastructure" [in Hebrew], mod.gov.il.

105 Israeli Ministry of Defense, "MAFAT."

106 "About us" [in Hebrew], Yuvan Ne'eman Workshop for Science, Technology, and Security, secyech.tau.ac.il.

107 This includes the Israeli Foreign Trade Administration at the Ministry of Economy and Industry, the Prime Minister's Office, the Ministry of Foreign Affairs, and the national cyber directorate, as well as ISDEF. The conference is sponsored by Israeli Aerospace Industries, among other Israeli weapons and security companies. ISDEF, "Past Highlights," isdefexpo.org; Cyber Week, "Cyber Week 23–27 June."

108 Nano Israel, "Nano Centers," "Companies," nanoisrael.org

109 Tel Aviv University, "Tel Aviv University Center for Nanoscience and Nanotechnology" [in Hebrew], *Scientific Report*, December 2018, nano.tau.ac.il; Hayadan, "Tel Aviv University is opening its micro and nano infrastructures for use by Israeli industry" [in Hebrew], July 27, 2010, hayadan.org.

110 Tel Aviv University, "MAFAT chief's award to Prof. Yosef Terkel for research with a special contribution to the security system" [in Hebrew], January 19, 2014, tau.ac.il.

111 Yasmin Yablonko, "A new acceleration program for the ISA and TAU Ventures of Tel Aviv University" [in Hebrew], *Mako*, May 9, 2018.

112 Yasmin Yablonko, "On the tech front: The accelerator program of the ISA and Tel Aviv University opens" [in Hebrew], *Globes*, July 4, 2018.

113 Yasmin Yablonko, "This is how the ISA nabs the future stars of the high-tech industry" [in Hebrew], *Globes*, August 14, 2018.

114 Avi Blizovsky, "The National Laboratory for the Development of Space Cameras was inaugurated at Elbit Systems El-Op" [in Hebrew], March 28, 2011, hayadan.org; Guy Yamin, "Kiryat Weizman: The Science Park leased 8,000 square meters of offices in recent months" [in Hebrew], *Globes*, March 5, 2006.

115 Ben-Gurion University of the Negev, "Researchers have found a method to identify a target photographed by a drone from an encrypted video transmission" [in Hebrew], January 15, 2018, bgu.ac.il; Blizovsky, "The National Laboratory for the Development of Space Cameras."

116 Nick Kolyohin, "Has Be'er Sheva become a major player in the high-tech arena? The data shows otherwise" [in Hebrew], *Maariv*, May 6, 2017; Gav-Yam Negev, "About the park" [in Hebrew], gavyam-negev.co.il.

117 Ben-Gurion University of the Negev, "Rafael will establish a research and development branch in the high-tech park in Be'er Sheva as part of the company's strategy" [in Hebrew], September 12, 2017, bgu.ac.il; Elbit Systems and Lockheed Martin also currently operate offices at the park: "Expanding in the network: Lockheed Martin deepens its cooperation with Israel" [in Hebrew], *New Tech Military Magazine*, December 23, 2014, new-techonline.com.

118 Ben-Gurion University, "Rafael will establish a research and development branch."

119 Talniri, "Rafael and Ben-Gurion University announce a strategic research cooperation agreement" [in Hebrew], January 29, 2019, talniri.co.il. This has already generated results. One example is information security company Morphisec, founded by Ben-Gurion University graduates and whose technology and patents are based on academic research developed at the university. The company is headquartered at Gav-Yam Negev and has already established cooperation with the US Department of Homeland Security. Morphisec, "Prevention-First Security," morphisec.com.

120 Gali Weinreb, "Yissum CEO seeks to connect academia and industry" [in Hebrew], *Globes*, October 18, 2017.

121 In 2018, Israel announced that it is the second-leading nation in technology transfer worldwide, as measured by revenues from intellectual property sales, and surpassed only by the United States. Most of these university patents were commercialized with Israeli industry, particularly those related to the security industry that were sold to weapons companies. Eytan Halon, "Yissum Launches Licensing Campaign to Boost Hebrew University Innovation," *Jerusalem Post*, October 24, 2018; Knesset Science and Technology Committee, "Outline of policy and protection of intellectual property in research and development institutions in Israel" [in Hebrew], May 7, 2012, knesset.org.

122 Zuri Dar, "Yissum established a division for the advancement and commercialization of projects in the field of combating terrorism" [in Hebrew], *Ha'aretz*, April 22, 2004.

123 Oded Hermoni, "Researchers in Israeli academia are developing methods to fight terrorism" [in Hebrew], *Ha'aretz*, June 22, 2004.

124 Israel Defense, "New research cooperation" [in Hebrew], October 6, 2014, israeldefense.co.il.

125 BGN Technologies Ltd., "Industry—BGU Cooperation" [in Hebrew], bgu.ac.il; Talniri, "Rafael and Ben-Gurion University."

126 BIRAD, "BIRAD: Research and Development Company Ltd." [in Hebrew], birad.biz; "When science comes to life" [in Hebrew], February 2018, birad.biz.

127 BIRAD, "Technologies developed by Bar-Ilan University researchers attract the attention of Elbit Systems" [in Hebrew], May 7, 2019, birad.biz.

128 Ibid.

129 The flagship course offered training in security exports, advertised as including practical, legal, and international knowledge essential to the field. While the course has since been officially discontinued, in part due to mobilizing by Israeli activists, much of its content was incorporated into an academic program titled "Import, Export, and International Trade."

130 Technion Magazine, "Guns and officers: The engine of Israeli exports" [in Hebrew], November 15, 2015, technion.ac.il.

131 Ibid.

132 Ibid.

133 Ibid.

134 Rafael, "About"; Neve Gordon, "The Political Economy of Israel's Homeland Security/Surveillance Industry," Surveillance Studies Centre, Queen's University, New Transparency Project Working Paper III, 2009; Stephen Graham, *Cities Under Siege: The New Military Urbanism* (New York: Verso, 2010).

4. Epistemic Occupation

1 "An Israeli lecturer in the USA: Israel conducts weapons tests—on Palestinian children" [in Hebrew], *Mako*, February 17, 2019, mako.co.il.

2 Ibid.

3 Just a few weeks after Shalhoub-Kevorkian presented her criminological research at a panel in 2021, clips from her presentation once again made the national news in Israel. A letter of complaint was sent to Minister of Education Yifat Shasha-Biton, whose response was cutting and swift. "I denounce the blasphemous words of the lecturer against the state of Israel," she said in a statement, announcing that she has called for Hebrew University to open a disciplinary proceeding against Shalhoub-Kevorkian. Hebrew University joined in on the condemnations, issuing a statement that it "disavows the words said by Professor Nadera Shalhoub-Kevorkian." Channel 13, "Chapter six" [in Hebrew], July 8, 2021, 13tv.co.il.

4 See, for example, Nadera Shalhoub-Kevorkian and Shahrazad Odeh, "Arrested Childhood in Spaces of Indifference: The Criminalized Children of Occupied East Jerusalem," *Canadian Journal of Women and the Law* 30, no. 3 (December 1, 2018): 398–422; Nadera Shalhoub-Kevorkian, "The Occupation of the Senses: The Prosthetic and Aesthetic of State Terror," *British Journal of Criminology* 67 no. 6 (November 2017): 1279–3000; Nadera Shalhoub-Kevorkian, "Gun to Body: Mental Health against Unchilding," *International Journal of Applied Psychoanalytic Studies* 17, no. 2 (June 2020): 126–45.

5 Nadera Shalhoub-Kevorkian, "Indigenizing Feminist Knowledge: Palestinian Feminist Thought Between the Physics of International Power and the Theology of Racist 'Security,'" in *Arab Feminisms: Gender and Equality in the Middle East*, ed. Jean Said Makdisi, Noha Bayoumi, and Rafif Rida Sidawi (London: I. B. Tauris, 2014), 205–16.

6 Amnesty International, "Israel's Apartheid Against Palestinians: Cruel System of Domination and Crime Against Humanity," February 1, 2022, amnesty.org; Human Rights Watch, "A Threshold Crossed: Israeli Authorities and the Crimes of Apartheid and Persecution," April 27, 2021, hrw.org; Eyal Hareuveni, "This Is Jerusalem: Violence and Dispossession in al 'Esawiyah," B'Tselem, May 2020, btselem.org; Yael Stein, "Unprotected: Detention of Palestinian Minors in East Jerusalem," B'Tselem, October 2017, btselem.org.

7 Rafael, "About" [in Hebrew], rafael.co.il; Neve Gordon, "The Political Economy of Israel's Homeland Security/Surveillance Industry," Surveillance Studies

Centre, Queen's University, New Transparency Project Working Paper III, 2009; Tariq Dana, "A Cruel Innovation: Israeli Experiments on Gaza's Great March of Return," *Sociology of Islam* 8, no. 2 (May 1, 2020): 175–98; Erella Grassiani, "Commercialised Occupation Skills: Israeli Security Experience as an International Brand," in *Security/Mobility: Politics of Movement*, ed. M. Leese and S. Wittendorp (Manchester: Manchester University Press, 2017), 57–73; Stephen Graham, *Cities Under Siege: The New Military Urbanism* (New York: Verso, 2010).

8 Lana Tatour, "Citizenship as Domination: Settler Colonialism and the Making of Palestinian Citizenship in Israel," *Arab Studies Journal* 27 no. 2, (2019): 8–39.

9 Ibid.; Areej Sabbagh-Khoury, "Citizenship as Accumulation by Dispossession: The Paradox of Settler Colonial Citizenship," *Sociological Theory* 40, no. 2 (June 2022): 151–78; Nadim N. Rouhana, "Introduction," in *Israel and Its Palestinian Citizens: Ethnic Privileges in the Jewish State*, ed. Nadim N. Rouhana (Cambridge University Press, 2017); Nadim N. Rouhana and Areej Sabbagh-Khoury, "Settler-Colonial Citizenship: Conceptualizing the Relationship Between Israel and Its Palestinian Citizens," *Settler Colonial Studies* 5, no. 3 (July 3, 2015): 1–21.

10 Nimer Sultany et al., "Forum," *Israel Studies Review* 27, no. 2 (January 2012): 190–200; Sabbagh-Khoury, "Citizenship as Accumulation by Dispossession."

11 Uri Ram, "The Colonization Perspective in Israeli Sociology: Internal and External Comparisons," *Journal of Historical Sociology* 6, no. 3 (September 1993): 327–50; Areej Sabbagh-Khoury, "Tracing Settler Colonialism: A Genealogy of a Paradigm in the Sociology of Knowledge Production in Israel," *Politics and Society* 50, no. 1 (March 2022): 44–83.

12 Sabbagh-Khoury, "Tracing Settler Colonialism."

13 See, for example, Yael Berda, *Living Emergency: Israel's Permit Regime in the Occupied West Bank* (Stanford, CA: Stanford University Press, 2018); Anat Matar, *The Poverty of Ethics* (London: Verso, 2022); Haim Yacobi, *The Jewish-Arab City: Spatio-Politics in a Mixed Community*, Routledge Studies on the Arab-Israeli Conflict 5 (London: Routledge, 2009); Hillel Cohen, *The Israeli Security Agencies and the Israeli Arabs, 1948–1967* (Berkeley: University of California Press, 2011); Yehouda Shenhav, *Beyond the Two-State Solution: A Jewish Political Essay* (Cambridge, UK: Polity Press, 2012); Gadi Algazi, "Matrix in Bil'in: A story about colonialist capitalism in today's Israel" [in Hebrew], *Theory and Criticism* 29 (Spring 2006): 173–91; Eilat Maoz, *Living law: Police and sovereignty in an occupation regime* [in Hebrew] (Jerusalem and Tel Aviv: Van Leer Press and Hakibbutz Hameuhad, 2020); among others.

14 This is evident not only in the research produced in these departments and the harassment of critical scholars but also in the scholars permitted entry. These social science and humanities departments often have no more Palestinian scholars than their disciplinarily and politically conservative counterparts. Many of them have only one or two Palestinian faculty members on the tenure track, and some have none at all. While some of these departments have slightly more Mizrahi representation among their permanent faculty, others have marginal or no such representation. See, for instance, the departments of sociology and anthropology at Hebrew University and Tel Aviv University and the departments of gender studies at Bar-Ilan University and Tel Aviv University.

15 Ari Shavit, "Waiting for the barbarians" [in Hebrew], *Ha'aretz*, January 5, 2004.

16 Ilan Pappé, "Fifty Years Through the Eyes of 'New Historians' in Israel," *Middle*

East Report, 207 (1998): 14–23; Avi Shlaim, "The War of the Israeli Historians," *Annales* 59, no.1 (2004): 161–7.

17 Avi Shaim, "Quick Thoughts: Avi Shlaim on Israel's New Historians, Hamas, and the BDS Movement," *Jadaliyya*, October 23, 2017.

18 Pappé, "Fifty Years Through the Eyes of 'New Historians.'"

19 Ilan Pappé, *The Making of the Arab-Israeli Conflict 1947–1951* (London: Tauris, 1992); Benny Morris, *The Birth of the Palestinian Refugee Problem, 1947–1949* (Cambridge, UK: Cambridge University Press, 1998); Avi Shlaim, *Collusion across the Jordan: King Abdullah, the Zionist Movement, and the Partition of Palestine* (New York: Columbia University Press, 1988).

20 Ibid.; Shlaim, "The War of the Israeli Historians." See, for example, Nur Masalha, *Expulsion of the Palestinians: The Concept of "Transfer" in Zionist Political Thought, 1882–1948* (Washington, DC: Institute for Palestine Studies, 1992).

21 Ilan Pappé, "The new history of the 1948 war" [in Hebrew], *Theory and Criticism*, no. 3 (1993): 99–114.

22 As Pappé shows, this approach is exemplified by prominent historian Israel Kolet, who openly called for the preservation of an Israeli historiography that would use the past to serve present needs and for the adoption of a "particularist Zionist historiography." It is also exemplified in the ahistorical terminology used by Israeli historians, such as *halutziut* (pioneering) and *aliya* (Jewish immigration), among others, that are both ideologically Zionist and particularistic to Israeli use. Ibid., 104.

23 Ilan Greilsammer, "The New Historians of Israel and Their Political Involvement," *Bulletin du Centre de recherche français à Jérusalem* 23 (2012): 1–9.

24 Ibid.; Jonathan Tepperman, "An Israeli Who Got Everybody Outraged," *New York Times*, April 17, 2004; Neil Caplan, "The 'New Historians,'" review of *The Making of the Arab-Israeli Conflict, 1947–1951* by Ilan Pappé, and *Israel's Border Wars, 1949–1956: Arab Infiltration, Israel Retaliation, and the Countdown to the Suez War* by Benny Morris, *Journal of Palestine Studies* 24, no. 4 (July 1995): 96–103.

25 Shavit, "Waiting for the barbarians."

26 Ibid.

27 Ari Shavit, "Survival of the Fittest," *Ha'aretz*, January 8, 2004.

28 Ilan Pappé, "An Indicative Archive: Salvaging Nakba Documents," *Journal of Palestine Studies* 49, no. 3 (Spring 2020): 22–40; Akevot, "Silencing: Malmab activities to classify archival documents" [in Hebrew], July 2019, akevot.org.il.

29 Knesset Science and Technology Committee, "Making historical archival materials accessible to researchers and the general public" [in Hebrew], protocol no. 12, May 15, 2023, knesset.gov.il.

30 Hagar Shezaf, "Burying the Nakba: How Israel Systematically Hides Evidence of 1948 Expulsion of Arabs," *Ha'aretz*, July 5, 2019.

31 Pappé, "Fifty Years Through the Eyes of 'New Historians.'"

32 See Walid Khalidi, ed., *All That Remains: The Palestinian Villages Occupied and Depopulated by Israel in 1948* (Washington, DC: Institute for Palestine Studies, 1992); Mustafa al-Wali, "The Tantura Massacre, 22–23 May 1948," *Journal of Palestine Studies* 30, no. 3 (Spring 2001): 5–18; Elias Shoufani, "The Tantura massacre within the historical context of the Judaization of Palestine" [in Arabic], *Majallat al-Dirasat al-Filastiniyya* 43 (Summer 2000): 101–17.

33 Ilan Pappé, *Out of the Frame: The Struggle for Academic Freedom in Israel* (London: Pluto Press, 2010).

34 Ilan Pappé, "The Tantura Case in Israel: The Katz Research and Trial," *Journal of Palestine Studies* 30, no. 3 (Spring 2001): 19–39; see more at Zochrot, "Al Tantura," zochrot.org.

35 Salman Abu Sitta and Terry Rempel, "The ICRC and the Detention of Palestinian Civilians in Israel's 1948 POW/Labor Camps," *Journal of Palestine Studies* 43, no. 4 (Summer 2014): 11–38.

36 Ibid.

37 Khalidi, *All That Remains*; al-Wali, "The Tantura Massacre"; Elias Shoufani, "The Tantura massacre within the historical context."

38 Pappé, *Out of the Frame*; Pappé, "The Tantura Case in Israel."

39 Ilan Pappé, "The Katz and Tantura affair: History, historiography, law and academia" [in Hebrew], *Theory and Criticism* 20 (2002): 191–218; Pappé, *Out of the Frame*.

40 The journalist interviewed Palestinians from the villages, faculty at the university of Haifa, and members of the Alexandroni brigade. Palestinians confirmed the massacre, and even some faculty at the university affirmed that it was a war crime. Pappé, "The Katz and Tantura affair."

41 Rana Barakat, "How to Read a Massacre in Palestine: Indigenous History as a Methodology of Liberation," *AlMuntaqa* 5, no. 2 (September/October 2022), 29.

42 Ibid.; Pappé, *Out of the Frame*; see also Pappé, "The Tantura Case in Israel."

43 Ibid.

44 *Tantura*, directed by Alon Schwarz (Israel: Reel Peak Films, 2022).

45 Tom Segev, "Ilan Pappé in the sights" [in Hebrew], *Ha'aretz*, May 23, 2002; David Ratner, "Historian who supported Teddy Katz will not be terminated" [in Hebrew], *Ha'aretz*, May 21, 2002; Pappé, *Out of the Frame*, 92; Lizette Alvarez, "Professors in Britain Vote to Boycott 2 Israeli Schools," *New York Times*, May 8, 2005.

46 Ben-dror Yemini, "The theory of stages" [in Hebrew], *NRG*, April 28, 2005; Ariana Melamed, "We will fight about history" [in Hebrew], Ynet, November 23, 2007.

47 Schwarz, *Tantura*.

48 Gur Alroey, "Theodore Katz's thesis: The academic point of view" [in Hebrew], University of Haifa Rector's Office, June 7, 2022.

49 Barakat, "How to Read a Massacre."

50 Ibid.; Khalidi, *All That Remains*; al-Wali, "The Tantura Massacre"; Shoufani, "The Tantura massacre within the historical context."

51 Im Tirtzu, "About us" [in Hebrew], imti.org.il.

52 This is in reference to the Theodore Herzl quote concerning the formation of the state of Israel, "If you will it, it is no dream."

53 It was created in 2006 as a nonparliamentary arm of the Likud party, at the time vying for a return to power. Following an introduction made by Benjamin Netanyahu himself, Im Tirtzu was funded by US evangelical Christian donors and maintained close ties to Likud officials after the party formed a new government in 2009. Raviv Drucker, "Exposed: The document that 'Im Tirtzu' wrote to Netanyahu in 2007—this is how we will lead to Olmert's resignation" [in Hebrew], *Drucker10*, April 25, 2017; Shahar Shay, "The auditor will examine:

'Forbidden connection between "Im Tirtzu" and the Likud on the eve of the 2015 elections'" [in Hebrew], Ynet, October 10, 2018. The founder of Im Tirtzu went on to work as Prime Minister Netanyahu's speechwriter and served as advisor and spokesperson for Likud headquarters: Tal Schneider, "Im Tirtzu gets to the Likud" [in Hebrew], *N12*, January 6, 2015; Erez Tadmor, "As some of you already know, yesterday I assumed the position of consultant and spokes-man for the Likud's *hasbara* headquarters. I promise to act to the best of . . ." [in Hebrew], Twitter, January 22, 2019.

54 Im Tirtzu, "The academic department" [in Hebrew], imti.org.il.

55 Im Tirtzu, "Incitement, exclusion, and anti-Zionist bias in universities" [in Hebrew], May 2010, imti.org.il. This happened after 2008, when the Institute for Zionist Strategies published a report on the approach to Zionism across Israeli universities: Neve Gordon, "An Assault on Israeli Academic Freedom—and Liberal Values," *Chronicle of Higher Education*, August 26, 2010. The report, which claimed syllabi disproportionately assigned texts critical of Zionism and scholars who theorized nationalism as a modern construct, was submitted to Israel's president for review.

56 Im Tirtzu, "Incitement, exclusion, and anti-Zionist bias."

57 Talila Nesher, "This is how the Council for Higher Education adopted the conclusions of 'Im Tirtzu'" [in Hebrew], *Ha'aretz*, December 2, 2011.

58 Ibid.

59 Im Tirtzu claimed that there remained an anti-Zionist bias in the syllabi and that tenured faculty members are associated with the "radical left": Im Tirtzu, "Politicization at Ben-Gurion University" [in Hebrew], November 2011, imti .org.il; Communist Party of Israel, "The minister of education wants to fire a lecturer from Ben-Gurion University" [in Hebrew], October 20, 2012, maki .org.

60 Or Kashti, "'Im Tirtzu' movement to Ben-Gurion University: Fire left-wing lecturers or we will drive away donors" [in Hebrew], *Ha'aretz*, August 17, 2010.

61 Nesher, "How the Council for Higher Education."

62 See, among others, Gordon, "An Assault on Israeli Academic Freedom."

63 Committee for the Evaluation of Political Science and International Relations Programs, *Ben-Gurion University Department of Politics and Government Evaluation Report* (Council for Higher Education, September 2011), che.org.il. After the international committee charged with assessing the political science departments at Israeli universities was assembled, its composition was altered, replacing Professor Ian Lustick—suspected of leftist affiliations—with Professor Abraham Diskin, formerly of the Institute for Zionist Strategies, which was responsible for the first 2008 report on the department and has close ties to Im Tirtzu. Nesher, "How the Council for Higher Education"; Or Kashti, "Right-wing groups join forces to fight 'anti-Zionist Bias' in Israeli academia" [in Hebrew], *Ha'aretz*, August 10, 2010.

64 In 2002, the CHE authorized the department's organization as an interdiscipli-nary unit. However, the report criticized this interdisciplinary focus and demanded that the department "corrects its current weaknesses in its core disci-pline of political science in terms of number of faculty, curriculum, and research." One committee member, Professor Galia Golan, claimed that some of the committee members tried to fail the department. Committee for the Evaluation of Political Science, *Ben-Gurion University Department of Politics*

and Government Evaluation Report; Nesher, "How the Council for Higher Education."

65 Council for Higher Education, "The recommendation of the sub-committee for quality assurance dated 9/12/4 regarding the implementation of the evaluation committee's recommendations" [in Hebrew], September 5, 2012, math .haifa.ac.il. This was despite the department taking steps to meet recommendations, including hiring of faculty representing additional methodological approaches and making changes to the academic program. Adi Ofir, "Critical moment for the future of higher education" [in Hebrew], *Haokets*, September 21, 2012.

66 Michal Reshef, "The Department of Administration in Ben-Gurion will get another chance" [in Hebrew], *Walla*, October 30, 2010. The CHE initially gave the university three weeks to present a plan to implement the committee's recommendations. Council For Higher Education, "The Council for Higher Education: 'Ben-Gurion University must present within three weeks a commitment to correct the deficiencies as presented by the chairman of the international committee'" [in Hebrew], October 30, 2012, che.org.il.

67 "APSA to the CHE: No Action Should Be Taken That Would Compromise Freedom of Inquiry and Teaching," *Israeli Academia Under Attack* (blog), October 4, 2012, isacademyunderattack.wordpress.com. The Association of American Geographers, the American Sociological Association, the Association for Israel Studies, and the Middle East Studies Association of North America also issued statements, posted on the same blog: "Letter from the Association of American Geographers," September 22, 2012; "American Sociological Association: Recommendation Based on Political Disagreements Rather than Academic Quality," October 6, 2012; "MESA to the Minister of Education: The Recommendation Has Little to Do with Academic Matters," September 25, 2012.

68 Oren Ziv, "An internal investigation in 'Hebrew University': The soldier was not attacked, the lecturer was not reprimanded" [in Hebrew], *Local Call*, January 8, 2019.

69 Oren Ziv, "The soldier who the professor 'humiliated' was previously an outstanding activist with 'Im Tirtzu'" [in Hebrew], *Local Call*, January 6, 2019; Haggai Matar, "The lecturer is right: There is a difference between soldiers and civilians" [in Hebrew], *Local Call*, January 7, 2019.

70 Inbar Twizer, "A lecturer at the Hebrew University in a confrontation with a soldier: 'You came in uniform, you will be treated accordingly'" [in Hebrew], Ynet, January 2, 2019.

71 Noam Dvir and Hanan Greenwood, "Students demand: Fire the professor that reprimanded the soldier" [in Hebrew], *Israel Hayom*, January 13, 2019.

72 Shira Kadari-Ovadia, "The Hebrew University apologized for the 'unusual incident' between the lecturer and a student in uniform" [in Hebrew], *Ha'aretz*, January 7, 2019.

73 Ziv, "An internal investigation in 'Hebrew University'"; Shira Kadari-Ovadia, "A lecturer at the Hebrew University is under threats following a false publication about reprimanding a female soldier in uniform" [in Hebrew], *Ha'aretz*, January 6, 2019.

74 Concerned faculty members from Hebrew University and from Academia for Equality published statements criticizing the Hebrew University administration for failing to uphold its commitment to Professor Hilfrich's and all students and

faculty's freedom of expression in the face of incitement and persecution by Im Tirtzu. David Enoch, "As a faculty member, I no longer trust the management of the Hebrew University" [in Hebrew], *Mekomit*, January 7, 2019; Academy for Equality, "Letter to Professor Asher Cohen, Hebrew University President and Professor Barak Medina, Hebrew University Rector" [in Hebrew], January 6, 2019.

75 In response to criticism about including an explicitly political movement as a social welfare organization, the university stated that Im Tirtzu is not affiliated with a political party and met the requirements of an organization promoting social change. The university let credits stand through the end of 2020. Shira Kadari-Ovadia, "The Hebrew University will award academic credits for volunteering with 'Im Tirtzu'" [in Hebrew], *Ha'aretz*, February 13, 2020.

76 Im Tirtzu, "Know the Israel hater" [in Hebrew], imti.org.il. Im Tirtzu's criteria for inclusion on the list include demonstrated direct or indirect support for the BDS movement, support for conscientious objection in Israel, participation in protest or activist activity critical of Israeli policy in the Occupied Palestinian Territory, "disrespecting state symbols," or engaging in leftist political activity on campus. Shira Kadari-Ovadia, "'Im Tirtzu' put up a website with contact details of lecturers with left-wing opinions" [in Hebrew], *Ha'aretz*, May 13, 2019.

77 Kadari-Ovadia, "'Im Tirtzu' put up a website."

78 For more on Kasher and the Israeli military's ethical code, see chapter 2.

79 Yarden Skop, "The full code of ethics for the academy: Do not deviate from the syllabus, political expression is an abuse of authority" [in Hebrew], *Ha'aretz*, June 9, 2017.

80 Ibid.

81 Im Tirtzu, "The 'Im Tirtzu' movement in response to the promotion of the ethical code in academia" [in Hebrew], imti.org. Joining their praise, "The Israelis" student movement affiliated with the far-right party Yamina started a petition in support of the ethical code. Shlomo Pyutrekovsky, "Students: The ethics code is meant to protect us" [in Hebrew], *Arutz Sheva*, June 12, 2017.

82 Some faculty questioned the code's definition of what is deemed "political" and therefore impermissible and pointed to the code's rendering Israel's occupation and Palestinian self-determination taboo. Sharon Luzon, "Welcome to Asa Kasher's course: An introduction to the Erdoğanization of Israel" [in Hebrew], *Local Call*, June 12, 2017.

83 Omri Zerachovitz, "The Council for Higher Education formulated an abbreviated code of ethics for the university; it shelved the Asa Kasher version" [in Hebrew], *Globes*, March 25, 2018; Adir Yanko, "The heads of the universities: The code of ethics—silencing" [in Hebrew], Ynet, March 25, 2018.

84 Zerachovitz, "The Council for Higher Education formulated"; Council for Higher Education, "Public statement of principles regarding proper conduct in institutions of higher education in the areas of overlap between academic activity and political activity" (Ethical code for the academy) [in Hebrew], May 29, 2018, che.org.il.

85 While the language of the last four prohibitions appears neutral, the context in which the principles were adopted and the fact that they follow the first prohibition of calling for a boycott leave little doubt as to what the CHE has designated as prohibitively "partisan" and which types of student "political views" faculty

cannot critique. Council for Higher Education, "Public statement of principles"; Zerachovitz, "The Council for Higher Education formulated."

86 Nadim N. Rouhana, "Decolonization as Reconciliation: Rethinking the National Conflict Paradigm in the Israeli-Palestinian Conflict," *Ethnic and Racial Studies* 41, no. 4 (March 16, 2018): 643–62; Tatour, "Citizenship as Domination"; Sabbagh-Khoury, "Citizenship as Accumulation by Dispossession."

87 Rouhana and Sabbagh-Khoury, "Settler-Colonial Citizenship."

88 Ibid., 13–14.

89 Association of Civil Rights in Israel, "The 'Nakba law'" [in Hebrew], May 5, 2011, acri.org.il.

90 Erez Tadmor and Erel Segal, *Nakba-Nonsense: The Booklet That Fights for the Truth* (Im Tirtzu, 2011), imti.org.il.

91 See chapter 5.

92 See, for example, Fayez Sayegh, *Zionist Colonialism in Palestine* (Beirut: Research Center, Palestine Liberation Organization, 1965).

93 Sabbagh-Khoury, "Tracing Settler Colonialism."

94 Ibid.

95 Sabbagh-Khoury, "Citizenship as Accumulation by Dispossession."

96 Khaled Jamal Furani, introduction to *Inside the leviathan: Palestinian experiences in Israeli universities* [in Arabic], ed. Khaled Jamal Furani and Yara Sa'di-Ibraheem (Jerusalem and Haifa: Van Leer Institute Press and Dar Laila, 2022), 5.

97 Ibid., 6.

98 Ayman Agbaria, "To be a Palestinian researcher at the Israeli university" [in Arabic], Fusha, December 15, 2017.

99 Sarab Abu-Rabia-Queder, "Epistemology of Surveillance: Revealing Unmarked Forms of Discipline and Punishment in Israeli Academia," *British Journal of Sociology* 73, no. 2 (March 2022): 387–401.

100 Agbaria, "To be a Palestinian researcher."

101 Abu-Rabia-Queder, "Epistemology of Surveillance."

102 Agbaria, "To be a Palestinian researcher."

103 Abu-Rabia-Queder, "Epistemology of Surveillance," 3.

104 Ibid., 9.

105 Ibid.

106 Ibid., 9.

107 Ibid.

108 Sarab Abu-Rabia-Queder, "The Dissipation of the Green Line in Palestinian Women's Research in Israel: Production of Ethical Knowledge and Research Justice," in *70 Years of Nakbah*, ed. Mohanad Mustafa (Haifa: Mada Al-Carmel, 2018), 23.

109 Ibid., 20.

110 Abu-Rabia-Queder, "Epistemology of Surveillance."

111 Abu-Rabia-Queder, "The Dissipation of the Green Line," 20.

112 Shalhoub-Kevorkian, "Indigenizing Feminist Knowledge."

113 Ibid.; Nadera Shalhoub-Kevorkian, "Palestinian Women and the Politics of Invisibility: Towards a Feminist Methodology," *Peace Prints: South Asian Journal of Peacebuilding* 3, no. 1 (Spring 2010).

114 Abu-Rabia-Queder, "Epistemology of Surveillance."

115 Central Bureau of Statistics, "Press release: Academic staff in higher education institutions in Israel, 2001/02–2021/22" [in Hebrew], June 27, 2022, cbs.gov.il.

116 Abu-Rabia-Queder, "Epistemology of Surveillance."
117 Furani, introduction to *Inside the leviathan*; Khalid Arar and Kussai Haj-Yehia, *Higher Education and the Palestinian Arab Minority in Israel* (Basingstoke, UK: Palgrave Macmillan, 2016).
118 Mada al-Carmel, "About Us," mada-research.org.
119 Mada al-Carmel, "Graduate Student Support Program," mada-research.org.
120 Furani, introduction to *Inside the leviathan*.
121 Ibid., 4.
122 Agbaria, "To be a Palestinian researcher"; Furani, introduction to *Inside the leviathan*.
123 Furani, introduction to *Inside the leviathan*.
124 Agbaria, "To be a Palestinian researcher."
125 Mada al-Carmel, "The Haifa Declaration," May 15, 2007, mada-research.org.
126 Ibid., 7.
127 Ibid., 8.
128 Edward W. Said, "Zionism from the Standpoint of Its Victims," *Social Text* 1 (1979): 7–58.
129 Ella Shohat, "Sephardim in Israel: Zionism from the Standpoint of Its Jewish Victims," *Social Text* 19/20 (1988): 1–35.
130 Ella Shohat, "The Invention of the Mizrahim," *Journal of Palestine Studies* 29, no. 1 (October 1999): 5–20.
131 Hanan Hever and Yehouda Shenhav, "The Arab Jews: The evolution of a concept" [in Hebrew], *Pe'amim: Studies in Oriental Jewry* 125–6 (2009), 4.
132 Ella Shohat, "Arab-Jews, Diaspora, and the Multicultural Feminism: An Interview with Ella Shohat by Evelyn Alsultany," in *Arab and Arab American Feminisms: Gender, Violence and Belonging*, ed. Rabab Abdulhadi, Nadine Naber, and Evelyn Alsultany (Syracuse, NY: Syracuse University Press, 2011), 46–59; Ella Shohat, *On the Arab-Jew, Palestine, and Other Displacements: Selected Writings of Ella Shohat* (London: Pluto Press, 2017).
133 Ella Habiba Shohat, "A Voyage to Toledo: Twenty-Five Years after the 'Jews of the Orient and Palestinians' Meeting," *Jadaliyya*, September 30, 2019; Shohat, "Arab-Jews, Diaspora, and the Multicultural Feminism."
134 Hever and Shenhav, "The Arab Jews," 6.
135 Yehouda Shenhav, *The Arab Jews: A Postcolonial Reading of Nationalism, Religion, and Ethnicity*, Cultural Sitings (Stanford, CA: Stanford University Press, 2006), 9.
136 Lital Levy, "Who is an Arab Jew? A comparative inquiry into the origins of the question, 1880–2008" [in Hebrew], *Theory and Criticism* 38–39 (Winter 2011): 101–35.
137 Tammy Riklis and Yonit Naaman, "The 'good' Mizrahim are not the problem" [in Hebrew], *Haokets*, November 7, 2015.
138 Bryan Roby, *The Mizrahi Era of Rebellion: Israel's Forgotten Civil Rights Struggle, 1948–1966* (Syracuse, NY: Syracuse University Press, 2015); Shlomo Swirski, *Orientals and Ashkenazim in Israel: The ethnic division of labor* [in Hebrew] (Tel Aviv: Segel Press, 1981); Ishak Saporta and Yossi Yonah, "Pre-vocational Education: The Making of Israel's Ethno-Working Class," *Race, Ethnicity and Education* 7, no. 3 (September 2004): 251–75; Moshe Lissak, *Mass immigration in the fifties: The failure of the melting pot policy* [in Hebrew] (Jerusalem: Bialik Institute, 1999).

139 Swirski, *Orientals and Ashkenazim in Israel*; Saporta and Yonah, "Pre-voca-
     tional Education."
140 Ibid.
141 Roby, *Mizrahi Era of Rebellion*.
142 Ibid.; Uri Cohen, *The mountain and the hill: The Hebrew university in Jerusalem
     during the pre-independence period and early years of the state of Israel* [in
     Hebrew] (Tel Aviv: Am Oved, 2006), 282.
143 While serving as head of the CHE Planning and Budgeting Committee in 2016,
     Tel Aviv University law professor Yaffa Zilbershats rejected the request to collect
     data on Mizrahi representation in higher education. "Enough with this," she
     dismissed the issue, claiming that ethnic definitions are "sterile" and inequality
     is no longer a problem. Rotem Shtarkman and Liorr Detel, "The Hebrew
     University has assets of 4 billion shekels. Their behavior hurts the students" [in
     Hebrew], *TheMarker*, October 29, 2016, themarker.com.
144 Nofar Moshe, "The Central Bureau of Statistics does not count the Mizrahim"
     [in Hebrew], *Kan*, August 4, 2017. After sustained pressure by grassroots
     campaigns, in 2022 the Israeli Bureau of Statistics announced it would add
     questions to track ethnicity within the Jewish population. Dr. Sigal Nagar-Ron,
     "Third-generation Mizrahim? From now on you're counted" [in Hebrew], Ynet,
     August 25, 2022, ynet.co.il. For an analysis of Israeli census policy and state
     racialization, see Sigal Nagar-Ron, "National statistics, ethnic categorization
     and measurement of inequality in Israel" [in Hebrew], *Israeli Sociology* 22
     (2021): 6–30.
145 Nagar-Ron, "National statistics."
146 The Bureau of Statistics found that students who grew up in cities and towns
     with medium or higher average income were significantly more likely to attend
     university and obtain graduate degrees than those in Israel's periphery with
     lower incomes. Lower-income students from Israel's development towns, origi-
     nally housing Mizrahi communities and currently immigrants from the former
     USSR and Ethiopia as well, attend local colleges in higher numbers than they do
     any of Israel's central universities. Yehouda Shohat and Moshe Schonfeld,
     "Double chance for a bachelor's degree: The educational gaps between students
     from the center and the periphery" [in Hebrew], Ynet, October 30, 2016, ynet
     .co.il. Among second-generation Jewish-Israeli citizens, Ashkenazim are nearly
     twice as likely to have a degree as their Mizrahi peers, and third-generation
     Ashkenazi Israelis remain 1.5 times more likely to obtain a degree as their
     Mizrahi peers. Or Kashti, "Even after a generation in the country: The ethnic
     racial gap in higher education continues" [in Hebrew], *Ha'aretz*, November 6,
     2015; Shahar Ilan, "Third generation for the ethnic demon: Ashkenazim have
     1.5 times more degrees than Mizrahim" [in Hebrew], *Calcalist*, February 19,
     2019; Yinon Cohen, Yitchak Haberfeld, and Tali Kristal, "Ethnicity and mixed
     ethnicity: Educational gaps among Israeli-born Jews," in *A view from below:
     Practices of difference in Israeli education* [in Hebrew], ed. Yossi Yonah, Nissim
     Mizrahi, and Yariv Feniger (Jerusalem: Van Leer Jerusalem Institute and
     Hakibbutz Hameuchad, 2013). A Bureau of Statistics study found that 28.8
     percent of Mizrahim versus 49.6 percent of Ashkenazim had university degrees,
     and the Tel Aviv University study found that between 41 percent and 48 percent
     of Ashkenazi adults had degrees, while only 17 percent of Mizrahim did.
     Another study found that 56.4 percent of third-generation Ashkenazim have a

degree versus 36 percent of Mizrahim: Yinon Cohen, Noah Lewin-Epstein, and Amit Lazarus, "Mizrahi-Ashkenazi Educational Gaps in the Third Generation," *Research in Social Stratification and Mobility* 59 (February 2019): 25–33; Riklis and Naaman, "The 'good' Mizrahim."

147 Israel Blechman, "Research report: On the ethnic composition of research universities in Israel" [in Hebrew], *Theory and Criticism* 33 (Fall 2008): 191–7; Riklis and Naaman, "The 'good' Mizrahim." This also holds true for Israeli colleges, even those based in the Israeli "periphery" and intended to serve local Mizrahi communities. Moti Gigi, Einat Yehuda, and Sigal Nagar-Ron, "Shades in the academy: National, ethnic, gender and spatial diversity among faculty and students at Sapir academic college" [in Hebrew], 2020. sapir.ac.il.

148 Tammy Riklis and Yonit Naaman, "'Defining yourself as Mizrahi was suicide': The story of Mizrahi expatriates" [in Hebrew], *Haokets*, June 23, 2020; Calanit Tsalach, "So what happened? Auto-ethnography of macroaggressions due to ethnicity" [in Hebrew], *Theory and Criticism* 46 (Summer 2016): 67–90; Yali Hashash, *Who's daughter are you? Ways of speaking Mizrahi feminism* [in Hebrew] (Tel Aviv: HaKibbutz Hameuhad, 2022); Iris Zarini, "Academic periphery, social periphery: Mizrahi women professors in Israel," in *For my sister: Mizrahi feminist politics* [in Hebrew], ed. Shlomit Leer (Tel Aviv: Babel, 2007), 143–51; Henriette Dahan Kalev, "You are so beautiful, you don't look Moroccan," in *Teachers in Israel: A feminist perspective* [in Hebrew], ed. Michal Zellermayer and Pnina Peri (Tel Aviv: Hakibbutz Hameuchad, 2002), 174–86; Itzhak Benyamini, "Persian" [in Hebrew], *Theory and Criticism* 32 (Spring 2008): 171–4.

149 Noa Borstein Hadad, "Serious allegations about the lack of diversity in the gender department in Tel Aviv led to the resignation of a lecturer" [in Hebrew], *Politically Corret*, January 16, 2019, politicallycorret.co.il.

150 Hashash, *Who's daughter are you?*. Hashash herself resigned in protest from the Tel Aviv University Gender Studies Program in 2019, following what she and a number of her students described as the persistent absence of institutional support for Mizrahi feminist thought in tenure lines and course offerings. Borstein Hadad, "Serious allegations about the lack of diversity."

151 Pnina Mutzafi-Heller, "You have an authentic voice: Anthropological research and politics of representation outside and within the researched community" [in Hebrew], *Theory and Criticism* 11 (Winter 1997): 81–98; Tsalach, "So what happened?"; Sigal Nagar-Ron, "Orientalism, southern epistemology and 'ethnic blindness' in Israeli academia" [in Hebrew], *HaKivun Mizrah* 38 (2020): 127–39; Smadar Lavie, "Cultural property rights and the racial construction of the Mizrahi as a trademark: Notes on the revolving door of Israel's academe-regime" [in Hebrew], *Mahbarot Kolno'a Darom* [South cinema notebooks] 2 (2007): 161–6.

152 Ella Shohat, *Taboo Memories, Diasporic Voices* (Durham, NC: Duke University Press, 2006).

153 Biton Commission, "Biton Commission report to strengthen the heritage of the Sephardic and the Eastern Jewry in the education system" [in Hebrew], June 29, 2016, education.gov.il; Shirit Avitan Cohen, "History at CHE: For the first time, the field of Judaism in Spain and the Islamic countries was recognized as an academic discipline" [in Hebrew], *Globes*, February 2, 2022. This declarative decision follows decades of advocacy by Mizrahi scholars to recognize Mizrahi Studies as a field and has yet to be translated into an actionable plan with

tangible financial and institutional support. But in principle, universities can now create dedicated academic tracks for Sephardi and Middle Eastern Jewish studies. Shohat, "Invention of the Mizrahim"; Or Kashti, "The Council for Higher Education recognized Jewish studies in Spain and the Middle East as an independent academic field" [in Hebrew], *Ha'aretz*, February 22, 2022.

154 Biton Commission, "Biton Commission Report."

155 See exceptions of this in Yali Hashash, "We're all Jews: On 'white trash,' Mizrahim, and intersectionality within the hegemony" [in Hebrew], *Theory and Criticism* 48 (Summer 2017): 249–64; Smadar Sharon, *How to occupy a homeland: The planning and settlement of Hevel Lakhish in the 1950s* [in Hebrew] (Haifa: Pardes, 2018). See also Sabbagh-Khoury, "Tracing Settler Colonialism"; Algazi, "Matrix in Bil'in."

156 Lana Tatour, "The Israeli Left: Part of the Problem or the Solution? A Response to Giulia Daniele," *Global Discourse* 6, no. 3 (July 2016): 487–92.

157 For more on this, see Sabbagh-Khoury, "Tracing Settler Colonialism"; Hashash, "We're all Jews."

158 AMRAM, "The Yeminite, Mizrahi and Balkan children affair" [in Hebrew], edut-amram.org.

159 The scale and historical details of the affair remain debated. For more on this, see Daniel Demalach, "The investigation committee misled the public" [in Hebrew], *Haokets*, September 21, 2022; Daniel Demalach, "A peep hole into the system of concealment and deception in the case of the Yemeni children" [in Hebrew], *Haokets*, April 6, 2022; Shoshana Madmoni-Gerber, *Israeli Media and the Framing of Internal Conflict: The Yemenite Babies Affair* (New York: Palgrave Macmillan, 2009); Meira Weiss, "The Children of Yemen: Bodies, Medicalization, and Nation-Building," *Medical Anthropology Quarterly* 15, no. 2 (June 2001): 206–21; Tova Gamliel and Nathan Shifriss, eds., *The children of the heart* [in Hebrew] (Tel Aviv: Resling, 2019).

160 For more on this, see Madmoni-Gerber, *Israeli Media and the Framing of Internal Conflict*; Gamliel and Shifriss, *The children of the heart*.

161 Naama Katiee, "Where is the criticism of the academy when it comes to the Yemeni children?" [in Hebrew], *Haokets*, July 6, 2017. Throughout these years of mobilization, Israeli universities have failed to facilitate or designate space or funding for research on the subject. Except for a single conference independently organized by Israeli scholars and held at Bar-Ilan in 2013, no Israeli university has agreed to house conferences on the subject or offered to fund scholarships or grants dedicated to researching the affair. Shoshana Madmoni-Gerber is one such scholar, who recounted her experience of leaving the Israeli university system in an interview: "It was clear to me that a critical work that challenges the Zionist discourse—and from a Mizrahi point of view—can only be written outside of Israel." Riklis and Naaman, "'Defining yourself as Mizrahi was suicide.'"

162 Yuval Sarel, "The involvement of health professionals in the case of the disappearance of children of Yemen, Mizrah and the Balkans" [in Hebrew], Israeli Ministry of Health, 2021.

163 Liat Kozma, "Between testimonies and medical ethics in the case of the Yemenite, Mizrahi, and Balkan children's affair" [in Hebrew], *Ha'aretz*, June 30, 2022.

164 Ibid.; Shifra Shvartz, "Evaluation of a draft report on the involvement of health professionals in the case of the 'disappearance' of children of Yemen, Mizrah, and the Balkans" [in Hebrew], December 1, 2021, knesset.gov.il.

165 Demalach, "The investigation committee"; Demalach, "A peep hole into the system"; Tom Mehager, "Where are the children and where are the MKs of Meretz?" [in Hebrew], *Haokets*, February 28, 2022; Tamar Kaplansky, "Who tampered with the assessment that was intended to bury the report in the case of the Yemeni children?" [in Hebrew], *Ha'aretz*, September 20, 2022; Hadas Ziv, "Multidisciplinary assessment: From covering up a historical injustice to building trust between the medical establishment and the affected communities" [in Hebrew], *Ha'aretz*, July 2022; Academia for Equality, "Academia for equality's statement of support for exposing the Yemenite, Mizrahi, and Balkan children affair" [in Hebrew], September 21, 2022.

166 Katiee, "Where is the criticism?" While Israeli academic journals have recently published articles by researchers that challenge testimonies of Mizrahi families and broadly back the state's denial of any systemic role in the affair, most critical scholarship continues to be published in Israeli nonacademic publications and presses or abroad. See, for example, Gamliel and Shifriss, *The children of the heart*; Madmoni-Gerber, *Israeli Media and the Framing of Internal Conflict*.

167 Knesset Science and Technology Committee, "Making historical archival materials accessible."

168 Ibid.

5. Students Under Siege

1 Ian Lustick, *Arabs in the Jewish State: Israel's Control of a National Minority* (Austin: University of Texas Press, 1980), 68.

2 Ahmad Sa'adi, *Through Surveillance: The Genesis of Israeli Policies of Population Management, Surveillance and Political Control Towards the Palestinian Minority* (Manchester: Manchester University Press, 2013).

3 Adam Raz, "The recommendations for dealing with the Arabs: 'Prevent as much as possible the formation of a broad stratum of educated people'" [in Hebrew], *Ha'aretz*, March 20, 2019.

4 Ibid.

5 Ibid.

6 Lana Tatour, "Citizenship as Domination: Settler Colonialism and the Making of Palestinian Citizenship in Israel," *Arab Studies Journal* 27 no. 2, (2019): 8–39.

7 Ibid., 14.

8 Ibid., 10. See also Nadim N. Rouhana and Areej Sabbagh-Khoury, "Settler-Colonial Citizenship: Conceptualizing the Relationship Between Israel and Its Palestinian Citizens," *Settler Colonial Studies* 5, no. 3 (July 3, 2015): 205–25.

9 Tatour, "Citizenship as Domination," 10.

10 Ismael Abu-Saad, "Palestinian Education in Israel: The Legacy of the Military Government," *Holy Land Studies* 56, no. 1 (2006): 21–56; Sa'di, *Through Surveillance*; Ibrahim Makkawi, "Community Engagement from the Margin: Zionism and the Case of the Palestinian Student Movement in the Israeli Universities," *Arab Studies Quarterly* 35, no. 2 (April 1, 2013); Lustick, *Arabs in the Jewish State*.

11 Abu-Saad, "Palestinian Education in Israel"; Saʿdi, *Through Surveillance*.
12 Ibid.; Hillel Cohen, *The Israeli Security Agencies and the Israeli Arabs, 1948–1967* (Berkeley: University of California Press, 2011).
13 Saʿdi, *Through Surveillance*.
14 Yair Bauml, *A blue and white shadow: The Israeli establishment's policy and actions among its Arab citizens: The formative years 1958–1968* [in Hebrew] (Haifa: Pardes, 2007); Yara Saʿdi, "Representations of the Spatial Experience in Mount Scopus Campus: Jerusalem in Palestinian Students' Discourse" (master's thesis, Hebrew University, 2015); Yara Saʿdi-Ibraheem, "Indigenous Students' Geographies on the Academic Fortress Campus: Palestinian Students' Spatial Experiences at the Hebrew University of Jerusalem," *Journal of Holy Land and Palestine Studies* 20, no. 2 (November 2021): 123–45.
15 Saʿdi, *Through Surveillance*.
16 Ibid.
17 Ibid.
18 Adalah, "A demand to cancel the Shabak's intervention in appointments in Arab schools" [in Hebrew], adalah.org
19 Ibid.
20 Adir Yanko, "The planner was exposed: A meeting between Shabak representatives and the director general of the Ministry of Education about the Arab students" [in Hebrew], Ynet, February 13, 2020, ynet.co.il.
21 Ibid.
22 Saʿdi, *Through Surveillance*; Bauml, *A blue and white shadow*; Hillel Cohen, *Israeli Security Agencies*.
23 Nir Hasson, "Policemen studying at Hebrew University arrested Palestinian students on the grounds that they were singing nationalist songs" [in Hebrew], *Haʾaretz*, March 28, 2022.
24 Ibid.
25 Ibid.
26 See chapter 2.
27 Diana Dolev, "Architecture, education and belligerence: A feminist view of the Hebrew University campus on Mount Scopus," in *Militarism in Education* [in Hebrew], ed. Hagit Gur (Tel Aviv: Babel, 2005); Ilan Gur-Zeev, "The 31st floor: University tower and Zionist phallocentrism" [in Hebrew], *Theory and Criticism* 16 (Spring 2000); Haim Yacobi, "Academic Fortress: The Planning of the Hebrew University Campus on Mount Scopus," in *Global Universities and Urban Development: Case Studies and Analysis*, ed. Wim Wiewel and David C. Perry (London: Routledge, 2015); Amnon Bar Or, "How the ruins of Shaykh Muwannis tie the academy and the army [in Hebrew], *Haʾaretz*, July 8, 2021.
28 Eyal Clyne, *Orientalism, Zionism, and Academic Practice: Middle East and Islam Studies in Israeli Universities* (New York: Routledge, 2019).
29 Saʿdi-Ibraheem, "Indigenous students' geographies."
30 Ibid.; Yael Maayan, "Two cases of racialized academic space" [in Hebrew], White Academy Conference, March 21, 2021.
31 Maayan, "Two cases of racialized academic space"; Clyne, *Orientalism, Zionism, and Academic Practice*.
32 Saʿadi, *Through Surveillance*.
33 Maayan, "Two cases of racialized academic space."
34 See also Saʿdi-Ibraheem, "Indigenous students' geographies."

35 Central Bureau of Statistics, "Press release: Higher education in Israel—selected data for the academic year 2018/19 on the occasion of the opening of the academic year" [in Hebrew], October 23, 2019, cbs.gov.il.

36 Shahar Ilan, "The treasury: Contrary to the claims of the budgetary and planning committee the integration of Arab students is on the decline" [in Hebrew], *Calcalist*, May 29, 2019.

37 Ibid.; Central Bureau of Statistics, "Press release: Higher education in Israel."

38 Zeev Kril and Najib Amaria, "Barriers to the integration of the Arab population in the higher education system" [in Hebrew], Israeli Ministry of Finance, 2019.

39 Ibid.

40 Ibid.

41 Council for Higher Education, "Statistical data files about higher education in Israel" [in Hebrew], che.org.il.

42 Council for Higher Education, "Accessibility of higher education to the Arab population" [in Hebrew], October 10, 2021, che.org.il; Council for Higher Education, "The 2020/21 academic school year is marked by the Corona pandemic" [in Hebrew], September 10, 2021, che.org.il.

43 Central Bureau of Statistics, "Press release: Academic staff in higher education institutions in Israel, 2001/02–2001" [in Hebrew], June 27, 2022, cbs.gov.il.

44 Nohad 'Ali and Rima'a Da'as, *Higher education among the Palestinian Arab minority in Israel: Representation, mapping, barriers and challenge* [in Hebrew] (Tel Aviv: Resling, 2018).

45 Arar and Haj-Yehia, *Higher Education and the Palestinian Arab Minority in Israel*. Human Rights Watch has shown that for decades Palestinian students have faced institutional discrimination from kindergarten through university education, and have been denied access to adequately resourced, physically accessible schools, resulting in a far higher drop-out rate than Jewish students: Human Rights Watch, "Second Class: Discrimination Against Arab Children in Israel's Schools," September 30, 2001, hwr.org. See also more recent reports by Amnesty International, the Palestinian civil rights organization Adalah and Mossawa, and Israeli organizations such as the Taub Center for Social Policy Studies: Amnesty International, "Israel's Apartheid Against Palestinians," February 2022, amnesty.org; Adalah, "Inequality Report: The Palestinian Arab Minority in Israel," February 2011, adalah.org; Mossawa Center, "Analysis of the Ministry of Education's Budget for 2016," mossawa.org; Nachum Blass et al., "Education inequality in Israel: From research to policy" [in Hebrew], Taub Center for Social Policy Studies in Israel, December 2019, taubcenter.org.il.

46 Nohad Ali, *Representation of Arab Citizens in the Institutions of Higher Education in Israel* (Haifa and Jerusalem: Sikkuy, November 2013); National Union of Israeli Students, *The psychometric exam as a tool for selection of applicants to higher education: For and against* [in Hebrew] (Tel Aviv: 2012); Arar and Haj-Yehia, *Higher Education and the Palestinian Arab Minority*; 'Ali and Da'as, *Higher education among the Palestinian Arab minority*.

47 Benny Nuriely and Liat Kozmeh, "Intersections of exclusion and inclusion: The Hebrew University School of Medicine, 1949–1970" [in Hebrew], White Academy Conference, March 21, 2021.

48 Raeli Saar, "In-demand departments were filled with Arabs and not with people from development towns—and the admissions method was changed" [in Hebrew], *Ha'aretz*, November 26, 2003.

49 Ibid.
50 Ibid.
51 For more on this, see Arar and Haj-Yehia, *Higher education and the Palestinian Arab minority*.
52 Adalah, "Objection to the age limit set by Tel Aviv University for studies in the faculty of medicine" [in Hebrew], adalah.org.
53 Council for Higher Education, "The principle issue with the age limit for admission to medical studies and paramedical studies in institutions of higher education" [in Hebrew], July 22, 2014, che.org.il.
54 Meirav Arlosoroff, "Ben Gvir adopts a European antisemitic policy—and uses it against Arab students" [in Hebrew], *Ha'aretz*, December 29, 2022.
55 Arar and Haj-Yehia, *Higher education and the Palestinian Arab minority*.
56 Kril and Amaria, "Barriers to the integration of the Arab population."
57 In 2018, over 8,000 Palestinian citizens were enrolled in universities in the West Bank, with enrollment exponentially rising. Yasser Waked, "Israeli campus in the West Bank: More Israeli Arabs than Palestinians study at Jenin University" [in Hebrew], *Ha'aretz*, March 20, 2018; Arar and Haj-Yehia, *Higher education and the Palestinian Arab minority*.
58 Ibid.
59 Among Jewish physicians, only 15 percent were trained abroad. Osama Tanous, "Covid-19 Fault Lines: Palestinian Physicians in Israel," *Journal of Palestine Studies* 49, no. 4 (August 1, 2020): 36–46.
60 Ibid.; Kril and Amaria, "Barriers to the integration of the Arab population."
61 Sarab Abu-Rabia-Queder and Khaled Arar, "Gender and Higher Education in Different National Spaces: Female Palestinian Students Attending Israeli and Jordanian Universities," *Compare: A Journal of Comparative and International Education* 41, no. 3 (May 2011): 353–70; Arar and Haj-Yehia, *Higher education and the Palestinian Arab minority*.
62 Waked, "Israeli campus in the West Bank"; Abu-Rabia-Queder and Arar, "Gender and Higher Education."
63 Arar and Haj-Yehia, *Higher education and the Palestinian Arab minority*.
64 Waked, "Israeli campus in the West Bank."
65 Wiam Belaoum and Yara Sa'di, "Obedience courts: Disciplinary committees as a mechanism to suppress the political activity of Arab students in Israeli universities" [in Arabic], Arab Culture Association, March 2013, alrasedproject.com.
66 Khaled Anabtawi and Yara Sa'di, "Outside the dorms: Racism in the eligibility criteria for student housing for Arab students in Israeli universities" [in Arabic], Arab Culture Association, March 2013, alrasedproject.com; Dirasat: The Arab Center for Law and Policy, *Obstacle course: Challenges and directions for the substantial integration of Arab citizens into Israel's higher education system* [in Hebrew] (Nazareth: Council for Higher Education, 2011); Ali, *Representation of Arab Citizens*.
67 Adalah, "Adalah Submits Petition to District Court Challenging Haifa University's Discriminatory Student Housing Policy," October 31, 2005, adalah .org.
68 Ibid.; Gilad Grossman and Itamar Inbari, "Discrimination with receipts" [in Hebrew], NRG, August 20, 2006.
69 Adalah, "A demand to cancel the use of military service as a criterion for assigning a room in the student dormitories at the University of Haifa" [in Hebrew],

adalah.org; Tamara Traubmann, "The Supreme Court: Preference for military veterans in dormitories will continue in 2008" [in Hebrew], *Ha'aretz*, April 10, 2007.

70 Anabtawi and Sa'di, "Outside the dorms"; Dirasat, "Obstacle course"; Ali, *Representation of Arab Citizens*; Arar and Haj-Yehia, *Higher education and the Palestinian Arab minority.*

71 Mohammed S. Wattad, "The legal status of the Arabic language following the Nation-State Basic Law" [in Hebrew], Icon-S Israel blog, January 7, 2020, israeliconstitutionalism.wordpress.com; Thair Abu Rass and Yael Maayan, *Arabic and Arab Culture on Israeli Campuses: An Updated Look* (Haifa: Sikkuy and Dirasat, 2014).

72 Muhammad Amara, Smadar Donitsa-Schmidt, and Abd Al-Rahman Mar'I, "Arabic Language in the Israeli Academy: Historical Absence, Current Challenges, Future Possibilities," Sikkuy and Dirasat 2017, sikkuy-aufoq.org.il; Abu Rass and Maayan, *Arabic and Arab Culture on Israeli Campuses*; Maayan, "Two cases of racialized academic space."

73 Abu Rass and Maayan, *Arabic and Arab Culture on Israeli Campuses.*

74 Maayan, "Two cases of racialized academic space"; Shira Kaderi-Ovadia, "Tel Aviv University refuses to establish a permanent prayer room for Muslims on campus" [in Hebrew], *Ha'aretz*, May 19, 2019.

75 Campus Rabbi–University of Haifa, "Campus rabbi" [in Hebrew], synagogue .haifa.ac.il.

76 Adalah, "Adalah's 2005 Annual Report of Activities," April 2006, adalah.org.

77 Cymbalista Synagogue and Jewish Heritage Center Tel Aviv University, "The synagogue" [in Hebrew], heritage.tau.ac.il; Moran Zelikovich, "Outrage: Tel Aviv University opens a mosque in the dormitories" [in Hebrew], Ynet, October 27, 2004.

78 Zelkovich, "Outrage."

79 Shira Kaderi-Ovadia, "After the publication in *Ha'aretz*, Tel Aviv University will establish a permanent prayer room for Muslims on campus" [in Hebrew], *Ha'aretz*, May 30, 2019.

80 Sa'di-Ibraheem, "Indigenous students' geographies."

81 Council for Higher Education, "Integrating the Arab society into higher education" [in Hebrew], che.org.il; Abu Rass and Maayan, *Arabic and Arab Culture on Israeli Campuses*; Ayala Hendin, "The integration of Arab students into the Israeli higher education system" [in Hebrew] (master's thesis, Hebrew University, 2009); Ali, *Representation of Arab Citizens.*

82 Alice Speri, "Israeli Forces Deliberately Killed Palestinian American Journalist, Report Shows," *Intercept*, September 20, 2022; Office of the UN High Commissioner for Human Rights, "UN Experts Demand Justice for Al Jazeera Journalist on One Year Anniversary of Her Killing," May 11, 2023, ohchr.org.

83 Bar Peleg and Deiaa Haj Yahia, "A student from Ben-Gurion was arrested on campus on suspicion of online incitement" [in Hebrew], *Ha'aretz*, May 15, 2022.

84 Ibid.

85 Ibid.

86 Sa'di, *Through Surveillance*; Bauml, *A blue and white shadow.*

87 Equity, Diversity and Community Commission, "Vision and goals" [in Hebrew], diversity.tau.ac.il.

Notes for pages 161 to 165

88 Diversity and Inclusion, Hebrew University, "Diversity policy for the Hebrew University of Jerusalem" [in Hebrew], diversity.huji.ac.il.

89 Andre Mazawi, "Education as Spaces of Community Engagement and a 'Capacity to Aspire,'" in *Educator of the Mediterranean: Up Close and Personal*, ed. R. G. Sultana (Malta: Sense Publishers, 2011). See also Makkawi, "Community Engagement from the Margin"; Abu-Saad, "Palestinian Education in Israel."

90 Makkawi, "Community Engagement from the Margin."

91 Yair Ettinger, "Haifa University: The Arabs were punished, the right-wingers were not" [in Hebrew], Walla, August 15, 2002.

92 Tamara Traubmann, "Students held a memorial rally for those killed in October 2000—and will face disciplinary actions" [in Hebrew], *Ha'aretz*, February 20, 2008.

93 State Comptroller, "The handling of disciplinary offenses in institutions of higher education" [in Hebrew], mevaker.gov.il.

94 Ibid.; Belaoum and Sa'di, "Obedience courts."

95 The Association for Civil Rights in Israel, "Minsky's appeal against the University of Haifa" [in Hebrew], March 9, 2014, law.acri.org; Yarden Skop, "The University of Haifa reduced the ban on political demonstrations on campus" [in Hebrew], *Ha'aretz*, January 20, 2016.

96 Talila Nesher and Revital Hovel, "Three hours before the event: The University of Haifa canceled an event commemorating the Nakba, even though it received all approvals" [in Hebrew], *Ha'aretz*, May 16, 2012.

97 Yarden Skop, "The University of Haifa has suspended the activities of left-wing and Arab groups on campus" [in Hebrew], *Ha'aretz*, May 15, 2014.

98 Yarden Skop, "Lecturers and students against the University of Haifa: 'Undemocratic conduct' on Nakba Day" [in Hebrew], *Ha'aretz*, May 19, 2014.

99 Adalah, "An appeal against Haifa University's decision to freeze the activity of student groups" [in Hebrew], May 27, 2014, adalah.org.

100 Adalah, "Following Adalah's appeal to the Supreme Court: The University of Haifa withdraws from the freezing of the Arab student groups" [in Hebrew], June 8, 2014, adalah.org.

101 Dean of Students Office, "Public activity regulations 2022: Update" [in Hebrew], Haifa University, 2022, haifa.ac.il.

102 Communist Party of Israel, "'Hadash' party student group at the Hebrew University: The administration is seriously harming freedom of expression" [in Hebrew], May 13, 2014, maki.org.

103 Sapir Sluzker Amran, "Second day of the fight between Hebrew University students on the right to protest" [in Hebrew], *Local Call*, May 1, 2014.

104 Yehuda Shavit, "Dean of Students office: Letter" [in Hebrew], Hebrew University of Jerusalem, May 4, 2014.

105 *Ha'aretz* editorial board, "Weak-kneed at Hebrew University" [in Hebrew], *Ha'aretz*, May 15, 2017.

106 Maya Avis, "Students: Ben Gurion University is harassing an exhibition about the demolition of houses in the Negev" [in Hebrew], *Local Call*, December 17, 2017.

107 Ibid.

108 Yarden Zur, "Tel Aviv University prevents students from carrying out pro peace activities for bureaucratic reasons" [in Hebrew], *Ha'aretz*, May 28, 2018.

109 Nati Yefet, "Ben-Gurion University disqualified singers for fear of incitement; the celebration of the Arab students was canceled" [in Hebrew], *Ha'aretz*, December 6, 2022.

110 Academic Secretariat, "General information" [in Hebrew], Tel Aviv University, January 24, 2023, tau.ac.il.

111 Ran Shimoni, "Three Arab students arrested during Nakba protests in Tel Aviv University" [in Hebrew], *Ha'aretz*, May 15, 2022.

112 Nati Yefet and Shira Kaderi-Ovadia "The mayor of Beersheba protested the waving of Palestinian flags at Ben Gurion, the university: Proud of the students" [in Hebrew], *Ha'aretz*, May 23, 2022.

113 Zo Haderekh editorial board, "A member of the Hadash chapter secretariat at Ben-Gurion University will face disciplinary proceedings due to her participation in a demonstration and her political activity" [in Hebrew], July 24, 2022, zoha.org.il.

114 Shira Kaderi-Ovadia, "Ben-Gurion University convicted a student in disciplinary proceedings for saying 'martyrs' at an event on campus" [in Hebrew], *Ha'aretz*, October 23, 2022.

115 Zo Haderekh editorial board, "Another hearing for a Hadash activist student who mentioned the word 'martyrs' at a rally in Ben-Gurion University" [in Hebrew], March 5, 2023, zoha.org.il; Shira Kaderi-Ovadia, "About 400 faculty members demand to overturn the conviction of a student at Ben-Gurion who said 'martyrs' at a rally to commemorate the Nakba" [in Hebrew], *Ha'aretz*, November 15, 2022.

116 Shira Kaderi-Ovadia, "Ben-Gurion University canceled the disciplinary proceedings against a student who said 'martyrs' on campus" [in Hebrew], *Ha'aretz*, March 8, 2023.

6. Academia Against Liberation

1 Addameer Prisoner Support and Human rights Association, "IOF Launch Mass Arrest Campaign Against Birzeit University Students Visiting Site of Israeli Home Demolition," July 18, 2021, addameer.org.

2 Ibid.; "Israel Carries Out Mass Arrests of Birzeit University Students," Palestine Chronicle, July 15, 2021, palestinechronicle.com.

3 Ibid.; Palestinian Information Center, "They Were Kidnapped by IOF Following Visit to Prisoner's Family: 13 Birzeit Students in Israeli Jails since Mid-July," August 14, 2021, palinfo.com.

4 Yara Hawari, "Defying Fragmentation and the Significance of Unity: A New Palestinian Uprising," *Al-Shabaka*, June 29, 2021.

5 MEE Staff, "Sheikh Jarrah: Israel Supreme Court Postpones Decision on Evictions," *Middle East Eye*, May 6, 2021.

6 "Israeli Police Fire Stun Grenades Inside Al-Aqsa Mosque," Al Jazeera, May 7, 2021, aljazeera.com; Stephen Farrell and Rami Ayyub, "Israeli Police, Palestinians Clash at Jerusalem's Al-Aqsa, Scores Injured," Reuters, May 7, 2021.

7 Oliver Holmes and Peter Beaumont, "Israeli Police Storm Al-Aqsa Mosque Ahead of Jerusalem Day March," *Guardian*, May 10, 2021.

8   Masha Averbuch, "Right before fulfilling my dream of becoming an engineer—I became a criminal" [in Hebrew], *HaMakom*, May 24, 2021.

9   Ibid.

10 OCHA, "Escalation in the Gaza Strip, the West Bank and Israel," May 20, 2021, ochaopt.org; Amnesty International, "Israeli Police Targeted Palestinians with Discriminatory Arrests, Torture and Unlawful Force," June 24, 2021, amnesty.org.

11 Dana El Kurd, "The Unity Intifada: Assessments and Predictions," *Arab Studies Journal* 29, no. 2 (Fall 2021): 134–43; Lana Tatour, "The 'Unity Intifada' and '48 Palestinians: Between the Liberal and the Decolonial," *Journal of Palestine Studies* 50, no. 4 (October 1, 2021): 84–9.

12 "In Pictures: In Show of Unity, Palestinians Go on Strike," Al Jazeera, May 18, 2021, aljazeera.com.

13 Jack Khoury, "Arab-Israelis to strike amid surge in Gaza violence; Fatah and Hamas declare 'day of rage'" [in Hebrew], *Ha'aretz*, May 18, 2021.

14 Tatour, "The 'Unity Intifada' and '48 Palestinians"; El Kurd, "The Unity Intifada."

15 Tatour, "The 'Unity Intifada' and '48 Palestinians."

16 Ibid.

17 Khaled Jamal Furani, introduction to *Inside the leviathan: Palestinian experiences in Israeli universities* [in Arabic] (Jerusalem and Haifa: Van Leer Institute Press and Dar Laila, 2022).

18 Ed Vulliamy, "In Gaza, the Schools Are Dying Too," *Guardian*, January 10, 2009.

19 Birzeit University, "History of Birzeit University," birzeit.edu.

20 The isolation of Palestinian students in the OPT was part of a broader Israeli campaign to sever them from Palestinian refugee student organizers and contain the Palestinian student movement and its articulation of revolutionary anticolonial politics. See Loubna Qutami, "Reborn as Fida'i: The Palestinian Revolution and the Making of an Icon," *International Journal of Communication* no. 16 (2022): 4659–83.

21 Antony T. Sullivan, "Palestinian Universities in the West Bank and Gaza Strip," *Minerva* 29, no. 3 (September 1991): 249–68; Gabi Baramki, *Peaceful Resistance: Building a Palestinian University under Occupation* (New York: Pluto Press, 2010).

22 Birzeit University, "History of Birzeit University."

23 Israel's military government compelled Birzeit University to apply for permits to expand beyond its associate's degree programs, and to report on academic programs and students. Birzeit was ultimately granted a permit by Israel solely for the academic year of 1972–73, which the university's administrators refused to apply to renew, and simply asserted their rights to continue operation thereafter. Baramki, *Peaceful Resistance*.

24 Edward Said, "Birzeit University: A Foundation Stone of Palestinian Civil Society Under Siege," *Washington Report on Middle East Affairs* (January/February 1999): 11, 88; Penny Johnson, "Protests, Prisoners and Palestinian Studies," in *Universities and Conflict: The Role of Higher Education in Peacebuilding and Resistance*, ed. Juliet Millican (New York: Routledge, 2019); Eileen Kuttab, "Reflections on Education as Political Practice," in Millican, *Universities and Conflict*.

25 Johnson, "Protests, Prisoners and Palestinian Studies"; Baramki, *Peaceful Resistance*; Ido Zelkovitz, *Students and Resistance in Palestine: Books, Guns and Politics* (London: Routledge, 2019).

26 Birzeit University's enrolling of Palestinian citizens of Israel was an issue the administration was repeatedly interrogated about by the Israeli military government for decades. Baramki, *Peaceful Resistance*.

27 Birzeit University, "History of Birzeit University"; Birzeit University, "University Closure History," birzeit.edu.

28 Baramki, *Peaceful Resistance*.

29 Birzeit University, "Dr. Hanna Nasir," birzeit.edu.

30 Rema Hammami, "On the Importance of Thugs: The Moral Economy of a Checkpoint," *Middle East Report* 231 (2004): 16–28; Sullivan, "Palestinian Universities in the West Bank"; Johnson, "Protests, Prisoners and Palestinian Studies"; Abdul-Rahim Al-Shaikh, "In Solidarity with Birzeit: The Black, the White, and the Gray," *Curriculum Inquiry* 52, no. 3 (2022): 351–72.

31 Birzeit University, "History of Birzeit University"; Right to Education Campaign, "History of the Campaign," right2edu.birzeit.edu.

32 Baramki, *Peaceful Resistance*.

33 Ibid.

34 Ibid.; see also Lee Davidson, "Nielson Pressures Israel to Reopen Closed Colleges," *Deseret News*, June 17, 1990; "Palestinian Education under Occupation," C-Span, June 16, 1990, c-span.org.

35 Amira Hass, "High Court Rejects Gaza Students' Petition to Study in West Bank," *Haaretz*, September 27, 2012.

36 Hammami, "On the Importance of Thugs."

37 Scholars at Risk Network, "2014-06-22 Birzeit University, Arab American University, Al-Quds University, Palestine Polytechnic University," scholarsatrisk.org; Birzeit University, "Birzeit University Condemns Storming of Its Campus by Israeli Occupation Forces," June 19, 2014, birzeit.edu.

38 "Army Invades Birzeit University, Illegally Confiscates Computers," IMEMC News, December 14, 2016, imemc.org; Scholars at Risk Network, "2017-12-14 Al-Quds University, Birzeit University," scholarsatrisk.org; "Israeli Soldiers Raid Birzeit University Campus, Seize Banners," WAFA, December 14, 2017, wafa.ps; Jacob Magid, "IDF Seizes 'Incitement Materials' at West Bank Universities," *Times of Israel*, December 14, 2017.

39 "15 Students Injured by Israeli Fire at Tulkarem University," IMEMC News, December 16, 2015, imemc.org.

40 "Special Focus: Palestinian Universities Subject to IOF Attacks," Al-Haq, November 30, 2015, alhaq.org; "Al-Quds University Campus Sabotaged by Israeli Forces," IMEMC News, November 20, 2016. imemc.org; "15 Students Injured by Israeli Fire"; "UPDATE: Ten Students Injured during Tulkarm University Protests over Trump's Announcement," WAFA, December 12, 2017.

41 "Israeli Forces Attack Students of Hebron Technical University," WAFA, March 4, 2018, wafa.ps; "Israeli Soldiers Close Kadoorie University's Entrances, Injure Four Students," IMEMC News, April 26, 2018, imemc.org.

42 Magid, "IDF Seizes 'Incitement Materials'"; "Israeli Soldiers Close Kadoorie University's Entrances." In 2015, for example, over 175 students and staff were injured by rubber bullets and 513 suffered from tear gas inhalation during Israeli military raids on campus: "Special Focus: Palestinian Universities." In 2016, the Israeli military raided an exhibition at the Faculty of Medicine, destroying the exhibit and seizing documents and electronic equipment: "Al-Quds University Campus Sabotaged." In 2017, The Israeli military raided

the student union and other offices on campus, confiscating banners and other political materials: Scholars at Risk Network, "2017-12-14 Al-Quds University"; Magid, "IDF Seizes 'Incitement Materials.'" The motivation for the raid became clear when exhibits for the campus museum about the experiences of Palestinian prisoners were destroyed and removed along with hundreds of books: Nick Riemer, "The Attack on Palestinian Universities," *Jacobin*, December 30, 2018.

43 "Israel Bans Palestinian Academic Conference in Jerusalem," IMEMC News, July 18, 2018, imemc.org; "Member of PLO Denounces Israeli Closure of Hind Al-Husseini College in East Jerusalem," WAFA, July 14, 2018, wafa.ps.

44 Global Coalition to Protect Education from Attack, "Education under Attack 2014: Israel/Palestine," February 27, 2014.

45 "Educational Toll of Gaza War: At Least 3 Universities, 148 Schools," Al-Fanar Media, August 3, 2014, al-fanarmedia.org.

46 Global Coalition to Protect Education from Attack, "Education Under Attack 2014."

47 OCHA, "Gaza: Initial Rapid Assessment," August 27, 2014, ochaopt.org.

48 "Educational Toll of Gaza War." See also Haidar Eid, "Gaza: Signposts on the Road to Liberation," *Electronic Intifada*, July 12, 2014.

49 Lizzie Dearden, "Israel-Gaza Conflict: University Hit as Palestinians Endure More than 200 Strikes in 24 Hours," *Independent*, August 2, 2014.

50 "Educational Toll of Gaza War"; "A Gaza Vocational College Devastated by the War," Al-Fanar Media, August 7, 2014, al-fanarmedia.org.

51 Asmaa al-Ghoul, "Gaza Universities Struggle to Stay Afloat," *Al-Monitor*, December 12, 2014.

52 OCHA, "Gaza Strip: Escalation of Hostilities 10–21 May 2021," May 22, 2021, ochaopt.org; Palestine Academy for Science and Technology, "War on Gaza: Targeting Civilians, Including School and University Students as Well as Members of Administrative and Teaching Staff—Statements," May 21, 2021, palast.ps.

53 OCHA, "Gaza Strip: Escalation of Hostilities."

54 Human Rights Watch, "Gaza: Israel's May Airstrikes on High-Rises," August 23, 2021, hrw.org.

55 Ibid.; B'Tselem, "In the May 2021 Fighting, Israel Bombed Four Towers in Gaza, Leaving Dozens of Families Homeless and Business Owners Jobless," December 15, 2021, btselem.org; OCHA, "Escalation in the Gaza Strip"; Scholars at Risk Network, "2021-05-18 Islamic University of Gaza," scholarsatrisk.org.

56 OCHA, "Gaza Strip: Escalation of Hostilities."

57 Nour Abu Aisha, "Libraries, publishing houses and cultural centers. Israel's 'targets bank' in Gaza—(photos)" [in Arabic], *Al-Quds Al-Arabi*, May 24, 2021; Linah Alsaafin and Ashraf Amra, "Gaza Recycles Rubble as Israel Upholds Ban on Construction Goods," Al Jazeera, June 17, 2021.

58 Abu Aisha, "Libraries, publishing houses and cultural centers."

59 Taghreed Ali, "Gaza's Largest Library Shakes Off Dust of War, Reopens Doors," *Al-Monitor*, March 6, 2022.

60 Amr EL-Tohamy, "Palestine's Education Institutions Are Victims of Conflict Again," Al-Fanar Media, May 18, 2021.

61 Ibid.

62 Ibid. For more on the psychological effects of the 2021 offensive on university students in the Gaza Strip, see Abdal-Karim Said Radwan et al., "Post-Traumatic

Stress Disorder among Palestinian University Students Following the May 2021 War," preprint, March 30, 2022.

63 El-Tohamy, "Palestine's Education Institutions."

64 Human Rights Watch, "Gaza: Israel's 'Open-Air Prison' at 15," June 14, 2022, hrw.org.

65 Ibid.

66 Ibid.; UNRWA, "Gaza: 15 Years of Blockade," unrwa.org.

67 GISHA, "The Impact of the Separation Between the Gaza Strip and the West Bank on Higher Education," May 2010, gisha.org.

68 Mona Jebril and Simon Deakin, "The Political Economy of Health in the Gaza Strip: Reversing De-development," *Journal of Global Health*, April 2, 2022; Mark Griffiths et al., "Israel's International Mobilities Regime: Visa Restrictions for Educators and Medics in Palestine," *Territory, Politics, Governance*, July 2022: 1–19.

69 Ibid. See also Hass, "High court rejects Gaza students' petition"; Razan Shamallakh, "Blockade on Dreams: Gazan Students Barred from Starting University Abroad," Albawaba, September 30, 2017.

70 Scholars at Risk Network, "2019-11-13 Bisan Center for Research and Development," scholarsatrisk.org; Bisan, "Bisan Center for Research and Development," bisan.org.

71 Amnesty International, "Israel/Occupied Palestinian Territories: NGO Director in Administrative Detention: Ubai Aboudi," November 22, 2019, amnesty.org.

72 Yuval Abraham, Oren Ziv, and Meron Rapaport, "Secret Israeli Document Offers No Proof to Justify Terror Label for Palestinian Groups," *Intercept*, November 3, 2021.

73 Ibid.; Isaac Scher, "CIA Unable to Corroborate Israel's 'Terror' Label for Palestinian Rights Groups," *Guardian*, August 22, 2022.

74 United Nations, "Outraged over Israel's Designation of Six Civil Society Groups as Terrorists, Speakers Tell Palestinian Rights Committee Harassment against Human Rights Defenders Must End," December 7, 2021, press.un.org; Scher, "CIA Unable to Corroborate"; Miriam Berger, "Israel Shutters Palestinian Rights Groups, Drawing Diplomatic Backlash," *Washington Post*, August 18, 2022; United Nations, "Israel/Palestine: UN Experts Call on Governments to Resume Funding for Six Palestinian CSOs Designated by Israel as 'Terrorist Organisations,'" April 25, 2022, ohchr.org.

75 See also Right to Education Campaign, "Ongoing Israeli Policies to Disrupt and Isolate Palestinian Higher Education," January 13, 2018, right2edu.birzeit.edu.

76 Many of these Israeli-designated "international faculty" are Palestinians, born abroad or who have lost their resident status in the West Bank, including East Jerusalem, because of Israeli policies. Amira Hass, "Due to the tightening of entry procedures: Foreign lecturers at universities in the West Bank are forced to leave" [in Hebrew], *Ha'aretz*, July 12, 2019.

77 Ibid.

78 Adalah, "Israel Forcing International Lecturers Out." Beyond security deposits, faculty have been subjected to Israeli restrictions on their movement, such as being banned from using Israeli airports, and have been granted tourist and not work visas, forcing them into precarious contracts. Hass, "Due to the tightening of entry procedures."

79 Adalah, "Israel Forcing International Lecturers Out."

80 Ibid.
81 Attorneys from Al-Haq and Adalah also pointed out how Israeli restrictions also threaten Birzeit's ranking among universities worldwide, which is determined in part by the proportion of international faculty and students. Birzeit University President Abdullatif Abuhijleh put the escalation in visa restrictions in context, explaining that blocking Birzeit's right to engage international academics is "part of an ongoing effort by the Israeli occupation to marginalize Palestinian institutions of higher education." Adalah, "Israel Forcing International Lecturers Out"; Birzeit University, "QS World University Rankings," birzeit.edu.
82 These included the American Anthropological Association, the American Political Science Association, the Middle East Studies Association of North America, the Modern Language Association, the National Women's Studies Association, and the Society for Architectural Historians. Middle East Studies Association of North America, "Letter to Israel Authorities about Restrictions on International Academics Working in Palestinian Universities," September 12, 2019, mesana.org.
83 Ibid.
84 Coordination of Government Activities in the Territories, "Procedure for entry and residence of foreigners in the Judea and Samaria Area" [in Hebrew], February 20, 2022, gov.il.
85 Birzeit University, "Call to Action: Birzeit University Rejects Israeli Measures Against Academic Freedom," March 12, 2022, birzeit.edu.
86 Middle East Studies Association of North America, "Letter Protesting New Israel Government Directive Regarding Selection of International Scholars and Students to Teach and Study in Palestinian Universities," April 5, 2022, mesana .org; American Anthropology Association, "AAA Opposes Israeli Restrictions on 'Foreign' Faculty and Students in Palestinian Institutions," April 1, 2022, americananthro.org; British Society for Middle Eastern Studies, "Prime Minister Naftali Bennett—Letter," April 6, 2022, brismes.ac.uk; Scholars at Risk Network, "Protect and Promote International Academic Travel to the West Bank," April 27, 2022, scholarsatrisk.org.
87 Human Rights Watch, "West Bank: New Entry Rules Further Isolate Palestinians," January 23, 2023, hrw.org.
88 US Embassy in Israel, "COGAT Statement by US Ambassador to Israel Tom Nides," September 4, 2022, useembassy.gov; Tovah Lazaroff, "US Concerned by Israel's New West Bank Restrictions for Foreigners," *Jerusalem Post*, October 19, 2022.
89 Coordination of Government Activities in the Territories, "Procedure for entry and residence."
90 Baramki, *Peaceful Resistance*; Sullivan, "Palestinian Universities in the West Bank."
91 Al-Shaikh, "In Solidarity with Birzeit."
92 Ibid.; Neve Gordon, "In Their Silence, Israeli Academics Collude with Occupation," *Chronicle of Higher Education*, June 2, 2014.
93 Gordon, "In Their Silence."
94 Amira Hass, "The Committee of University Heads: We will not act against discrimination in higher education in the West Bank" [in Hebrew], *Ha'aretz*, August 28, 2019.
95 Birzeit University, "Call to Action."

96 Tamar Trabelsi Haddad, "'Visit quotas' for Palestinian universities? 'Don't give ammunition to BDS'" [in Hebrew], Ynet, June 28, 2022.
97 Ibid.
98 Birzeit University, "Call to Action."
99 Letter from the General Assembly of Hebrew University, June 23, 2022; letter from the Scientific Council of the Weizmann Institute of Science, June 23, 2022.
100 In their letter to the Civil Administration regarding the 2022 directive, for instance, Academia for Equality do amplify the demand from Palestinian universities to cancel the directive. But they have not consistently campaigned, as Palestinian universities do, for the Israeli military governance of universities to be dismantled, nor for Israel to be held accountable by the international community until the academic freedoms of Palestinian universities are upheld.
101 Tatour, "The Unity Intifada and '48 Palestinians."
102 "Father of Captive Abu-Ghosh: 'We Did Not Recognise Her Due to Atrocity of Torture,'" MEMO, January 4, 2020, middleeastmonitor.com; Linah Alsaafin, "Palestinian Student Released from Israeli Jail after 15 Months," Al Jazeera, December 1, 2020.
103 Scholars at Risk, "2019-08-28 Birzeit University," scholarsatrisk.org
104 Alsaafin, "Palestinian Student Released."
105 Addameer, "Mais Abu Gosh Sentenced to 16 Months in Prison and a Fine," March 3, 2020, addameer.org.
106 Alsaafin, "Palestinian Student Released."
107 Right to Education Campaign, "Statement about the Israeli Occupation's Arrest of Birzeit University Students, Faculty Members," January 23, 2020, right2edu .birzeit.edu.
108 Birzeit University, "Israeli Forces Kidnap University Students, Storm Campus in Violation of Campus Sanctity," March 26, 2019, birzeit.edu; Scholars at Risk, "2019-03-26 Birzeit University," scholarsatrisk.org.
109 "Two Palestinian Women Moved to Israeli Administrative Detention," Al Jazeera, December 17, 2019, aljazeera.com. Two previous heads of the Birzeit student council before Hassan were also arrested. Omar Kiswani, was arrested on campus by undercover Israeli military soldiers in March 2018. Kiswani endured interrogations and torture and was prevented from seeing his lawyer for several weeks. In November 2019, Yehya Rabie was arrested at his home and kept in administrative detention. Birzeit University, "Israeli Forces Kidnap University Student, Fire Shots on Campus in Broad Daylight," March 7, 2018, birzeit.edu; Right to Education Campaign, "Our Students Imprisoned Away from Sunlight," April 18, 2018, right2edu.birzeit.edu; Scholars at Risk, "2018-11-19 Birzeit University," scholarsatrisk.org.
110 Addameer, "LPHR and Asdameer Statement on the Release of Birzeit University Female Student Union Council Head, Shatha Hassan, and Ongoing Targeting of Palestinian University Students," June 4, 2020, addameer.org; Scholars at Risk, "2019-12-12 Birzeit University," scholarsatrisk.org.
111 Addameer, "Commemorating the International Day of Education by Highlighting the Reality of the Right to Education for Palestinian Political Prisoners," January 24, 2023, addameer.org.
112 Birzeit University, "Israeli Forces Kidnap University Student, Fire Shots"; Jacky Khoury, "Documented: An undercover unit arrested the head of the student union in Birzeit, who is affiliated with Hamas" [in Hebrew], Haaretz, March 7, 2018.

113 Addameer, "Suspended Graduation: The Targeting and Political Detention of Palestinian University Students," February 3, 2020, addameer.org.

114 Ibid.

115 Ibid.

116 Ibid.

117 B'Tselem, "Administrative Detention," btselem.org. For more on administrative detention, see Addameer, "Administrative Detention as a Tool of Oppression and Domination," October 5, 2022, addameer.org.

118 Addameer, "Administrative Detention," July 2017, addameer.org; "UN Special Rapporteur on OPT Calls on Israel to Comply with International Law on Detention," Al-Haq, May 24, 2017, alhaq.org.

119 Addameer, "Israel's Designation of the Democratic Progressive Student Pole an 'Unlawful Association' Is Another Manifestation of Its Apartheid Regime," December 8, 2020, addameer.org.

120 Addameer, "Birzeit University Student Layan Nasir Targeted Amid Israel's Broader Silencing Campaign Against Palestinian Students," August 3, 2021, addameer.org.

121 Addameer, "Palestinian Students under Suspended Detention," January 24, 2023, addameer.org.

122 UN Human Rights Council, "Opinions Adopted by the Working Group on Arbitrary Detention," June 7, 2021, A/HRC/WGAD/2021/8.

123 Addameer, "Commemorating the International Day of Education."

124 Addameer, "Undercover Israeli Occupation Forces Storm Birzeit University, Arresting Five Palestinian Students and Shoot Live Ammunition," January 12, 2022, addameer.org.

125 Addameer, "Commemorating the International Day of Education."

126 Reported in interviews with author.

127 Masha Averbuch, "The escalation reached the academy: Students were arrested, others are afraid to return to the dormitories" [in Hebrew], *Hamakom*, May 14, 2021.

128 Ibid.

129 Jonathan Cook, "Palestinians in Israel Now Face Far Right Mob Violence Backed by the State," *Middle East Eye*, May 14, 2021.

130 Josh Breiner et al., "Also tonight, Jews and Arabs attacked each other throughout the country, a 19-year-old soldier was seriously injured in Jaffa" [in Hebrew], *Ha'aretz*, May 13, 2021.

131 Yaron Carmi, "Jewish rioters attacked and wreaked havoc on Allenby Street in Haifa" [in Hebrew], *Haipo*, May 13, 2021.

132 Bar Peleg and Tomer Appelbaum, "More than twenty attackers were recorded in a lynching in Bat Yam. Only four were arrested" [in Hebrew], *Ha'aretz*, May 24, 2021.

133 Jonathan Cook, "Palestinians in Israel."

134 Adalah, "The 'law and order' arrest operation directed at the Arab population" [in Hebrew], May 27, 2021, adalah.org.

135 Ibid.; Josh Breiner, "The police: 2,142 people have been arrested since the beginning of the 'Guardian of the Walls' operation, 91 percent of them Arabs" [in Hebrew], *Ha'aretz*, June 3, 2021.

136 Adalah, "The 'law and order' arrest operation"; Amnesty International, "Israeli Police Targeted Palestinians with Discriminatory Arrests, Torture

and Unlawful Force," June 24, 2021, amnesty.org; Adalah, "What Happened in the 'Torture Room' at Israel's Police Station in Nazareth?," June 7, 2021, adalah.org.

137 Hagar Shezaf and Yanal Jabarin, "Exposed to attacks and incitement, Arab students stay away from the campuses and return to their families" [in Hebrew], *Ha'aretz*, May 19, 2021.

138 Palestinian student organizers have assembled hundreds of screenshots of such online incitement, which were reported in interviews and shared with the author. See also ibid.

139 Reported in interviews by Palestinian students with the author.

Epilogue

1 Edward Said, *Representations of the Intellectual* (New York: Vintage Books, 1994), 98.

2 See Gurminder K. Bhambra, Dalia Gebrial, and Kerem Nişancıoğlu, eds., *Decolonising the University* (London: Pluto Press, 2018); Linda Tuhiwai Smith, Eve Tuck, and K. Wayne Yang, eds., *Indigenous and Decolonizing Studies in Education: Mapping the Long View* (New York: Routledge, 2019); Kate McCoy, Eve Tuck, and Marcia McKenzie, eds., *Land Education: Rethinking Pedagogies of Place from Indigenous, Postcolonial, and Decolonizing Perspectives* (New York: Routledge, 2017).

3 Caitlin P. A. Harvey, "The Wealth of Knowledge: Land-Grab Universities in a British Imperial and Global Context," *Native American and Indigenous Studies* 8, no. 1 (2021): 97–105.

4 Ibid.; Robert Lee et al., "Land Grab Universities," *High Country News*, landgrabu.org.

5 Margaret A. Nash, "Entangled Pasts: Land-Grant Colleges and American Indian Dispossession," *History of Education Quarterly* 59, no. 4 (November 2019): 437–67.

6 Lee et al., "Land Grab Universities."

7 Craig Steven Wilder, *Ebony and Ivy: Race, Slavery, and the Troubled History of America's Universities* (New York: Bloomsbury, 2013).

8 Harvey, "The Wealth of Knowledge"; Sharon Stein, *Unsettling the University: Confronting the Colonial Foundations of US Higher Education* (Baltimore, MD: Johns Hopkins University Press, 2022).

9 Maori land seizure funded the development of a number of universities, while other universities were strategically placed to expand settlement. Te Wharepora Hou, "Universities Continue to Benefit from Colonial Land Confiscations," tewhareporahou.wordpress.com; Harvey, "The Wealth of Knowledge."

10 Pedro Mzileni and Nomalanga Mkhize, "Decolonisation as a Spatial Question: The Student Accommodation Crisis and Higher Education Transformation," *South African Review of Sociology* 50, no. 3–4 (October 2, 2019): 104–15.

11 Harold Wolpe, "The Debate on University Transformation in South Africa: The Case of the University of the Western Cape," *Comparative Education* 31, no. 2 (1995): 275–92; Ian Bunting, "The Higher Education Landscape under

Apartheid," in *Transformation in Higher Education: Global Pressures and Local Realities in South Africa*, ed. N. Cloete et al. (Dordrecht: Kluwer Academic Publishers, 2004), 35–52.

12 Mzileni and Mkhize, "Decolonisation as a Spatial Question," 105.

13 Harvey, "The Wealth of Knowledge"; Eve Tuck, "Indigenous Land and Decolonization Curriculum," in *The SAGE Guide to Curriculum in Education* (Thousand Oaks, CA: SAGE, 2015); McCoy, Tuck, and McKenzie, *Land Education*.

14 Bhambra, Gebrial, and Nişancıoğlu, *Decolonising the University*; McCoy, Tuck, and McKenzie, *Land Education*.

Afterword

1 Robert Barnes, "Supreme Court Rejects Race-Based Affirmative Action in College Admissions," *Washington Post*, June 29, 2023; Taifha Alexander et al., *CRT Forward: Tracking the Attack on Critical Race Theory* (Los Angeles: UCLA Critical Race Studies, 2023); Henry A. Giroux, *Insurrections: Education in an Age of Counterrevolutionary Politics* (London: Bloomsbury Academic, 2023); Divya Kumar, "Florida Bill Would End Diversity Programs, Ban Majors, Shift Power at Universities," *Tampa Bay Times*, February 23, 2023; Ishena Robinson, "Anti-CRT Mania and Book Bans Are the Latest Tactics to Halt Racial Justice," Legal Defense Fund, naacpldf.org; Michelle Goldberg, "This Is What the Right-Wing Takeover of a Progressive College Looks Like," *New York Times*, April 29, 2023; "New College Faculty Turnover Is 'Ridiculously High' after DeSantis Takeover," *Orlando Sentinel*, July 18, 2023.

2 Ginia Bellafante, "She Attacked Israel and the N.Y.P.D. It Made Her Law School a Target," *New York Times*, June 2, 2023; "JLSA Statement in Support of Fatima," Google Doc, May 21, 2023, https://docs.google.com/document/d/1YuEmcjfra01kftXhi9Ui4Yb0-8v1uF9MO3asayp7rq0/edit; Stop Anti-Semitism on College Campuses Act, H.R. 3773, 118th Cong. (2023). Specifically, the bill uses the International Holocaust Remembrance Alliance (IHRA) definition of anti-Semitism, which extends to criticisms of Israeli state policies even if they violate international law, the Geneva and Hague Conventions, or the UN Charter and its various conventions on racism, apartheid, torture, human rights, and the like. "Human Rights and Other Civil Society Groups Urge United Nations to Respect Human Rights in the Fight Against Antisemitism," Human Rights Watch, April 20, 2023, hrw.org.

3 Alexis Grenell, "Does Fatima Mousa Mohammed Oppose Israel's Very Existence?," *Nation*, June 8, 2023; David Samel, "'Nation' Article Promotes Jewish Fears over Palestinian Equality in Attack on Fatima Mohammed," Mondoweiss, June 22, 2023, mondoweiss.net. A month later, the *Nation* did run a rejoinder to Grenell's incredibly ill-informed essay, though it is worth mentioning that Grenell is a regular columnist for the magazine. Hebh Jamal, "Fatima Mousa Mohammed Deserves to Be Defended, Not Smeared," *Nation*, June 13, 2023.

4 "Netanyahu's Cabinet Ministers in Race to See Who Is Most Fascist," *Ha'aretz*, May 28, 2023; Usaid Siddiqui and Federica Marsi, "Israel Judicial Crisis Live:

Parliament Ratifies Divisive Bill," Al Jazeera, July 24, 2023; Jonathan Guyer, "What the Siege of Jenin Signals about the Future of Israel and Palestine," *Vox*, July 6, 2023, vox.com; Mohammed Najib, "250 Palestinian Students Leave Their Universities Citing Israeli Incursions in West Bank," *Arab News*, March 18, 2023, arabnews.com; "Statement from Press Secretary Karine Jean-Pierre on the Visit of President Isaac Herzog of Israel," July 13, 2023, whitehouse.gov.

5 In addition to the myriad incidents discussed in *Ivory and Steel*, there is the case of Professor Rivka Feldhay of Tel Aviv University who, in 2012, was banned from participating in a scientific conference in Berlin because she signed a petition four years earlier supporting Israeli soldiers who refused to serve in the West Bank. See Associated Press in Jerusalem, "Israeli Academic Banned from German Conference by Netanyahu," *Guardian*, December 6, 2012.

6 Menachem Fisch et al., "Academic Freedom: For Whom?" (2008), right2edu .birzeit.edu.

7 Committee on Academic Freedom, "Detention and Sentencing of Palestinian Student Activist Ola Marshoud," Middle East Studies Association blog, mesana .org; Nick Riemer, "The Attack on Palestinian Universities," *Jacobin*, December 30, 2018, jacobin.com.

8 See, for example, Michael S. Roth, "Boycott of Israeli Universities: A Repugnant Attack on Academic Freedom," *Los Angeles Times*, December 19, 2013, and my rebuttal, "Defending Zionism Under the Cloak of Academic Freedom," Mondoweiss, January 4, 2014), mondoweiss.net. Dozens of statements by university presidents, administrators, academic organizations, and the like opposing the academic and cultural boycott of Israel can be found here: "University Statements Rejecting Divestment and the Academic Boycott of Israel," Jewish Virtual Library, jewishvirtuallibrary.org.

9 Brian Hauss, "The Right to Boycott Is Under Threat," ACLU, October 11, 2017, aclu.org.

10 "Ron DeSantis Slams CIA and Accuses 'Anti-Israel' UN of Fomenting Terrorism," *Middle East Eye*, July 17, 2023; "West Bank 'Not Occupied' Territory, Says Ron DeSantis," Al Jazeera, July 17, 2023.

11 "Governor Ron DeSantis Receives Honorary Fellowship from Ariel University," press release, May 27, 2019, flgov.com; "Governor Ron DeSantis Applauds Historic Memorandum of Understanding Agreement between Florida Atlantic University and Ariel University," press release, May 27, 2019, flgov.com.

12 The original series of essays appeared in the *New York Times Magazine*, August 14, 2019, but since then it has expanded into a book-length collection of essays by an even more varied group of scholars. See Nikole Hannah-Jones et al., eds., *The 1619 Project: A New Origin Story* (New York: Random House, 2021). C. A. Bridges, "What Is 'The 1619 Project' and Why Has Governor DeSantis Banned It from Florida Schools?," *Tallahassee Democrat*, January 27, 2023, tallahassee .com.

13 Florida Department of Education, "Florida's State Academic Standards—Social Studies, 2023," fldoe.gov.

14 Ben Samuels, "From BDS to Settlements: Where DeSantis Stands on Israel and the Jewish Community," *Ha'aretz*, May 22, 2023.

Index

National and University House of
Books (formerly Israeli
National Library), 62, 63–4
National Laboratory for the
Development of Space
Cameras, 109
National Security College
(University of Haifa), 100–1
Native American and Indigenous
Studies Association,
adoption of BDS resolution
by, 5
Nawaja, Nasser, 24–5, 27
Negev, Avraham, 26
Negev, Judaization of, 77–81
Netanyahu, Benjamin, 84, 87
New College, 197–8
new historians, as challenging
dominant narrative about
establishment of Israel,
119–21
New Zealand, universities in as
built through seizure of
Indigenous territory, 194
Nides, Tom, 182
1948 war, limits placed on study
of, 132
Nisreen (faculty member), 136

occupation (by Israel)
civil resistance to, 174
in Gaza Strip. See Gaza Strip
Hebrew University's role in, 57
limits placed on study of, 127,
128, 132, 145
self-censorship by Jewish-
Israeli faculty whose
scholarship critically
explores, 131
in West Bank. See West Bank
Occupied Palestinian Territory
(OPT), 2, 10, 14, 15, 16, 29,
30–2, 35, 38, 40–1, 46, 47, 48,
49, 59, 81, 82, 83, 85, 86, 87,
95, 103, 104, 116, 117, 127,
130, 132, 156, 162, 164, 168,
172–3, 174, 175, 179, 180,
187
Odeh, Ayman, 144
Ofer, Avi, 31
Ohio House of Representatives,
visit to Israel by delegation
of, 98
Old City of Jerusalem, 32, 33, 71
Olmert, Ehud, 22–3
"Operation Law and Order," 189
oppression (of Palestinians), 3–4,
5, 7, 8, 10, 11, 12, 15, 115–17,
116, 118, 135, 149, 195, 196,
201

Palestine Archaeological
Museum, 28–9, 30

Palestine Polytechnic University,
raid on, 175
Palestine Technical University,
raids on, 176
Palestinian Academic Freedom
Network, 175
Palestinian Campaign for the
Academic and Cultural
Boycott of Israel (PACBI), 5,
6, 195
Palestinian Federation of Unions
of University Professors and
Employees, 16
Palestinian Human Rights
Organizations Council, 11
Palestinian Liberation
Organization (PLO), 11
Palestinian Minister of
Communication, 178
Palestinian Ministry of Justice, 11
Palestinian NGO Network, 11
Palestinians
access to education. See
education
as asserting national identity,
133
campaign to curb discussion of
Palestinian rights in Israeli
academy, 128
and development of
anticolonial politics, 133
interest of in their history, 132,
137–8
Israeli citizenship for, 117, 147
mass exodus of from campuses,
191
oppression of. See oppression
(of Palestinians)
percentage of among students
summoned before
disciplinary committees,
162–3
percentage of as leaving Israel
in pursuit of higher
education, 155
as percentage of bachelor's
degree students, 153
as percentage of faculty at
Israeli universities, 137
as percentage of first-year
bachelor's degree students,
152
as percentage of Israeli citizen
population, 137
as percentage of master's degree
students, 153
as percentage of PhD students,
153
percentage of practicing
Palestinian citizen physicians
trained abroad, 155
as percentage of students,
stagnation of, 153

as percentage of university age
population in Israel, 152
as percentage of university
faculty, 153
pursuit of higher education by,
155, 173
racial hatred against students,
191
repression of. See repression
scholars as challenging
foundational myths of state
of Israel, 139
student enrollment of, 152
targeting of. See targeting
trials of in Israeli military
courts, 41
underfunding of schools, 153
unofficial caps on enrollment in
medical fields, 154
Palestinian universities. See also
specific universities
defined as military targets,
178
detention of students at. See
detention
as governed by Israeli military,
15–16
isolating of, 179
Israeli universities as remaining
silent as Israeli policies stifle
Palestinian universities, 182
raids on, 175, 176, 185, 187
restrictions on, 183
targeting of, 174–5, 176
Pappé, Ilan, 119, 120, 122, 123–4
"Path of the Pilgrims," 33–4
Perry, Simon, 43–4
petitions, 27, 63, 71, 87, 130, 149,
151, 154, 156, 158, 163,
180–1, 182, 183, 199
Physicians for Human Rights–
Israel, 104
Prawer-Begin Plan (2012–17), 78
"Procedure for Entry and
Residence of Foreigners in
Judea and Samaria Area"
(Israeli Civil
Administration), 181
protests, ix, 2, 71, 74, 94, 95, 103,
129, 149, 150, 156, 160, 162,
163, 164, 165, 167, 168, 170,
170–1, 171, 172, 174, 176, 181,
182, 187, 187–9, 188, 189, 191
Puda, Eli, 50

Rabi, Uzi, 48
Rabin, Yitzhak, 56–7
Rabinowitz, Dan, 6
Rafael, 15, 92–3, 105, 106, 107,
109, 110
Ramle, 189
rebellion, universities as sites of,
174–5, 200